MAD AS THE MIST AND SNOW

Mad as the Mist and Snow

Exploring Oregon Through Its Cemeteries

Johan Mathiesen

www.AshlandCreekPress.com

Mad as the Mist and Snow: Exploring Oregon Through Its Cemeteries

Johan Mathiesen

Published by Ashland Creek Press

www.ashlandcreekpress.com

© 2011 Johan Mathiesen

All rights reserved. No part of this book may be reproduced or transmitted, in any form or by any means, without written permission of the publisher.

ISBN 978-0-9796475-5-0

Library of Congress Control Number: 2011932007

All maps and directions in this book were created with information available at the time of writing and are subject to change.

Excerpts on pages 260-261 are from the Center for Columbia River History (www.ccrh.org) and are used with permission.

Printed in the United States of America on acid-free paper. All paper products used to create this book are Sustainable Forestry Initiative (SFI) Certified Sourcing.

Cover photo and all interior photos by Johan Mathiesen.

Cover and book design by John Yunker.

To My Kay

For whom this journey has been a long exercise in Patience,

And without whom there would have been no journey, at all.

"Too loved to be forgotten"

Contents

A Word Before We Begin 1

Explorations and Observations 5
   A Little History 7
   Sacred Ground and Digital Archaeology 12
   Finding Graveyards 16
   The Odd Fellows and the Masons 19
   Woodmen of the World 24
   The Lord Is My Cowboy 28

Epitaphs 33
   A Word Before You Go 35
   Die Laughing 39
   Say Again 48
   The Full Measure 55
   Old Soldiers Do Die 66
   Borrowed Memories 70
   The Bible Told Me So 79
   Curtain Call: Going Out with the Bard 87
   Parting Wisdom 90
   Long Day's Journey Into Night 99
   Death Is Always Out of Season 103

Best Cemeteries of Oregon 107
    The Best Cemeteries of Oregon 109

Guide to Oregon Cemeteries 119
    How To Use This Guide 121
    Basin & Range 125
    Central Prairies 137
    Clackamas & the Highlands 159
    Columbia Plateau 169
    Columbia River 181
    Far East 199
    Grande Ronde & Wallowa Valleys 209
    John Day Country 219
    North Coast 227
    Pine Belt 247
    Portland Metro 253
    Santiam Basin 281
    Siskiyous 293
    South Coast 301
    Tualatin River Valley 307
    Umpqua Drainage 319
    Upper Willamette 325
    Yamhill Valley 345

A Word Before We Begin

It started with two shepherds stopping to eat lunch. It's thought that they picked some local watercress to augment their sandwiches, not knowing the cress was poisonous. When the bodies were found, they hadn't been robbed or attacked. Just dead. No one claimed the bodies and, because they'd been dead some days before discovery, no one wanted to truck them anywhere distant.

Why not just bury them where they are? someone suggested.

Done.

And that's how the International Order of Odd Fellows (IOOF) Cemetery in Lakeview began.

Which is more or less how many cemeteries began. Someone died, and they needed a place to bury him/her. Once governments formed, burial sites were selected more formally, but initially most cemeteries were carved out of someone's Donation Land Claim (DLC). Once one person had been buried on the back forty, it made sense to bury one's neighbors there when they died, too. Propitious plots tended to become cemeteries for the general public and were often donated to the IOOF, Masons, or local authorities.

The beauty of this system is that, as a consequence, countless pioneer cemeteries are secreted away on back roads that rarely, if ever, see a tourist. These remain places known only to local teenagers, the sheriff, and the UPS driver. Tracking them down becomes an exercise in geo-sleuthing and an excuse to visit nooks and crannies that one would never have reason to visit otherwise.

I hope you'll be entertained by the stories here, but I hope even more that your interest will be piqued to visit some of these sanctuaries yourself—the more obscure, the better because the real reason to head into the bush after cemeteries is simply to head into the bush; the cemeteries are merely an excuse. We have but one chance to see the show before we return to dust.

About the Book

The book is divided into four sections. The first is a collection of explorations and observations, most of which originally appeared in Blogging a Dead Horse (http://bloggingadeadhorse-dmt.blogspot.com). The next section is a selection of epitaphs from my database of some 1,700 epitaphs, arranged into eleven themes. Following this section is a listing of what I have found to be the best cemeteries of Oregon, across fourteen categories.

The final and largest section is a gathering of vignettes and profiles of these 200-plus Oregon cemeteries, arranged into eighteen regions. There is no attempt to be definitive or exhaustive; it is meant to whet the appetite.

Dead Man Talking

Once your appetite is thoroughly whetted and you want to hear about more cemeteries, visit my Flickr site: Dead Man Talking (http://www.flickr.com/photos/deadmantalking). Once you're at the site, click on "collections"; from there it's obvious.

Oregon is one of five states for which I maintain collections, but only the Oregon and Washington collections are of any size, and Washington is limited and regional in scope. There are some 14,000 (and counting) cemetery photos posted. Each region in this book is mirrored in the Oregon Collection of Dead Man Talking. All the photos for every cemetery in this book, plus those for the hundreds of other cemeteries in the collection, are available for online viewing. Furthermore, each photo is "geo-located" and accompanied by a map/aerial-photo display. I strongly suggest you visit the Flickr site before heading out to look for the cemeteries in this book if you have any questions about the written directions. It will eliminate the guesswork and vastly increase the number of cemeteries available to you.

~

Exactly why we should care about a body after a person's dead is somewhat of a mystery, but we do, as do other animals. Whatever the reason, disposing of dead people involves solemn ritual in every society. Cemeteries are common but by no means universal. They excel at providing a locus for rituals surrounding death. In our society, this usually includes burial of the body, erection of some form of memorial, and often subsequent visitation and embellishment of the grave site. That being said, there's a considerable range of practices within that general format. Many cemeteries restrict the kind of memorials allowed and/or prohibit embellishments, so the use of cemeteries varies considerably as well. Sometimes restrictions are made on economic grounds, other times for cultural reasons. There is no uniform code of behavior for cemeteries, despite an overarching cultural similarity.

The cemeteries themselves are the core of this book. It is not a book about the people buried in the cemeteries, though we'll meet many of them along the way. It is not a history book, though there's a lot of history within these pages. It's not a travel book, despite descriptions of many places to visit. It's a book about cemeteries: how to find them, what to expect when you do, and glimpses of how they're used. If this book has a message, it's that a cemetery is not a place to bury bones but rather a place to celebrate the memory of those who have forged on ahead. It is an art gallery of grief through the lens of time. It reflects the hopes and aspirations of a community. It's a last breath, quivering for eternity.

These people in the graveyard—they're not dead. They're just half-dead. You still go there. I still go there. Together we read their stones. We squint at their kiln-fired portraits. Who are those people? How did they get here? We still think about them, if only in the slightest of whispers. Their bodies and their souls have long since slipped into starlight, but their memories linger like fog around their names. Cemeteries are not where people go when they die. It's where they go to stay alive.

About the Book's Title

W. B. Yeats wrote the poem *Mad as the Mist and Snow* in 1929, when he was sixty-three years old. I found it as the epitaph on the grave of John McArthur (1945–1998) in the diminutive, reclusive Jones Pioneer Cemetery. As with all good poetry, I've never quite understood what it meant, but it seemed to sum up life perfectly. It must have felt that way to Mr. McArthur, too.

> *And I seem to know*
> *That everything outside us is*
> *Mad as the mist and snow.*

Explorations and Observations

A Little History

Welcome to the stone forest where magical beings and amazing stories live. The star of this book—the protagonist, as it were—is the cemetery itself. We might stop and nod to people along they way—after all, they live here—but we're going to concentrate on their homes: the graveyards of their everlasting peace.

What we're interested in is not who's buried in a cemetery but *how* they're buried, how they are remembered. That Jim Morrison is buried in Père Lachaise Cemetery in Paris is of marginal interest. That people still come daily to lay flowers on his tomb is of significant interest.

Père Lachaise *is* important. It was the model after which modern cemeteries were drawn. For the most part, Americans traditionally followed European burial practices. Prior to Père Lachaise, cemeteries tended to be church affairs, and the word "cemetery" wasn't applied to them; "graveyard" sufficed. Municipalities might maintain burying grounds, though often they were reserved for paupers or people outside the grace of the ecclesiastical authorities. Given the lack of space in a churchyard, bodies inevitably began to pile on top of bodies, the solution being to raise the ground level and add a new layer, repeating as necessary.

Eventually, at the turn of the nineteenth century, one such Parisian cemetery gave way, spilling its contents into the basements of neighboring buildings. Enough was enough. The City of Paris decided something had to be done and created a new graveyard out in the countryside, beyond the urban press: Père Lachaise. They modeled *their* cemetery after the palatial estates of wealthy Englishmen.

The English, for their part, were fond of extensively landscaping their estates to make them look like idealized versions of nature—in contrast to what was already there—into which they liked to position sculptures, miniature classical buildings, and edifying follies. The Parisians hoped their new cemetery would look the same and draw visitors from the city who would be properly educated and uplifted. After some clever marketing, it worked, and a fad was born. Cemeteries would never be the same.

Cemeteries are, first and foremost, living spaces. Like any other cultural artifact—be it a school, factory, town, library, shopping center, state, what-have-you—each cemetery has a life of its own. Living cemeteries are those still in use. They are not static. Their changes may be slow and subtle, but they live on.

Dead cemeteries tend to disappear through neglect, forgetfulness, or conscious removal or destruction. Forgotten cemeteries continually reappear in the process of digging for foundations, road cuts, pipelines, etc., while other dead cemeteries are among the best preserved, and best known, structures on the face of the earth; the Pyramids, the Taj Mahal, and Stonehenge come quickly to mind. To be sure, given the considerable length of time humans have been here, most cemeteries have long been irretrievably lost. Nonetheless, long-lost burial grounds are constantly discovered. In rediscovered cemeteries, aside from the bodies themselves, the most important findings are the trappings left with the corpse: the grave objects. One can often make the case that the single best window we have into an ancient culture comes through its grave offerings. Without them, our knowledge of the past would be much less full. And certainly when it comes to our most famous cemeteries, such as the Pyramids, the cemeteries and their attendant objects far outweigh the bodies in importance. King Tut's okay, but it's his paraphernalia that really excites and informs us.

But there's a disconnect between how we view ancient cemeteries and how we view our own, though the disconnect is not uniform across our culture. The disconnect is more than academic; it's led to enormous changes in our burial practices, which in turn are having a commensurate impact on the cemetery industry. A headline in *The Oregonian* from August 5, 2007, encapsulates the problem: "Oregon cemetery plots go begging." The problem, author Anna Griffin contended, was that "more and more, particularly on the West Coast, consumers are choosing cremation over burial."

In Oregon, Griffin wrote, the cremation rate was then 65 percent, which corresponded to the 67 percent that Metro (an Oregon agency that oversees local pioneer cemeteries) reported. Just forty years ago, the rate was 5 percent. The problem affects virtually all the state's major cemeteries, with the notable exception of the Veterans Affairs (VA) cemeteries, which are constantly looking to expand. Their reason is simple: They give away their plots and pick up the burial tab. It's an offer veterans and their families find hard to refuse.

Even in non-VA cemeteries, the incidence of government-supplied markers often dominates the graveyard, but even that hasn't stemmed the drain away from using the major cemeteries that service the cities of the region. The stark truth is that cemeteries are now competing for a severely shrunken market. Not only do a mere 35 percent of people now opt for burial, but many of those come from cultures that frown upon not being able to have upright, visible grave markers and hence shun the major cemeteries, which are invariably lawn cemeteries. Portland's River View announced in 2011 it was selling half of its nearly 300 acres.

But it is a mistake to think that cremation is the sole cause of cemeteries' problems. The cemeteries' problems are self-inflicted, and cremations are a response; at worst, they're a symptom. There is nothing that prevents cremains from being buried. The problems are related to the disconnect, and much of the secret lies in the cultural response that requires some people to have upright monuments versus flush memorials. What might seem a minor cultural eccentricity affecting a minority of Americans is, in truth, symptomatic of an underlying yearning of many people that is not being satisfied in conventional lawn cemeteries—a yearning that drives potential customers away from cemeteries and paradoxically toward cremation. There is, in fact, a whole class of cemeteries largely unaffected by the switch to cremation—the vernacular cemeteries.

Cemeteries for the most part can be divided into two classes: designer and vernacular, vernacular cemeteries having developed organically from the local community, and designer cemeteries being developed specifically as cemeteries. Père Lachaise was the first designer cemetery. It was the first time anyone had tried to place the dead in a landscaped park designed especially for that purpose. (In fact, the idea for parks came out of cemetery design.) The first such cemetery built in the United States was Mount Auburn in Cambridge, Massachusetts, in 1831; this and many similar early ventures were started by horticultural societies. They were extremely successful, with thousands of people streaming to visit them on fine weekends, to such as extent that traffic rules often had to be promulgated to contend with the throngs, with sometimes only plot-owners allowed to bring horses or carriages onto the grounds. Both Portland's Lone Fir and Eugene's Masonic Cemetery, for example, had city trollies come to their front gates.

Two things stemmed that tide of popularity. One was the invention of parks, which drew away former cemetery visitors. That invention might have altered the use patterns of cemeteries but wouldn't alone have significantly affected the primary role of the cemetery, that of memorial ground, had not cemeteries gone through further design changes that drastically altered their function.

By 1855, Spring Grove Cemetery in Cincinnati had begun the process of consolidating management of the cemetery under one person, in this case Adolph Strauch, who introduced the idea of clustering large monuments on the side of open lawn areas, the size of which he also increased. The process reached its apogee some fifty-eight years later when Hubert Eaton opened Forest Lawn Memorial Gardens in Glendale, California, doing away with family upright markers altogether and turning the entire operation into a lawn cemetery, with stones flush to the ground for ease of maintenance.

Eaton was following the time-honored American tradition of streamlining his business, making it more profitable and cutting costs. But he took his idea one step further, one that exacerbated the problem begun with the implementation of the flush marker. Neither Eaton nor Strauch knew that in their efforts to maximize their profits and minimize their costs, they were sowing the seeds of their own destruction.

Eaton eliminated not only the monuments to death that dominated the early designer cemeteries, which can still be seen in cemeteries such as Portland's Lone Fire or Cottage Grove's Fir Grove, but he tried to eliminate the very idea of death itself, as witnessed by the name change. "Cemetery" carried too much of the burden of death with it, so he opted for "memorial garden," which immediately became code for the new style of cemetery to such an extent that sometimes older cemeteries changed their names to accommodate the new nomenclature, such as Rest Lawn Memorial Park outside Junction City, a pioneer cemetery that subsequently adopted the "memorial garden" tag. You can be sure that any cemetery you find with the name "memorial garden" attached will be a lawn cemetery. In cases such as Rest Lawn and many other vernacular cemeteries, one can see land developed prior to and after the invention of the lawn cemetery. Many pioneer cemeteries mistakenly adopted this approach, and in many, a charming wooded spot now sits next to a barren open plot.

Eaton didn't stop there, though. Instead of shroud-draped statues and lamentations for the departed, Eaton erected his own monuments that avoided any mention of death, most often classical reproductions or Christian statuary. Eaton's goal, essentially, was to chase death from the graveyard, and in this he pretty much succeeded. But in the process, he chased away its raison d'être. He could call his place a "memorial garden," but if there was nothing to remember, why end up there? Slowly, as memorial gardens spread, more and more people took up cremation. It's not that they necessarily preferred cremation, but given the exorbitant cost of funerals, what was the point if there was no place to go to remember your loved one? One flush stone next to another in a limitless lawn is hardly conducive to visitation and rumination. The very reason to visit a cemetery was largely eliminated. Coupled with a cost explosion resulting from the American post–Civil War predilection for embalming and the sales insistence of the funeral industry into more and more expensive coffins, traditional funerals and burials became exceedingly expensive while the product offered was in equal part diminished. People paid a lot of money for something they didn't use much, and, subsequently, began pulling out of the lawn cemeteries altogether. Unless, of course, they were free.

Sacred Ground and Digital Archaeology

I work with sacred ground: cemeteries. There are other types of sacred ground—churches and the like, battlefields, virgin springs—but cemeteries are pretty much universally accepted as sacred ground. At least if it's your cemetery. If it's somebody else's cemetery, they're fair game for looting. The world's museums are stuffed with artifacts stolen from cemeteries, up to and including the bodies themselves. But if it's your grandma and grandpa, hands off. And if the looting is done publicly and at a decent time remove, it's called archaeology.

A cemetery is composed of dead bodies and their associated artifacts. Among other things, the artifacts tell you the cemetery is there. Without them, the bodies belong to the nameless stream of dead people long since disappeared. The most important artifact in a cemetery is the one that tells you that it is there. If it's lasted for any length of time, it's probably stone. It's called a tombstone. The rich can build their whole tombs out of stone; then it's called a mausoleum. A mausoleum is a glorified tombstone.

All cemeteries are at risk of being robbed. For some reason, human skulls have a value all their own, as do burial offerings. Public theft—that done by archaeologists—has the virtue of a) keeping the artifacts in the public eye, and b) if we're lucky, advancing our knowledge.

When an archaeologist studies a grave, he or she, aside from looking at the body itself, inventories the associated artifacts, which we commonly call the "grave offerings," though they all don't serve the same purpose that the word "offerings" implies. Some artifacts are more for decoration than offerings to the dead or to the spirits of the dead; perhaps "ephemera" might be a better term to cover both. Traditionally, of course, the artifacts are simply taken back home with the archaeologist to his or her university or other supervising institution, the better to preserve and study them.

Just exactly what the purpose and understanding of ephemera are, though, is a matter of interpretation, and, undoubtedly, many different forces come into play; but when food offerings are found at a grave site, for instance, it's not clear whether the people who left them actually intended them to be used by the deceased or whether they were left as a symbolic gesture. One has to presume that the concept of symbolism dates to very early human existence. For the observer, it's not important that the ephemera are not meant for the deceased's actual use; they're significant because they indicate what the survivors—and presumably other people of their time and place—thought important. Grave ephemera, then, reflect the people and times in which they are offered. That's what the stuff found with King Tut does: It helps explain Egyptian life in those times. Archaeologists try to make sense of peoples and times through what they throw away and what they leave for their dead. It's a very time-consuming task.

The first "offering," as it were, is the marker itself, the object that tells you a grave is there. The marker is important because without it people wouldn't know where to come to remember the deceased, and ultimately cemeteries are not about stashing the dead somewhere but about not letting people die. Cemeteries are where the connections between the quick and the dead are maintained. No one in a cemetery, if he or she has a marker, is truly dead. The marker can be considered "the permanent offering." It's the offering that's not ephemeral. Its importance is that it locates the place of remembrance and the place to which temporary offerings are brought. Without the permanent marker, everything quickly fades. Cemeteries, if they don't obviate the process, at least slow it down.

American grave ephemera include anything left at a grave site excepting the monument, from a simple flower or a pebble to complex assemblages of hundreds of items. Through a combination of decay, cleanup, and theft, grave site ephemera disappear relatively quickly, and from times past we have no record of what was left at our graves. We can find grave ephemera from other eras and places where ephemera were buried with the deceased, but for the most part that has never been an American custom; consequently, almost everything ever left at our graves has long since vanished.

Interestingly enough, while grave ephemera from other cultures—Peru or Egypt, say—excite great interest and study, to my knowledge local ephemera has routinely been ignored. Which means that vast amounts of information have been lost and that the opportunities are still endless. (The worry being, inevitably, that the opportunities will continue being ignored.) With the advent of digital photography, it's become economically feasible to amass large collections of ephemera—pictures dripping with anticipation that someone will come and sort them. My only regret is that we don't know what people left behind at graves in the 1940s, much less the eighteenth century. We only know what the Egyptians left behind.

Grave offerings open tremendous windows into the deceased, their cultures, and their times. They tell us more about those who left them than about those for whom they were left. The amount of cultural information packed into one picture of grave site ephemera is quantum leaps above the information conveyed by tombstones alone. Unfortunately, though, it's a case of being unable to see the forest for the trees. Current ephemera is too much under our nose to pay attention to it, and once it's gone we never knew it was there in the first place.

With tombstones, the corollary to ephemera is "personalization," which is jargon for anything carved into a stone other than names and dates. There has always been some degree of personalization of tombstones, a practice that has waxed and waned in popularity depending on custom, technology, and materials. And there have always been "handmade" markers as well as professional ones. Some limited academic attention has been paid to professional representations in recent tombstone personalization, largely anecdotal rather than analytical and in small databases.

I collect grave site offerings, permanent and ephemeral. I am a digital archaeologist. I record objects brought to sacred ground in order to bask in and add to the spiritual powers present there. I don't loot any graves. I don't take anything away to display or to sell. What I do is record a world that will be gone tomorrow. Like the river that is never the same whenever you step into it twice, the cemetery you visit will not be the same one I saw. I'm showing you the soft inside of the culture of the Oregon Territory as it stands at the beginning of the twenty-first century. It will never be seen again.

Finding Graveyards

One of the great mysteries of the world is: How does one find graveyards? It's not as easy as one would think. There is no master list of graveyards. Sure, big cemeteries in big cities are easy to find with a gas-station map, but small, rural ones can be much trickier, though the situation is improving. Oregon has a magnificent tome, *Oregon Burial Site Guide* by Dean Byrd, et al., that lists thousands of such grave sites even if they can no longer be found, often with directions limited to section-and-range numbers. Nothing like tramping around someone's back forty: "Don't mind me; I'm just looking for a cemetery," you shout with a friendly wave.

On a national scale, the United States Geological Survey (USGS) (www.usgs.gov) maintains a list of geographical features, including cemeteries, for every place in the Union. Its website has a form for searching that database, where you can look for all the cemeteries in a given county—or, more accurately put, all the cemeteries in the USGS database for any given county, and that is by no means all the cemeteries for any given county.

From where the USGS gets its data is somewhat of a mystery as well, though most of the Oregon data originally comes from an Oregon Department of Transportation (ODOT) study from 1978 by the aforementioned Dean Byrd (which led him to do his subsequent volume). Regardless of from where the USGS data comes, it's woefully inadequate, more so in some places than others, but always with both significant and minor cemeteries being ignored. In other words, it's a good place to start, but it's never wise to leave it at that.

Google Maps is currently the best site for cemetery searching. Google continually refines its product; information that was not there last year shows up this year. They've begun to routinely mark cemeteries on their maps. Google is consistently more accurate than the USGS, though by no means perfect, and the maps now show property lines as well. But they still miss major cemeteries as well as small ones. As their aerial photo resolution improves, it's easier and easier to spot cemeteries from the photographs. One should always compare the map to the aerial photo.

Once into Google Maps, there are other tricks for finding cemeteries. One is to search for roads named "Cemetery Road," which will turn up lists of roads that include the word "cemetery" within them, such as "Iman Cemetery Road." There are three cemeteries in Skamania County, Washington, for example, that are accessed by roads bearing their names and the word "cemetery," none of which are listed by the USGS but all of which show up in a Google Map search.

Searching Google Maps using the word "cemetery" and the name of any county and any state will bring up a map full of cemetery locations, some more real than others, but it's a good place to start. Again, it's always advisable to compare aerial photographs with maps.

Other sources include local history societies and genealogical groups, which occasionally compile cemetery lists, but they're highly erratic and rarely have adequate directions. "Find a Grave" lists a lot of cemeteries, but because it's not the organization's priority, few of them are mapped, and when I checked the location of three sample cemeteries, all three were incorrectly located. I've also run across personal cemetery websites that may list thousands of cemeteries but in the end adequately describe very few. In other words, grandiose expectations can lead to disappointing results.

What's definitely true is that while random driving around the countryside may whet one's appetite for cemeteries, it will never provide a full meal; they're too well hidden. Finding them takes sleuthing.

Unless, of course, you live in or visit this part of the Oregon Territory, where you can find cemeteries by visiting the Flickr site of Dead Man Talking (www.flickr.com/photos/deadmantalking).

Furthermore, through photos and text, I let you know what to expect once you get there. Every cemetery in this book is on that site.

In addition, most of the cemeteries profiled in Part III have been mapped in a custom Google Map, excerpted below:

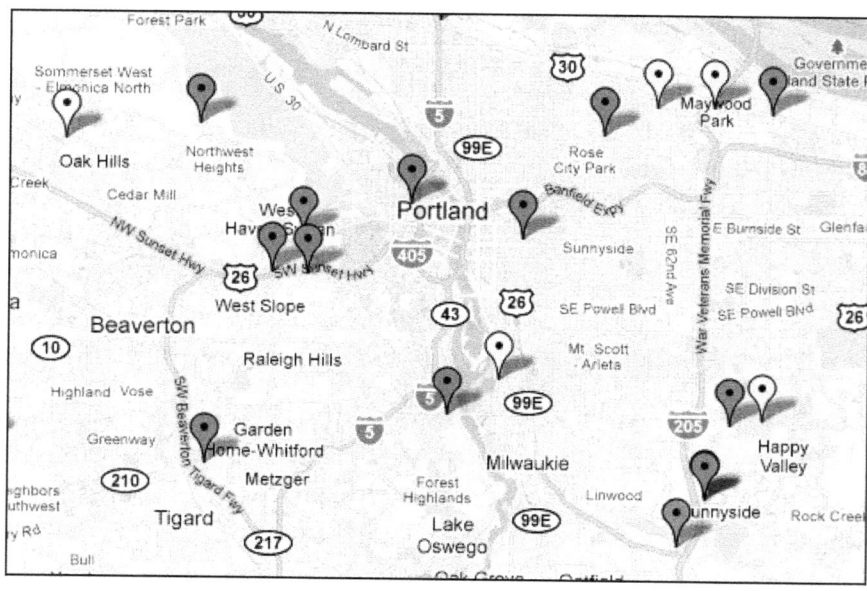

You can find a link at www.ashlandcreekpress.com/books/madasmist.html.

The Odd Fellows
and the Masons

Grass Valley Cemetery

The Odd Fellows and the Masons are still out there, but few of us remember what they used to mean to American life, how they dominated American society. We don't remember it because we never knew it. We only know they have halls here and there in some towns, halls as often falling to the wrecking ball as not. If it weren't for the Shriners' circus, most Americans would know nothing of the Masons.

Yet telltale traces of the pervasive influence that these fraternal organizations (known in England as "friendly societies"), the Odd Fellows and the Masons in particular, had on American life are scattered throughout the landscape: the cemeteries. As always, cemeteries are the archaeologist's treasure trove, and in this case the very names of the cemeteries leave a memory of a time when fraternal organizations played a central role in our culture. It was a time when people were trusting their eternity to their chosen fraternity, something previously reserved for the church. How and why this transformation occurred and why it as quickly disappeared are enduring mysteries. There are volumes written about fraternal organizations, but they rarely get covered in high school civics. Their place in our history is largely forgotten, and were it not for the halls and cemeteries, the knowledge of their very existence would soon vanish.

Nestucca Valley Cemetery

Both Masons and Odd Fellows are, as their names would suggest, evolutions of ancient trade guilds that spread from Europe to America and were going particularly strong at the time of the American Revolution. Freemasons were, arguably, of higher status than Odd Fellows, but in their prime, the Odd Fellows easily numerically outstripped the Masons, which is reflected in the number of cemeteries they provided. In the Dead Man Talking Oregon Territory database, Odd Fellow cemeteries outnumber Masonic cemeteries almost two to one.

(In days of yore, trades were divided up by rank, with masters being at the top. Independent tradesmen [they were, invariably, male] not under the direct tutelage of a master, i.e., neither apprentice nor journeyman, were referred to as "fellows." Often in smaller towns there weren't enough members of a given trade to form its own local guild, so these independent fellows would sometimes join together and form their own guild of mishmash professions, hence the name Odd Fellows.)

Needless to say, trade unions of any stripe have often been looked on with a jaundiced eye by the powers that be, as proletarian associations evoke political suspicion. Guilds were formed to provide protection of one's craft in the marketplace, both by setting standards and providing economic safeguards for its members. It's in the latter duty that the Odd Fellows have shined in American life.

By the nature of the Odd Fellows being a collection of people from diverse crafts, it could never have the role of setting professional standards, so that aspect of guild fellowship was never a burden; they could concentrate on fiscal protection for their members, which is reflected in their mission statement: "To visit the sick, relieve the distressed, bury the dead and educate the orphan."

It was their boast that "no Odd Fellow or Odd Fellow's dependent *ever becomes a public charge*" (emphasis theirs, from Ira Wolfe's 1927 book *Album of Odd Fellows Homes*).

Harrisburg IOOF Cemetery

For a while, at least, they took those responsibilities very seriously. By 1927, the Odd Fellows were operating sixty-two "homes" across America, an inspired combination of caring for old, indigent members under the same roof as an orphanage, while using the accumulated wisdom and energy to operate a farm. It's a model to which we could well return.

They did not, though, surround their homes with cemeteries. For that they selected other locations. Unfortunately, I've yet to find a history of their cemetery involvement. Their website doesn't mention cemeteries, but it doesn't mention the old homes, either. Advancing social legislation, especially that of the New Deal, put the kibosh on the Odd Fellows' communal philanthropy. It may have been better for the country, but not necessarily for the Odd Fellows.

For the most part, the IOOF (Independent Order of Odd Fellows) has given up the cemetery business. I have no idea when the last Odd Fellow cemetery was founded, but I'd vote for prior to mid-twentieth century. Some are still maintained by IOOF chapters, but the majority have long since been handed over to other authorities, often with a name change that disguises their origins. Likewise with the Masons.

(For the record: An analysis of a 670-cemetery Oregon Territory database returned fifty-one Odd Fellow cemeteries versus twenty-six Masonic. The same survey recorded fifty-five Catholic cemeteries and seventy-two with ties to other Christian religions. Nine were Jewish. Probably, the bulk of the remaining were Donation Land Claim cemeteries created by the claim holder and subsequently taken over by a civic authority. A few were started by municipal authorities themselves, something unheard of today. More recent cemeteries have been commercial endeavors.)

But the remnant in name or history of a cemetery with IOOF affiliation isn't just a record of the importance of those institutions in American life; their locations also mark previous prosperity. Many a disappearing community in Oregon that can no longer muster a gas station, much less a lodge hall, once had an Odd Fellows cemetery. If the town was really important, it might have a Masonic cemetery as well.

In Fossil, for example—population 470—the Odd Fellow and Masonic cemeteries are themselves fossils, as much as the bones that pop out of the ground. Their very presence testifies to the former glory of this rural wayside, a theme repeated over the entire state.

How this compares with the rest of the country, I have no idea. IOOF and Masonic cemeteries blanket the nation, but what percentage of them were founded by fraternal orders is unknown. In the Oregon Territory, the IOOF was connected with roughly 7.6 percent of its cemeteries. The Masons come in at 3.9 percent. Nobody's counting the rest of the country. In the end, the Odd Fellows weren't so odd after all. They simply disappeared.

Lorane IOOF Cemetery

Woodmen of the World

IOOF Cemetery, The Dalles

No one forgets their first Woodmen of the World (WOW) faux stump headstone. A cemetery novice tells you in an excited voice of an incredible find he or she made in a small cemetery near home. Yep, WOW. The stump—fallen tree and all that—is a traditional symbol of death and has been used informally both here and in Europe for a long time, but the Woodmen of the World, in its program of providing tombstones for its members, kicked the image into high gear.

Granite Hill Cemetery, Grants Pass

Information on WOW headstones is hard to come by; I don't think there's been a book about them yet (authors take note). Faux stumps were not the only motif the WOW used, but they were definitely the most notable. What's particularly notable is that, despite their popularity and ubiquity, as far as I can tell each one is unique.

My understanding is that orders and drawings were sent to local craftsmen to execute the monuments, who in turn interpreted the drawings as they saw fit. Whatever the cause, the result has been a windfall of unique monuments across the entire country.

Lone Fir Cemetery, Portland

The Woodmen of the World still exist—they'd be happy to sell you some insurance—but their policies, alas, no longer come with a tombstone. It's a pity, but we'll just have to suffer through. Carve your own.

Brownsville Pioneer Cemetery, Bellfountain

The Lord Is My Cowboy

Camp Polk Cemetery, Sisters

There is, arguably, no American image (Uncle Sam notwithstanding) more iconic than that of the cowboy. Clint Eastwood and John Wayne, for good or ill, have shaped the world's vision of America as much or more than anybody. I suspect one might find a cowboy image engraved on a tombstone anywhere in the United States, but the legitimacy of the image doesn't manifest itself until you reach the Great Plains and the West. Out here, the cowboy still exists and still looks pretty much like he (usually a he) always did, except that you're as apt to find him on an ATV or a pickup as on a horse. Without flogging a dead horse too much, I must point out that these engravings are all recent. We've had cowboys here for 150 years, but you'd never know it by gravestone markers; as far as they're concerned, cowboys have just arrived.

Alpine Cemetery, Alpine

Several of Oregon's most distinctive grave markers have a cowboy theme. The cowboy is universally recognized by his hat and his horse. An entire accompaniment of clothing, gear, and tack go along with the hat and horse, but those two elements are iconic and are almost always present.

IOOF #110 Cemetery, Fossil

The image of the cowboy is often paired with an image of his workplace: the vast Western landscape. To the extent that all people are molded by their surroundings, the dramatic landforms of the West are constantly part of its self-image. It's why so many of us had no choice but to follow the allure and climb aboard the Oregon Trail. The reproduction of the landscape on tombstones is faithful enough to local conditions that one can often get a good idea of location from the simple sketches available.

Saint Joseph Cemetery, Condon

Working details of a cowboy's life are often found among the etchings, including the kind of stock being tended. I have one etching of a horse leading a pack train, and several of bucking broncs. Dogs are often depicted as well, not only as companions but among the working images; they're integral to stock management in the Oregon Territory. The cowboy is often accompanied by a cowgirl, most assuredly his wife.

I've probably gotten into as much trouble in Oregon over what to call cowboys as I have over anything else. The first time was at a communal dinner table in French Glen, where it was explained to me by a ranch-hand that they were "buckaroos," thank you, "not cowboys." Later I had an equally impassioned Native American explain to me that her people were "Indian cowboys, not common buckaroos." Ignorance is neither an excuse nor blissful.

Religion isn't strongly represented in combination with cowboys, although it does crop up sporadically, one of my favorites being an etching of a cowboy riding herd on a mixed bunch of cows and calves, and carrying the epitaph, "The Lord is my shepherd." There's a certain irony in a cowboy surrendering himself to a sheep-herder.

Some of the most poignant and touching markers are ones with no human image at all. How can one not love a Cowboy Pastor, knowing that he's "Loved By God & Family"?

Or how can one not be moved by a single spur imbedded in cement or by the ubiquitous coil of rope? Many an old cowboy boot has found its final resting place in a graveyard as well. For poignancy it's hard to top a simple concrete marker in the eclectic Camp Polk Cemetery, one with plastic lettering pressed into cement and an outlined sketch of a hat. No name, just the declaration: "Cowboy/ 19 yrs/ Horse Kicked."

Epitaphs

A Word Before You Go

Le der nier cri de coeur

Who wrote the epitaph? It's not always easy to tell. Tombstones and epitaphs are not unlike historical markers alongside the highway. The chosen few words are tantalizing, as if you're given a snapshot of someone but only allowed to see a lock of hair and some buttons. You're to fill in the rest with your imagination. You can be sure that, whatever is written on a tombstone, it's not about that person. No matter who wrote it, it's a fictionalized sketch of how that person wanted to be presented or how someone wanted him or her remembered. It's not them.

It's about dreams.

The crushing paradox is that life is given meaning through death. In eternity, all things are meaningless; the inexorable mill of time grinds everything to a fine powder. There is no good or evil, no beginning or end. There are only infinite monkeys on infinite typewriters typing infinite Shakespeares. But we are not given infinity. We are given but one opportunity to be here now. That's why it's so very important to not blow it. We have only one chance. This is it.

We may hope, and we may sincerely believe, that somehow we continue on, but in our heart of hearts, when it's time to go, we want one last word with the people we're leaving because, no matter what we wish for, we know that, if nothing else, we were here. We had our life. It was good or bad by itself. There may or may not be an afterlife to judge us, but life will continue on. People will read our tombstones. If judgment is to be made, it will be made here.

Which is why the epitaph is chosen with such care. Because in the end, the person to whom one is speaking is not his or her best friend or lover or mother but rather the stranger a hundred years hence. For that, we invented cemeteries.

Cemeteries are not just places to store dead bodies. If that's all we wanted, volcanoes would do just fine. Not every society has cemeteries, but all societies have ways of honoring their dead, even if that means bringing the bones home and storing them on a shelf. One doesn't have to believe in an afterlife to want to communicate with the departed, and it seems to work best if we set aside a special place for it. It's not a power inherent in a place but one we give it—Descartes writ large: To think a place sanctified makes it so.

Cemeteries are those places in our society where we visit with the past. When we go there, we conjure the spirits to wander the gravestones with us. We are never alone. One by one, the dead rise before us and speak in voices half-shredded by moonlight. Voices so soft we have to bend close to the grave and read what they say. Epitaphs. A hundred years later, they're still talking to us. The last whisper.

There is no guarantee that cemeteries will be with us forever. Like the Postal Service—something one can't imagine life without—their time may be passing. Despite the recent flowering of funerary arts, cremation threatens to send this ancient tradition up in smoke. We may end up being one of those societies that forgoes cemeteries. They may become too expensive to maintain. Already in many European countries, one only rents cemetery space. After one's lease is up, the bones are dumped in a common ossuary.

Cremation does not necessarily mean no burial, no cemetery. Cemeteries are frantically trying to provide proper space for cremains, but the economics of keeping them at home or scattering them are compelling. Furthermore, there's a strong emotional compulsion to have one's ashes scattered at a particularly meaningful place. Both forces operate to the detriment of cemeteries. Little wonder that cemeteries such as Portland's Lone Fir have sold off major land holdings. On the other hand, many small rural cemeteries are reaching capacity. Maintaining them will always be a community expense. Unless, of course, they're allowed to disappear.

Perhaps there will always be cultural pressures to maintain cemeteries. Some groupings, some ethos, don't allow for cremation. They hold to standards that may not be relaxed for a long time. Others may eschew cremation for aesthetic principles. But what is already the case, and becoming more so, is that fewer and fewer people, both proportionally and in real numbers, are choosing traditional burial with headstones. The art of the epitaph is wilting.

Will it be replaced by the Internet? No memorial site on the Internet will convey the same message that an epitaph chiseled into rock can. The medium is definitely part of the message, if for no other reason than an epitaph, somewhat like a haiku, is constrained in how long it can be. The longest never run more than a paragraph or a stanza or two. One has to distill one's essence into an epitaph. It's a delicate art. Sites on the web have no space limitations. They can go on forever. Furthermore, they are usually interactive, so the site can continue growing, theoretically, forever. Or until the electronic shock wave from some future war wipes the Internet from the face of the earth. Once that happens, the old-fashioned, chiseled-in-stone epitaphs will be all that are left.

~

I once attended an international bakers' convention in Las Vegas. It's a quadrennial event that attracts vendors and customers from around the world. It was held in a cavernous hall the size of many football fields, inside which purveyors had built gigantic oven systems four stories high. The salesmen—and they were usually men—flitted from language to language like warblers in a berry bush. They would run off a list of facts in English, make a quick aside to a customer in Japanese, and schedule a meeting in Arabic, all without taking a breath. But when it came to counting money, they invariably reverted to their native language. Some things are too important to leave to simple error.

Likewise epitaphs. Take a stroll through almost any American cemetery—pioneer cemeteries tend to work well—and read the epitaphs. Chances are pretty good that soon you'll run into ones written in German or Norwegian or French. In some places they'll be in Chinese or Japanese or Russian. Chances are that most of those people lived in and dealt with America for years and years before passing, that they have children and grandchildren who still live in America. Yet their epitaphs are in foreign tongues. Because the heart only speaks in one's native language, an epitaph is too important to leave to simple error.

General Notes:

[ ] Brackets: Brackets mean I said it, not the stone.

Punctuation and spelling: I leave them as I see them. I correct nothing. The temptation is to "clean up" the epitaphs, insert those errant apostrophes, but who am I to tamper with folk art? While it's customary to point out uncorrected errors by following them in brackets with the word sic, meaning as written, I have elected to not follow that practice and let the epitaphs come through unadorned. The bereaved don't need English teachers.

Where famous quotations are recognizable, I've noted their original sources [in brackets] if the epitaph does not.

The epitaphs are drawn from the entire Oregon Territory database, not just Oregon cemeteries.

Die Laughing

Who knew that dying could be so much fun? My wife won't let me, but my choice of epitaph would be, "Your name here."

Anon
Lone Fir Cemetery

> *This wasn't in my schedule book*

Anon
Condon Cemetery

> *Do not disturb*
> *Taking a nap*

Anon
Coles Valley Cemetery

> *Blessed are those who clean up*

Anon
LONG CREEK CEMETERY

> *Here lies a town girl who became*
> > *a ranchers wife and right hand*
> *A passionate mother. A lover of*
> > *family*
> *A promoter of womens education*
> > *and a shopper*
> *Knew I would be asked*
> > *Yes Honey I will get the gate*

Fred Barnard (1918–1993)
RIDGEFIELD CEMETERY

> *I have made many trades in my life,*
> *But I think I went in the hole on this one.*

Theodore (1931–2008) & Nedine (1932–1997) Barnhouse
MITCHELL CEMETERY

> *Raised four beautiful daughters*
> *with only one bathroom and*
> *still there was love*

Herman (d. 1986) & Agnes (d. 1992) Baxter
MT CALVARY CATHOLIC CEMETERY

> [his] *On the highway to heaven*
> [hers] *Drive like hell and you'll get there*

Mathew Beecher (1952–2001)
TUALATIN PLAINS PRESBYTERIAN CEMETERY

> *Always go to other people's funerals. Otherwise they won't go to yours.*
> *Yogi Berra*

Robin Boon (1913–2004)
AUMSVILLE CEMETERY

> *With the Lord, enjoying a good cup of Yuban*

Gertie Bunnell (1912–1983)
ESTACADA IOOF CEMETERY

> *Who should live so long?*

Rachael Burchard (1921–2004)
SOUTH YAMHIL CEMETERY

> *I wouldn't miss my only chance*
> *For omnipotent enlightenment*

Charlo Dick (1953–2006)
BRAINARD CEMETERY

> *All dressed up and no place to go*

Richard (1940–2005) & Colleen (b. 1941) Dohrn
OCEAN VIEW CEMETERY

> *Life is uncertain. Eat dessert first.*
> [Original quote from the writer Ernestine Ulmer]

Jim Everts (1940–1999)
AUMSVILLE CEMETERY

> *Tree hugger*
> *"left town" 1999*

Claude (b. 1922) & Frances (1923–1998) Friend
SCOTTSBURG CEMETERY

> *Tried to leave the woodpile a little higher than we found it.*

Eino Kangas (1932–1994)
UNION CEMETERY (UNION)

> *Plop plop*
> *fizz fizz*
> *Oh what a relief it is*

Seymour (d. 1990) & Edith (d. 1994) Lehman
HAVURAH SHALOM CEMETERY

> [his] *You're on your own*
> [hers] *Not any more*

Barbara Lockwood (1944–2007)
JOSEPH CEMETERY

> *Barbara stopped here*

Mildred Long (1931–1993)
CLIFFSIDE CEMETERY

> *Gone for the bait*

Esther Lyon (1914–2002)
SILVERTON CEMETERY

> *Well, I'm only curious*

Alma Markee (d. 1984)
SAINT MARY CATHOLIC CEMETERY

> *Death is a journey*
> *And you know how I like to travel*

Gloria Martin (1926–2002)
ROBERT BIRD CEMETERY

> *I told you I was sick*

Glen Myers (1980–1999)
FAIRVIEW CEMETERY

> *Where the sidewalk ends…*
> *True life begins.*
> *"What the hell…?"*

Edward Nielsen (1961–1997)
BAY CENTER CEMETERY

> *On the edge of passing days*
> *I rather thought Paradise would be like a library*

Times Arrow
Decendant of Chief Huckswelt
WEELAPA TRIBE OF THE CHINOOK'S

> *Death will always come out of season*

Mary Ogden (1920–2000)
ODD FELLOWS CEMETERY (DAYTON)

> *It's your mother*

Patricia (1928–2003)
LONE OAK CEMETERY

> *I'd rather be shopping at Nordstroms*

Porter Payne (1921–2005)
UNION CEMETERY (UNION)

> *I'm going to miss me*

Jan Peckham (1946–1999)
UNION CEMETERY (CEDAR MILLS)

> *It's always something*

Kristie Pergin (1976–1992)
WOODVILLE CEMETERY

> *The phone must be for you*
> *Smile*

Edith Porter (d. 2000)
KESSER ISRAEL CEMETERY

> *I have three wonderful sons, It's too bad you couldn't keep me a little longer.*

Stan Shattuck
IOOF Cemetery (Coburg)

> *Sam Shattuck was*
> *hung by mistake*

Alice Spear (1923–1989)
Coos River Cemetery

> *They said she was too different*
> *and she wrote too many tunes*

James Staven
Pleasant View Cemetery

> *Excavating on higher ground*

Dawn Vocé (1954–2004)
Stearns Cemetery

> *You put your right foot in*

Timothy Wilke (1973–2004)
Finley–Sunset Hills Cemetery

> *Don't cry Mom*
> *I'm fine*
> *It's only money*

David Williams (d. 1922)
PHILLIPS CEMETERY

For God, Country, and Old Wazzu

Say Again

The line between humorous epitaphs and enigmas can be thin. Sometimes one just doesn't know what was intended. The sheer number of quizzical epitaphs makes me want to rap on the tombstone with a pebble and ask, "Excuse me, would you repeat that?"

Anon
LEWIS AND CLARK CEMETERY

A fine young man ahead of us on the trail

Ruth "Penny" Arnold (1917–1998)
MOUNT PLEASANT CEMETERY

She was a webel

Bill (1929–2001)
MOON CREEK CEMETERY

> *Don't*
> *slam the doors*
> [Under an etching of a 1960s convertible]

John Crecelius (1936–2002)
WILLAMETTE NATIONAL CEMETERY

> *He loved his*
> *Dog Loki*

Drake (1934–2000)
JACKSONVILLE CEMETERY

> *Waiting for summer*

William Druery
ODD FELLOWS CEMETERY (DAYTON)

> *I once had a girlfriend like that*

Fenton Galer (b. 1929)
HOPEWELL CEMETERY

> *Be wise and Fentonize*

William Gilmore (1839–1937)
COOS RIVER CEMETERY

>   *The inheriet laws*
>   *matter is the crea-*
>   *tor of the universe*

Benjamin Grant (1983–2005)
ROCK POINT/GOLD HILL IOOF CEMETERY

>   *Sorry Guys, I had to bounce late.*

Micah Green (1985–2001)
GETHSEMANI CEMETERY

>   *I see dumb people*

Bruce Hayward (1952–1996)
JACKSONVILLE

>   *Got Jets!*
>   [Under an engraving of a pig adorned with a flower collar and standing atop a golf tee]

Edwin Herzog
EAGLE POINT NATIONAL CEMETERY

>   *Have you heard*
>   *the one about*

Alice Johnson (1914–1994)
MOUNTAINSIDE CEMETERY

> *I'm the boss*

Vernon Justen (1948–2003)
BUCK HOLLOW CEMETERY

> *There is no bush*
> *Too hard to push*

Richard Kariola (1937–2006)
BUNKER HILL CEMETERY

> *We love you, enjoy your pie.*

Sviatoslav Kudearoff (1930–1992)
MOUNT VERNON CEMETERY

> *Never satisfied—will be back*

William Lamb
SACRED HEART CEMETERY

> *Nothing stupid*

Nancy Lander (1868–1887)
CANYON HILL CEMETERY

>   *A woman is like the snow that falls upon the river,*
>   *White for a moment, and gone forever.*

Claire Luce (1923–1971)
FORT HARNEY CEMETERY

>   *Wife of Henry Luce III*
>   *Mother of Kenneth D. O'Sullivan*
>   *William M. Hurt and James H. Hurt*
>
>   *The truth shall*
>   *Make you free*
>
>   *Don't coddle me into the grave. I'm*
>   *Going to march into it. I'm a man,*
>   *After all.*

David Merrifield (1951–2003)
WILLAMETTE NATIONAL CEMETERY

>   *There is no spoon*

Kenneth Newton (1935–1995)
WESTSIDE CEMETERY

>   *Stay in the buggy*

Maxine Niebling (b. 1932)
FOREST LAWN CEMETERY

>*There once was a*
>*girl from Kelso...*

Violet Olson (1915–2005)
SKYLINE MEMORIAL CEMETERY

>*Why seek the living here*

Charles Reynold (1867–1914)
ZION MEMORIAL CEMETERY

>*I pray thee cease they counsel*

Malcolm Rogers (1928–1990)
ADAMS CEMETERY

>*Finished with engines*

Richard Roskopf (1936–1994)
FINLEY–SUNSET HILLS CEMETERY

>*You never know boys...*

Kay Shineflug (1939–1998)
EUREKA CEMETERY

>*Excuse me...*

Thomas Teel (1927–2002)
UNION POINT CEMETERY

> *Break, Air Duck.*

Shad Tyler
ROCK POINT/GOLD HILL IOOF CEMETERY

> *Shadrack*
> *Because I can*

Trudy Tyler (1949–2006)
ROCK POINT/GOLD HILL IOOF CEMETERY

> *Care authority*

Steven Weathers (1957–2005)
ANTIOCH CEMETERY

> *I can only imagine*

C. G. Wenders (d. 1857)
ROCK CREEK CEMETERY

> *Shortly before his death a white dove sat on the window sill of his father's sleeping room in Pennsylvania*

The Full Measure

Of all the epitaphs, arguably the most satisfying are those that describe, in the simplest of sketches, the essence of a life lived full, from detailed descriptions of family and work to those that exalt in having been present. Sometimes it is one facet of a life that resonates through the ages; other times it is the graceful span of its arc. For some, it truly may be a good day to die.

Anon
HUDSON CEMETERY

> *U.S.M.C. 1945–49 572555*
> *I.L.W.V. Local 21*
> *Crew member*
> *Kindergarten Cop*
> *Point Break*
> *Teenage Mutant Ninja III*
> *Father of Consuelo, Ramona, Cody*

Jerry Bogle (1936–2004)
KINDER CEMETERY

> *Started many AA meetings*
> *Saved many lives*

E Bristow (1788–1872)
PLEASANT HILL CEMETERY

> *A pioneer:*
> *The first settler in Lane Co. 1846*
>
> *A man's life is his monument*
> *His deeds are the inscription*

Grace Byrnes (b. 1921)
COVE CEMETERY

> *World War II B-17 Inspector*

Joseph Champion (1823–1891)
TILLAMOOK IOOF CEMETERY

> *The first white settler, the first county clerk, and taught the first school in Tillamook County.*
>
> *Joseph C. Champion lived at Kechis Point, on Tillamook Bay, April 1, 1851, having come from Astoria in a whale boat with two companions, who returned with the boat the next day. He lived in a hollow spruce tree, which he called his castle for the first three months.*

Benjamin Deutsch (1912–1994)
HAVURAH SHALOM CEMETERY

> *Pioneered the introduction*
> *of pastrami into the*
> *United States and Jewish culture*

Frank Ellis (1905–1966)
ROSE CITY CEMETERY

> *King of the Gypsies*

Guy Gravlin (1886–1955)
PIONEER MASONIC CEMETERY (GRANTS PASS)

> *Proprietor of Grants*
> *Pass last livery stable*

Ed Hart (1905–1997)
AMERICAN LEGION CEMETERY

> *Born Edward L. Hart*
> *in Oregon March 18, 1905*
> *Came to Twin Rocks in 1912*
> *Enjoyed the lumber Merchant*
> *Marine and cheese industries*
> *And everything God made*
> *Died Wheeler Oct. 18, 1997*

Samuel and Huldah (1823–1907) Colver
PHOENIX PIONEER CEMETERY

> *In*
> *Memory of*
> *Samuel and Huldah*
> *Colver*
> *Pioneers of 1850 who located*
> *this Donation Claim in 1851*
> *amid hostile Indians*
> *and who have seen*
> *the wilderness*
> *blossom*
> *as the*
> *rose*

Desire Griffin (1806–1884)
MASONIC CEMETERY (HILLSBORO)

> *Missionary to native tribes, 1839*
> *First white woman in*
> *Tualatin settlement, July, 1841.*
> *First white mother in same, Nov. 8, 1842*
> *Continued as helping missionary*
> *Till death, Sept. 22, 1884, in her 80th yr.*

Obediah Hines (1805–1853)
LEE MISSION CEMETERY

> *Drowned in Snake River west of Boise, Idaho, en*
> *route to Oregon with his family and his brothers' families*

Felix Iman (1828–1902)
IMAN CEMETERY

> Born DeKalb Co., Mo.
> Arrived at Cascades by ox team in 1852
> Married Margaret Windsor 1853
> 1854 built & owned steamer "Wasco"
> 1855 donation land claim of 323 acres
> 1858 worked on upper Cascades block house
> Built & owned 2 sawmills
> Built 1st school. For short time saloon owner.

Margaret Iman (1834–1924)
IMAN CEMETERY

> Born at Tippecanoe Co., Ind.
> 1852 Missouri to The Dalles on horse back
> Carried motherless babe 500 miles
> Took raft downriver to Cascades
> 1853 met and married Felix G. Iman
> Survived Indian War of Mar. 26, 1856
> Indians burned home
> Had 16 children, 9 boys, 7 girls

James Leabo (1823–1898)
MULTNOMAH PARK CEMETERY

> Was a pioneer of 1846, served in the
> Cayuse Indian War, and was one of the
> party who rescued the women and chil-
> dren who were taken prisoners by
> the Indians at the Whitman Massacre, which
> took place in the fall of 1847.

David Lenox (1807–1873)
WEST UNION BAPTIST CEMETERY

> *Captain of first wagon train*
> *to cross*
> *Rocky Mountains 1843*

Alton Lounsbury (1939–2006)
ROSEBURG NATIONAL CEMETERY

> *Just an old car painter*

Ralph Martin (1933–2005)
ROSEBURG NATIONAL CEMETERY

> *Fisherman skydiver cook*
> *71 and 420 friendly*

F. X. Matthieu (1819–1914)
BUTTEVILLE CEMETERY

> *Last survivor of the 52 persons that formed the first civil*
> *government west of the Rockies on May 2, 1843*

Frank McCully (1859–1939)
OLD CHIEF JOSEPH GRAVE SITE

> *Frank David McCully*
> *the Father of Wallowa County*
> *was buried in this Indian cemetery because of long*
> *friendship with Chief Joseph and his people.*

Peter Mcintosh (1861–1940)
HILLS CEMETERY

> *Father of the cheese industry in the Oregon Country*

Peter Skene Ogden (1794–1854)
MOUNTAIN VIEW CEMETERY (OREGON CITY)

> *Born in Quebec*
> *Died at Oregon City*
> *Fur trader and explorer*
> *in Old Oregon*
> *Arrived Columbia River 1818*
> *Clerk of North West Company*
> *Chief Factor Hudson's Bay*
> *Company at Fort Vancouver*
> *Rescued Survivors of*
> *Whitman massacre 1847*

Anna Pittman (1803–1838)
LEE MISSION CEMETERY

> *Beneath this sod*
> *The first ever broken in Oregon*
> *For the reception of a*
> *White mother and child*
> *Lies the remains of*
> *Anna Maria Pittman*
> *First wife of*
> *Rev. Jason Lee*
> *And their infant son*
> *She sailed from New York in July 1836*
> *Landed in Oregon June 1837*
> *Was married July 15, 1837*
> *And died*
> *June 26, 1838*

Frank Riddle
CHIEF SCHONCHIN CEMETERY

> *In memory of*
> *Frank Tazewell Riddle*
> *Native of Kentucky*
>
> *Miner, rancher, frontiersman,*
> *guide and interpreter during*
> *the Modoc War, 1872–1873*
>
> *Beloved husband of Winema*
>
> *Dedicated by*
> *Klamath County Historical Society*
> *October 1985*

Schonchin
CHIEF SCHONCHIN CEMETERY

> *Schonchin*
> *Head Chief of the Modocs*
>
> *His courageous loyalty to*
> *his treaty obligations*
> *kept the bulk of his tribe*
> *from the warpath and*
> *saved the Klamath settlements*
> *1872–3*
> *Marker erected by*
> *Eulalona Chapter, D.A.R.*
> *1932*

Thomas Shadden (1809–1894)
MASONIC CEMETERY (MCMINNVILLE)

> *Pioneer of 1842. Signer of the "Wolves Letter."*
> *Took his family to California with Lansford Hastings in 1843.*
> *Made his fortune during the gold rush of 1849.*
> *Brought his family back to Oregon in 1850.*
> *This cemetery is part of his original farm.*
> *His built his home of Baker Creek Road in 1859.*
> *It is still standing after nearly 150 years.*

Rachel Spalding (1808–1880)
MASONIC CEMETERY (HILLSBORO)

> *with her husband, Rev. H. H. Spalding*
> *was successful in modest*
> *but enduring labors among*
> *Native Tribes*
>
> *Let daughters of Oregon share the work*
> *and the Eternal rest*

Martha Sumner-Shadden (1814–1899)
MASONIC CEMETERY (MCMINNVILLE)

> *Pioneer of 1842 - mother of 13, including the first white child*
> *Born in California to a family that crossed the plains.*

Joseph Turnidge (1819–1857)
MILLER CEMETERY (MILLERSBURG)

> *First circuit rider in this area*
> *Emigrated to Oregon from Missouri in 1846*
> *on the first wagon train up the treacherous*
> *Southern Oregon route. Took a land claim on*
> *the Santiam. Organized the first churches of any*
> *faith in the valley. "Elder Joe," preacher, singer,*
> *farmer, father, faithfully rode circuit through*
> *rain, sickness and danger.*
>   *To honor his memory this memorial*
> *is erected by the Turnidge Clan*
>   *1973*

Leonard White (1835–1878)
LONE FIR CEMETERY

> *A pioneer of the 40s*
> *Sometimes called*
> *Father of Oregon Waters*

Winema
CHIEF SCHONCHIN CEMETERY

> *In memory of*
> *Winema, Modoc heroine*
> *Interpreter for Peace Commission*
> *Pensioned by Congress for courageous*
> *and loyal service — Modoc War, 1872–3*
>
> *Presented by Winema Chapter*
> *Placed by Eulalona Chapter*
> *Daughters of the American Revolution*
> *May 30, 1932*

OLD SOLDIERS DO DIE

One has to draw a line somewhere. There are no markers more plentiful than military markers, thanks to a generous government allowance covering their cost, and there are any number of ways they could be analyzed, not the least of which would be military occupations. This list is restricted to a handful of more unusual veterans' tombstones found in Oregon Territory cemeteries.

John Holman (1787–1861)
MASONIC CEMETERY (MCMINNVILLE)

> *Veteran of War of 1812*
> *Son of veteran of American Revolution*
> *Oregon pioneer 1843*

John Parkhill (1816–1910)
LONE FIR CEMETERY

> *A soldier in the Seminole War of 1837*
> *The Mexican War of 1846*
> *An Indian War veteran*

> *Cayuse War 1855*
> *also*
> *A volunteer fireman*
> *City of Portland, Oregon*
> *A friend to all*

Denton Rees (1907–1977)
WILLAMETTE NATIONAL CEMETERY

> *31st Infantry*
> *Bataan survivor*

Eugenia Rett-Wilczkowiak (1921–1983)
DANISH CEMETERY

> *Member Polish Underground Home Army*
> *Warsaw Uprising 1943*
> *Honor: Bronze Cross of Merit with Swords*
> *World War II 1939–1944*
> *Beloved*
> *Sister, Wife, Mother, Grandmother*

Merlin Ringering (b. 1922)
ROBERT BIRD CEMETERY

> *Gunners mate Third class M. H. Ringering was a 5 inch 38 caliber anti air craft specialist. In charge of a eleven man crew. In the Armed Guard he sailed to New Caledonia, Espiritu Santos, Samoa, Eniwetok, Solomon Island. Guadacanal, Saipan and Honolulu. On board a C2 cargo vessel anchored in Okinawa*

harbor near the city of Naha in the spring of 1945 he and his crew stayed in their gun tub 22 days and nights shooting down Japanese suicide planes coming in at all hours. 6 ships were sunk in the harbor, but his load of bombs, heavy equipment and barrels of gasoline were saved. His last voyage was aboard a T2 tanker with a cargo of B52 aircraft fuel sailing to the island of Tinian where the atomic bomb took off from.

John Smith (1839–1912)
COVE CEMETERY

> *Veteran of Battle*
> *of Nashville Tenn*
> *under Col. Grigsby*

Txhia Cha (1955–1995)
GETHSEMANI CATHOLIC CEMETERY

> *CIA scout for Free Laos*
> *American citizen*

D. C. A. Venville (1881–1900)
MILWAUKIE PIONEER CEMETERY

> *D. C. A.*
> *Venville*
> *Born*
> *Jan. 8, 1881*
> *Who was wounded*
> *and captured with*

Lieut. Gilmore
of the U. S. Navy, on
April 12, 1899
at Baler, Luzon, P. I.
and was treacher-
ously murdered
by order of Novicio,
an Insurgent Genl.
some time after
Feb. 20, 1990.

We know not where
his body lies,
but his spirit is
with God.

Steven Watson (Lieut.) (1828–1864)
VANCOUVER BARRACKS CEMETERY

> *Killed in battle with the Snake*
> *Indians xxx Crooked River, Ogn.*
> *May 13, 1864*

Xiong Pao Lee (1930–2003)
COLUMBIA MEMORIAL CEMETERY

> *Served in the*
> *Special Guerilla Units (SGU)*
> *Royal Armed Forces (FAR)*
> *in Laos from 1960 to 1975*
> *in the Vietnam War*

Borrowed Memories

The range of quotes, attributed or otherwise, found on tombstones is astounding. My sense is that (except in the case of small children) due to the familiar and intimate nature of quoted epitaphs, they are usually chosen by the interred.

Anon
Howell Prairie Cemetery

> *She has wandered into an unknown land and left us dreaming, how very fair it needs must be since she lingers there.*
> [Excerpt from a longer piece, seemingly without authorship, found often on tombstones]

Anon
Woodville Cemetery

> *The best and most beautiful things in the world cannot be seen or even touched. They must be felt with the heart.*
>   *Helen Keller*

Doreen Allen (1923–1997)
MOTHER JOSEPH CATHOLIC CEMETERY

> *She is handsome, she is pretty*
> *She is the belle of Belfast city*
> [Traditional Irish song]

George (1892–1982) & Laura (1892–1893) Appel
DAMASCUS CEMETERY

> *Blessed be the tie that binds*
> [Lyrics by John Fawcett 1740–1817]

James (1928–2000) & Dorothy (b. 1930) Ashbaugh
RIVER VIEW CEMETERY

> *Two roads diverged in a wood, and*
> *I took the one less traveled by,*
> *And that made all the difference.*
>   *Robert Frost*

Russell Bender
MOUNT JEFFERSON MEMORIAL PARK

> *"Away"*
>
> *I can not say & I will not*
> *Say that he is dead —*
> *He is just away.*

With a cheery smile & a wave of
The hand,
He has wandered into an unknown
Land.
           James Whitcomb Riley

Rosie (1933–1999) & Don (b. 1930) Bray
SPRING VALLEY PRESBYTERIAN CEMETERY

We built a sweet little nest, somewhere out in the west,
and let the rest of the world go by
[1919 Ernest Ball & J. Keirn Brennan song:
"Out there beneath a kindly sky
We'll build a sweet little nest somewhere in the west
And let the rest of the world go by."]

Orren Cary (1844–1874)
FRANKLIN BUTTE CEMETERY

Shed not for her the bitter tear,
Nor give the heart to vain regret;
'Tis but the casket that lies here,
The gem that filled it sparkles yet.
[Belle Starr was buried on her ranch (1889) with a marble headstone on which was engraved a bell, her horse, a star and this epitaph supposedly written by her daughter, Pearl. You'll note the date of Ms. Cary's death. I suspect that the epitaph associated with Belle Starr was a chapbook poem and not an original of her daughter.]

Melvin (1922–1981) & Cleo (b. 1926) Circle
WISNER CEMETERY

> *Lives of great men all remind us*
> > *We can make our lives sublime,*
> *And, departing, leave behind us*
> > *Footprints on the sands of time;*
> *Footprints, that perhaps another,*
> > *Sailing o'er life's solemn main,*
> *A forlorn and shipwrecked brother,*
> > *Seeing, shall take heart again.*
> > > *Henry Wadsworth Longfellow*

Carol "Ken" Davidson, Jr. (1926–1979)
LONE OAK CEMETERY

> *Crossing the Bar*
>
> *Sunset and evening star*
> *And one clear call for me.*
> *But such a tide as moving seems asleep*
> *And may there be no moaning of the bar*
> *When I put out to sleep.*
>
> *Too full for sound and foam*
> *When that which drew from out the*
> *Boundless deep*
> *Turns home again.*
>
> *Twilight and evening bell*
> *And after that the dark!*
> *And may there be no sadness of farewell*
> *When I embark.*

For tho from out our bourne of time
And place
The flood may bear me far,
I hope to see my pilot face to face
When I have crossed the bar.
[compare with Alfred Lord Tennyson's "Crossing the Bar"]

Dewey Davis (1929–2006)
ENTERPRISE CEMETERY

Home is the sailor, home from the sea...
And the hunter home from the hill
[Robert Louis Stevenson, "Requiem"]

Victoria de Garcia (1946–1997)
SAINT MATTHEW CATHOLIC CEMETERY

Full many a flower is born to blush unseen
And waste its sweetness on the desert air
[Thomas Gray, "Elegy Written in A Country Churchyard"]

Jacob Hayward (1971–1998)
MULTNOMAH PARK PIONEER CEMETERY

Life is like a tree.
When a strong wind blows,
The tree must sway
Or be torn from its roots.
        Chief Joseph

David & Althea Keyes
LYLE-BALCH CEMETERY

> *Here with a loaf of bread beneath the bough,*
> *A flask of wine, a book of verse — and thou*
> *Beside me singing in the Wilderness*
> *And wilderness is paradise now.*
> [Omar Khayyám]

James Mahin (1935–1995)
MOUNTAIN VIEW CEMETERY

> *My candle burns*
> *at both ends.*
> *It shall not*
> *last the night,*
> *but oh my foes*
> *and friends,*
> *it gives*
> *a lovely light.*
> [Edna Saint Vincent Millay, "First Fig"]

John McArthur (1945–1998)
JONES CEMETERY

> *Mad as the mist and snow*
> [From the W. B. Yeats poem of same name]

Patrick Moor (1943–1972)
FAIRVIEW CEMETERY

> *Yet sings, knowing that he*
> *hath wings.*
> [Victor Hugo]

Jermaine (1936–2002) & Walter (1937–1989) Murray
TENMILE UNITED METHODIST CEMETERY

> *At the going down of the sun and*
> *In the morning we will remember them*
> [Laurence Binyon, "For the Fallen"]

Bernice Pearson (1915–1992)
MOUNT UNION CEMETERY

> *I expect to pass this way but once.*
> *Any kindness I can show any fellow*
> *creature, therefore, let me do it*
> *now, for I shall not pass this way again.*
>   *Lucretius*
> [The quote is widely attributed to Étienne de Grellet: "I shall pass through this life but once. Any good therefore that I can do, let me do it now. Let me not defer or neglect it. For I shall never pass this way again."]

Martin Plamondon II (1945–2004)
SAINT JOHN'S CATHOLIC CEMETERY

> *The widest land*
> *Doom takes to part us,*
> *Leaves thy heart in mine*
> *With pulses that beat double.*
> E.[lizabeth] B.[arrett] B.[rowning]

David Quiring, Jr. (1905–1969)
EVERGREEN-WASHELLI CEMETERY

> *I have promises to keep*
> *And miles to go before I sleep*
> [Robert Frost, "Stopping by Woods on a Snowy Evening"]

Lee Read (1908–1973)
ANTIOCH CEMETERY

> *Do not go gentle into that good night*
> [Dylan Thomas poem of the same name]

Safotu
SISKIYOU MEMORIAL PARK

> *Til my trophies*
> *At last I*
> *Lay down*
> [George Bennard, "The Old Rugged Cross"]

Jane Smith (d. 2003)
RIVER VIEW CEMETERY

> *Bid me love and I will give*
> *A loving heart to thee*
> [Robert Herrick, "To Anthea Who May Command Him Anything"]

Barbara Strayer (1963–1982)
SOUTH YAMHILL CEMETERY

> *Of things, some are in our power and others are not.*
> *Epicieus*

Thomas Thornton (1922–1997)
SAINT JOHN'S CEMETERY (BARBERTON)

> *Hail thou star of the ocean*
> *Portal of the sky*
> *Ever Virgin Mother*
> *Of the Lord most high.*
> [Opening lines of "Ave Maris Stella"]

THE BIBLE TOLD ME SO

No book provides more epitaphs than the Bible, at least in Oregon. I'm sure I didn't exhaust the Biblical references in my 1,700-epitaph database; I only recorded the ones that leapt out at me. Here are a selection of those.

Anon
TURNER CEMETERY

> *Let me go for the day breaketh*
> [Genesis 32:26]

June Alaspa (1919–2001)
FERN PRAIRIE CEMETERY

> *and the greatest of all these is love*
> [I Corinthians 13:13]

Robert Allen (1966–2002)
LA CENTER CEMETERY

> *I thank my God every time I remember you.*
> *Philippians 1:3*

James (1934–1995) & Geraldine (b. 1935) Bogardus
BETHANY MEMORIAL CEMETERY

> *Love bears all things*
> *Believes all things*
> *Hopes all things*
> *Endures all things*
> *Love endures*
> [I Corinthians 13:7]

Catherine Browning (1957–1983)
NORTHWOOD PARK CEMETERY

> *May those who sow*
> *in tears reap with*
> *shouts of joy*
> [Psalm 126:5]

Minnie Burton (1936–2004)
FRANK ABEL CEMETERY

> *Wait on the Lord, Be of good courage*
> *and he shall strengthen thine heart*
> *Psalm 27:14*

Willie Dowell (1891–1918)
BELVIEU CEMETERY

> *Greater love hath no man than this,*
> *That a man lay down his life for*
> *His friends.*
> [John 15:13]

Wes Epperly (1966–1985)
YANKTON COMMUNITY CEMETERY

> *Oh sing to the Lord a new song*
> *For he has done marvelous things!*
> *His right hand and his holy arm*
> *Have worked salvation for him.*
> *Psalm 98:1*

Carole Galer (1930–2001)
HOPEWELL CEMETERY

> *Blessed are the peacemakers*
> [Matthew 5:9]

Dana Haynes (1950–2006)
BRAINARD CEMETERY

> *He finished well.*
> *Philippians 3:10*

Nona (1910–1999) & Emery (1908–1984) Headings
FAIRVIEW MENNONITE CEMETERY

> *The sleep of a labouring man is sweet.*
> *Ecclesiastes 5:12*

David Heller (1988–2005)
COLUMBIA MEMORIAL CEMETERY

> *Having become perfect in a short while,*
> *He reached the fullness of a long career;*
> *For his soul was pleasing to the Lord.*
> *Wisdom 4:13,14*

Virginia Hillyard (1989–1994)
AMBOY CEMETERY

> *But when the morning*
> *had now come, Jesus*
> *stood on the shore.*
> *John 21:4*

Johnston (1900–1902)
CIVIL BEND CEMETERY

> *Suffer little chil*
> *dren to come unto*
> *me and forbid*
> *   them not.*
> *[Luke 18:16]*

Waldo Johnson (1904-1905)
LOGAN–PLEASANT VIEW CEMETERY

> *He shall gather*
> *the lambs with*
> *His arm, and*
> *carry them in*
> *His bosom.*
>
> [Isaiah 40:11]

Gladys Mayden (1912–2004)
HOBSON-WHITNEY CEMETERY

> *Weeping may endure for a night*
> *but joy comes in the morning*
> [Psalm 30:5]

Juanita McGhee (1913–1998)
FERN RIDGE CEMETERY (SEAL ROCK)

> *Well done, good and faithful handmaiden.*
> *Enter into the joy of the Lord.*
> *Matthew 25:23*

Steven Olds (1965–2002)
ELSIE CEMETERY

> *They will soar high on wings like eagles. They will run and not grow weary. They will walk and not faint.*
> *Isaiah 40:31*

William (1942–1976) & Gayle (b. 1944) Raum
GLENDALE MEMORIAL CEMETERY

> *All the waters cannot quench love,*
> *Nor the floods drown it.*
> [Song of Solomon 8:7]

Edith (1900–1963) & Lawrence Reierson
ELSIE CEMETERY

> *I will lift mine eyes to the hills.*
> *Psalm 121:1*

Wayne (1921–2000) & Betty (b.1930) Roberts
PLEASANT HILL CEMETERY (PLEASANT HILL)

> *For he seldom considers the years of his life*
> *Because God keeps him occupied with the*
> *Gladness of his heart.*
> *Ecclesiastes 5:20*

James (b. 1926) & Maxine (1923–1996) Roherty
SACRED HEART CEMETERY (LAKE OSWEGO)

> *Jesus said, "Look at the birds of the air."*
> [Matthew 6:26]

Stephen Russell (1950–2002)
HOWELL PRAIRIE CEMETERY

> *Fear not, for I have redeemed you.*
> *I have called you by name; you are mine.*
> *Isaiah 43:1*

Mattie Smith (1855–1896)
KELLY CEMETERY

> *Watch therefore; for ye know not*
> *what hour your Lord doth come.*
> [Matthew 24:42]

Sussman-Fields
AHAVAI SHALOM CEMETERY

> *Set me as a seal upon they heart,*
> *As a seal upon they arm,*
> *For love is strong as death*
> *Song of Songs*
> [In the Christian Bible, "Song of Solomon" 8:6]

James Wilbur (1811–1887) & Lucretia Stephens (1812–1887)
LEE MISSION CEMETERY

> *Mark the perfect man, and*
> *Behold the upright. For the*
> *End of that man is peace.*
> [Psalm 37:37]

Irene (1930–2002) & Leslie (b. 1925) Wright
DRAIN-YONCALLA MASONIC CEMETERY

> *For the mountains may depart and the hills be removed,*
> *But my steadfast love shall not depart from you.*
> *Isaiah 54:10*

Steve Zimmerman
MOUNTAIN VIEW CEMETERY (CENTRALIA)

> *To every thing there is a*
> *season, and a time to every*
> *purpose under heaven*
> [Ecclesiastes 3:1]

CURTAIN CALL:
GOING OUT WITH THE BARD

No single author provides more epitaphs than William Shakespeare, the Bard of Avon. That could probably be said of quotes in general. I don't want to rank burials, but the Shakespeare readers are cut from pretty fine cloth. It's interesting to note that only two of the quotes are attributed and none name their source work.

Thomas Allen (1884–1964)
GRANDVIEW CEMETERY

> *I am constant as the northern star,*
> *Of whose true-fixed and resting quality,*
> *There is no fellow in the firmament.*
>   *Shakespeare*
> [Julius Caesar]

Sheila Box-Lee (1936–2006)
STEVENSON CEMETERY

> This above all: to thine own self be true.
> [Hamlet]

Samuel Goodman (1890–1984)
NEVEH ZEDEK CEMETERY

> Good night, sweet prince,
> And flights of angels sing
> thee to thy rest!
>   Shakespeare
> [Hamlet]

Jason Hatfield (1975–2003)
LONE FIR CEMETERY

> …and, when he shall die,
> take him and cut him out
> in little stars
> and he will make the face
> of heaven so fine
> that all the world will be
> in love with the night
> and pay no worship
> to the garish sun.
> [Romeo & Juliet]

Irma Hummasti (1911–1982)
SVENSEN PIONEER CEMETERY

> *Fear no more the heat o' the sun,*
> *   Nor the furious winter rages;*
> *Thou thy worldly task hast done,*
> *   Home art gone, and ta'en thy wages;*
> *Golden lads and girls all must*
> *As chimney-sweepers, come to dust.*
> [Cymbeline]

Henry S. Kranzler (1920–1999)
SCENIC HILLS MEMORIAL PARK

> *we are*
> *such stuff*
> *as dreams are made on*
> [The Tempest]

Parting Wisdom

Last minute instructions. Do I have the keys? Did I turn off the stove? Stop the mail? The newspaper? Oh yes, a note for the kids. Tell them to stay out of trouble and no big parties. That's the force behind these epitaphs: the desire to say one last word.

Anon
AMERICAN LEGION CEMETERY

> *The real Chief Seattle said, "There is no death, you just go to another world.*

Anon
LONE FIR CEMETERY

> *And early death?*
> *innocence is better*
> *than a long life of*
> *folly*

Anon
FALLS CITY CEMETERY

>*Be like this sundial*
>*Count only the sunny hours*

Robert Adolph (1926–1986)
FERN RIDGE CEMETERY

>*This world is not conclusion*
>*A sequel stands beyond*
>*Invisible, as music*
>*But positive as sound*
>[See Emily Dickinson, "The World Is Not Conclusion"]

William Bailey
OYSTERVILLE CEMETERY

>*The fish are rising*
>*children are laughing with joy*
>*Bon's free and at peace*

Lois Baker (1936–2000)
NORTH PALESTINE CEMETERY

>*Where did the time go*

George Bales (b. 1908)
AMERICAN LEGION CEMETERY

> *Now that we have said hello*
> *Lets take a walk on the beach*

Elsie (1917–1960) & Louie (1911–1977) Barnes
BELLFOUNTAIN CEMETERY

> *Now twilight lets*
> *Her curtain down*
> *And pins it with a star*
>
> [McDonald Clarke]

Elthea (1915–1994) & Edwin (1909–1994) Barrett
GREENCREST MEMORIAL PARK CEMETERY

> *I miss you most of all when day is done*

Bonnie (b. 1941) & F. Wayne (1940–2000) Benton
CANYON HILL CEMETERY

> *Behave yourself*

James Codega (1947–2001)
OYSTERVILLE CEMETERY

> *Deep peace of the running waves to you*

Marian Dingman (1920–1994)
PLEASANT HILL CEMETERY

>   *There is no kitten too little to scratch*

John Elsberry (1907–1957)
CROSS CUT CEMETERY

>   *He wandered - he returned*

Margaret Fisher (1915–1991)
PLEASANT HILL CEMETERY

>   *Raised on*
>   *Corn bread, beans and a lot of love*

Donna Friton (1968–2004)
ADAMS CEMETERY

>   *A whisper away*
>   *A lady knows when to say goodbye*

R. A. Gerity (1928–1998)
LONE PINE CEMETERY

>   *Listen to the wild…*
>   *It is calling you*
>   [Robert Service]

Shelby Haiek-Richey (1974–1990)
LOGAN–PLEASANT VIEW CEMETERY

> *Nothing compares 2 U SK8 forever*

Ho Yee (1927–1969) & Yin Sang Yu (b. 1927)
KNOX BUTTE CEMETERY

> *Ask, when appropriate*
> *Aid, when appreciated*

Cathy Horton (1957–2004)
SHAARIE TORAH CEMETERY

> *Because that's my job*

Michael House (b. 1948)
RIVER VIEW CEMETERY (PORTLAND)

> *Deep peace of the*
> *Shining stars to you*

Warren Jaeger (1944–2005)
ANTIOCH CEMETERY

> *It is what it is…*

A. Paul Jewell (1947–1997)
MONUMENT CEMETERY

The presence of your absence in everywhere

Leone Keil (1925–1991)
AURORA COMMUNITY CEMETERY

Bend and say you love me

Wade (1944–2001) & Diane (b. 1951) Kinney
SPRINGWATER CEMETERY

Don't drive faster than your guardian angel can fly

Elsie Mahler (1912–1991)
LONE FIR CEMETERY (PORTLAND)

There is always music among the trees

Jerry Noyes (1984–2002)
CONFEDERATED TRIBES OF GRAND RONDE CEMETERY

It's okay, Mom, we'll catch up

Delia Powers (1959–2003)
NORWAY CEMETERY

> *I follow the*
> *Rules of no man.*

Rebecca Schaeffer (1967–1989)
AHAVAI SHALOM CEMETERY

> *I am so wise*
> *To think love will prevail*
> *I am so wise*

Ernest Schoenborn (1941–1984)
MOLLALA MEMORIAL CEMETERY

> *He loved the woods… And there he died*

Sam Simpson (1845–1899)
LONE FIR CEMETERY

> *Onward ever,*
> *Lovely river,*
> *Softly calling to the sea,*
> *Time, that scars us,*
> *Maims and mars us,*
> *Leaves no track or trench on thee.*

> [Excerpt from poem, "Beautiful Willamette," by deceased]

James (1805–1887) & Elizabeth (1806–1889) Stephens
LONE FIR CEMETERY (PORTLAND)

> *Here we lie by consent, after 57 years 2 months and 2 days sojourning though life awaiting nature's immutable laws to return us back to the elements of the universe, of which we were first composed.*

Jack (b. 1927) & JoAnn (1932–2007) Stone
TAFT CEMETERY

> *Sit long, talk much, laugh often*

Hershel Tanzer (1926–2003)
AHAVAI SHALOM CEMETERY

> *It's nightfall on the trail*
> *My voice now still, encamped eternally*
> *Underneath a stately tree*
> *Atop this lovely hill*

Richard (b. 1934) & Gloria (b. 1932) Walker
ROCK POINT/GOLD HILL IOOF CEMETERY

> *Never slack down in a hard pull*
> *Arlie*

Beryl (1921–203) & Edna (1927–2008) Williams
MIDVALE-EASTSIDE CEMETERY

> *Here little Indian children played and here our children played*
> *We farmed here and God blessed us*

Steve Woodall (1944–2003)
APPLEGATE PIONEER CEMETERY

> *A brother in the wind*

Kara Zander (1978–2002)
EVERGREEN MEMORIAL CEMETERY

> *Knocking on doors before entering is always a smart thing to do. This is not just for the privacy of the owner of the room, but also for the person who wants to enter. What if someone was creating a surprise for another person and "hid" in a room to prepare it, and the other one barged in? The surprise and fun would be ruined. God is preparing a room for me up in heaven. The door is shut now, but when it is time for my soul to move on, I will knock and discover a glorious surprise beyond description. Lord, thank you for surprises and the fun associated with them. I am faithfully sure that yours will be awesome beyond words... like they always are. Amen.*

Long Day's Journey Into Night

Neither lives nor deaths are equal. Some deaths are too painful to bear, even at this remove. Is life fair? No, it simply is.

Anon
Pilot Butte/Greenwood Cemetery

> *Heaven doesn't seem*
> *so far away*
> *Since little Jim*
> *went there to stay.*

Anon
Turner Twin Oaks Cemetery

> *Thirteen once composed our number,*
> *Father, mother, sisters, brothers.*

Ah, well! for us all some sweet hope lies
Deeply buried from human eyes.

James Alva (1896–1918)
MOUNT ZION CEMETERY

> *Mother's only hope lies*
> *burried here*

Norad Coffin (1872–1889)
UNION CEMETERY (UNION)

> *Her last words:*
> *Oh Mother I hear the*
> *Angels singing and they*
> *Sing for you Mother*

Jane Doe
ADAMS CEMETERY

> *She died a tragic death and was unclaimed. As long as a stranger cares, she will always be remembered, She's in God's care.*

[Anonymous victim of a serial killer]

Charity Harris (1866–1892)
SHADYBROOK CEMETERY

> *Let her rest, let her sleep*
> *Where the lone willow weeps.*

William Holcomb (1888–1912)
EAGLE VALLEY CEMETERY

> *Just in the morning of his day*
> *In youth and love he died*

Austin Lindquist (1991–1998)
CLAGGETT CEMETERY

> *It'll be OK*

Destiny Maitland (1998–2006)
FOREST LAWN CEMETERY (GRESHAM)

> *We woke up at the Pearly Gates*

Edwin Miller (1942–1973)
CLIFFSIDE CEMETERY

> *Life's burden became*
> *Too much to bear.*
> *We understand, Ed.*

Matthew Webber (1962–1994)
ZION MEMORIAL CEMETERY

> *The little boat*
> *That sailed too far from shore*

Olive Wren (1871–1881)
CORNELIUS UNITED METHODIST CEMETERY

> *Her last words were do*
> *the girls know I am*
> > *going away*

Death Is Always Out of Season

Edward Nielsen (1961–1997, Bay Center Cemetery) provided the title of this chapter. A book could have been filled with children's deaths. I have limited this chapter to a handful of notable adult demises. Each of them leaves a void in the sunset.

Merlin Chooktoot (1920–1941)
BROWN CEMETERY

>*Assassinated Dec. 6, 1941*

Gerold Goff (1937–1971)
PLEASANT HILL CEMETERY

>*Whose plane was lost off*
>*Santo Domingo and*
>*was never found*

Dan Johnson (1946–1971)
ROSEBURG CEMETERY

> *Lost his life in an airplane crash near Arctic Village,*
> *Alaska, on April 3, 1971*

Robert Krug (1849–1919)
CAMP POLK CEMETERY

> *Murdered by A. J. Weston*

David Martin (1861–1893)
KELLY CEMETERY

> *Killed by a runaway team*

Andrew Pack (1976–2005)
FOREST LAWN CEMETERY

> *On a beautiful Indian Summer day, 11/16/1976*
> *in Sayre, PA, Andrew Gene Pack was born.*
> *He grew into a fine young man, earning a masters*
> *degree in physical therapy. He worked at*
> *Legacy Medical Center in Gresham.*
> *On 7/22/2005 in Ensenada, Mexico, four children*
> *8 years old and younger were caught in a riptide*
> *in the Pacific Ocean. Andy went in to help.*
> *All the children survived. Andy did not.*

Moses Weiss (d. 1943)
AHAVAI SHALOM CEMETERY

> *Died concentration camp*
> *Germany 1943*

Best Cemeteries of Oregon

The Best Cemeteries of Oregon

This guide includes profiles of more than 200 cemeteries, out of which I have selected some of the cemeteries I believe are most deserving of a visit. I've organized these cemeteries into a number of categories, ranging from cemeteries with the best view to the "most ghoulish" cemeteries. Included after each cemetery description is the name of the region that it can be found within. In the next section, you'll find a more in-depth profile of the cemetery, along with driving directions.

Best Pioneer Cemeteries

Clatsop Plains Cemetery

Built on rolling links land, sandwiched between Highway 101 and a military base, this cemetery nevertheless exudes antiquity. It hasn't been used in ages but is still maintained and worth a visit for the grave of Celiast, princess-daughter of Coboway, Chief of the Clatsops. (Region: North Coast)

Svensen Pioneer Cemetery

As sweet a little graveyard one could hope for, sheltered behind hedges and robustly cared for by a volunteer crew, nothing sets this cemetery apart so much as the care with which it's managed. (Region: Columbia River)

Best Catholic Cemeteries

Calvary Catholic Cemetery (Portland)

The largest Catholic cemetery in the state, its older sections follow the "garden" cemetery ideal of curving roads, impressive monuments, and opulent serenity. A large, fairly new Celtic cross guards the entrance. Sport your Irish colors when you visit. (Region: Portland)

Saint Mary's Cemetery (Corvallis)

Steep, hard to walk around, and thickly planted, this cemetery is a garden of much more than just gravestones. If you're lucky, the resident deer will accompany your tour. (Region: Upper Willamette)

Best Jewish Cemeteries

Havurah Shalom Cemetery

This cemetery takes some sleuthing to find, but it's a little gem once you locate it. Enfolded within Metro's Jones Pioneer Cemetery, the light here is especially graceful and the community of activists is uncommon. (Region: Portland)

Kesser Israel Cemetery

Unlike any other Jewish cemetery, this feels as if it could be in Eastern Europe. It sits cheek-by-jowl with a conventional Jewish cemetery; together, they are a cultural education. (Region: Portland)

Most Romantic Cemeteries

Moon Creek Cemetery

Not only is this a touching cemetery with a wonderful view of the John Day Valley and Aldrich Mountains, it also has that evocative name. Stop here for a tryst. Bring wine and cheese. (Region: John Day Country)

Carson Cemetery

Gnomes and elves inhabit this magical cemetery. Like many good cemeteries, it's a trick to find but worth the effort. It hardly looks as if the soil has been prepped for a cemetery at all, and the graves are wedged in between tree roots. (Region: North Coast)

Fort Harney Cemetery

If there's any cemetery that screams "Old West," this is it. Sparse, windblown, in the lee of a cliff overlooking the Malheur Basin, one expects the Cavalry to ride up at any moment. The new, intriguing sarcophagi only heighten the mystical aura of the place. Bring beer and sausages and a good hat. (Region: Basin & Range)

Cemeteries with the Best Views

Taft Cemetery

It's almost best to view this one sitting down. Dramatically perched above the Pacific, you can see China from here (squint). The collection of markers is outstanding, but the view tops everything. There's nothing like it on the coast—or anywhere, for that matter. (Region: North Coast)

Mosier Cemetery

Floating above cherry orchards, this cemetery is best viewed in spring when the trees are in blossom, but it's serene any time of the year. (Region: Columbia River)

Masonic Cemetery (Fossil)

Choosing the best view in Eastern Oregon is a fool's task; there are too many good ones. This cemetery is not as busy as the IOOF Cemetery across town, but it has, arguably, the better view of the surrounding uplands. In the late afternoon it is sublime. (Region: John Day Country)

MOST GHOULISH CEMETERIES

Sunset Pioneer Cemetery (Tigard Evangelical)

Aside from being abandoned, overgrown, and on a path to a bus stop, the most disturbing aspect of this cemetery is the deep holes in front of some tombstones. Oh yeah? Yeah! (Region: Portland)

Ramsey Cemetery

At the farthest reaches of outer Portland, this obelisk to one man is being overrun with berry bushes, and it also has a homeless camp at the bottom of the slope. (Region: Portland)

BEST URBAN CEMETERIES

River View Cemetery (Portland)

The queen, not just of Portland's cemeteries, but of Oregon's cemeteries. A grand cemetery in classic "garden/rural" style, it contains the cream of Portland society, at least these days. We don't do ostentation like other places, but we do dignity just fine. (Region: Portland)

Rose City Cemetery

Though nothing to write home about from outward appearances, the wealth of this cemetery is in its diverse community. Aside from prominent Gypsy graves, it has many Eastern Orthodox interred as well. And then, as if that weren't enough, it wraps itself around a Japanese Cemetery. (Region: Portland)

Masonic Cemetery (Eugene)

In a shining example of what can be done to a moribund graveyard, the caretakers have managed to revive the cemetery, restore the art deco mausoleum, and turn the place into a wildlife sanctuary in one bold stroke. Nothing embodies the spirit of Eugene better than this. (Region: Upper Willamette)

MOST ECLECTIC CEMETERIES

Meacham Cemetery

This forest of PVC pipe and boards is visually unlike anything in the state. How it got this way and who maintains it is not obvious, but it stands out in a crowd. Fortunately, it's easy to get to. (Region: Grande Ronde & Wollowa Valleys)

Jacksonville Cemetery

One of the all-time great cemeteries in the state, it's amazingly complex and large for such a small community. In truth, it's a collection of six cemeteries—including Jewish and Order of Red Men—strung along a wooded hillside and has both an interpretive center and signs. If you see just one thing in Jacksonville, make it this cemetery. (Region: Siskiyous)

BEST ETHNIC CEMETERIES

Agency Cemetery (Warm Springs)

This sprawling cemetery sits in a spectacular location, has a tremendous collection of handmade monuments, and is the biggest Native American cemetery in the state. (Region: Pine Belt)

Hilltop Cemetery

The only cemetery in the state containing graves in a Mexican style. While the state has a considerable Latino population, this is the only cemetery where that community puts on such a display. (Region: Upper Willamette)

Gervais Masonic Cemetery

The cemetery of choice for the Old Believer colony centered around Woodburn. The Eastern Orthodox cross is distinctive, and this is the state's largest collection. Many of the original crosses were made of PVC pipe, but they've largely been replaced. (Region: Central Prairies)

MOST BEAUTIFUL CEMETERIES

Paul Washington Cemetery

This is a beautiful and well-maintained cemetery any time of the year, but the Memorial Day decorations here are of a different order than anywhere else I've visited. They are simply gorgeous, using thousands of flowers in all. It's located on tribal headquarters grounds in Siletz. (Region: North Coast)

Mountain View Corbett Pioneer Cemetery

No cemetery sits higher on the flanks of Mount Hood than this cozy cemetery. Overlooking orchard pockets climbing the bobbing ridges of Oregon's iconic mountain, this is a delightful spot to contemplate eternity. Or the afternoon. Try to avoid windy days. (Region: Columbia River)

BEST MILITARY CEMETERIES

Fort Stevens Cemetery

The smallest of Oregon's military cemeteries, but arguably the sweetest, this cemetery is surrounded by deep forest, and the light lays in like a leaf falling through the branches. The least known of the military cemeteries as well, it guards its family with the formal dignity that only military cemeteries provide. Only the special are buried here. (Region: North Coast)

Eagle Point Cemetery

Not particularly large but with enchanting views, Eagle Point, bless her heart, uses traditional stone uprights. Their absolute symmetry mimicking the surrounding orchards enables their own sense of peace and order in an often chaotic universe. (Region: Siskiyous)

Willamette National Cemetery

By far the largest of the Oregon National Cemeteries, it is, unfortunately, a lawn cemetery. But, that said, it's unquestionably the best lawn cemetery in the state. Nothing else approaches it. The architecture and landscaping are superb. And the views are awesome. (Region: Portland)

Most Exuberant Cemeteries

Camp Polk Cemetery

Arguably the most fun cemetery in the state. A free-for-all of considerable proportion set on a hillock in the middle of a wildlife preserve, it's as colorful and entertaining as a cemetery can get, at least in this neck of the woods. Comes complete with fire pits and homemade benches. (Region: Pine Belt)

Pleasant Hill Cemetery

Two words: Ken Kesey. He isn't buried here, but his neighbors are. This was his turf, and the cemetery exudes the joy of the Merry Pranksters. No, it's not filled with outlandish stuff, just good vibes. (Region: Upper Willamette)

Best-Preserved Cemetery

Echo Cemetery

The entire town of Echo is a showcase for preservation, and the cemetery keeps up the high standards. The larger-than-life-size statues for the Cunha Family surpass anything similar anywhere in the state. Improvements are continually added. Plus, it's close to the freeway. (Region: Columbia Plateau)

Myrtle Creek Pioneer Cemetery

There's something almost too perfect about the way the light filters through the trees here. It's simple and unostentatious, but from the new gate to the glade of graves is a perfect balance of memory and nostalgia. (Region: Umpqua Drainage)

Union Cemetery

Is this the cream of Eastern Oregon cemeteries? Could be. The tiny, tiny chapel in the center is unique and oh-so-charming. Furthermore, it has a monument to which a mystery person brings new flowers annually. There are a lot of great cemeteries in the Grande Ronde Valley, but this is the flagship. (Region: Grande Ronde & Wollowa Valleys)

Best Churchyard

Tualatin Plains Presbyterian Cemetery

You don't have to be a believer to feel close to God in this exquisite cemetery. The church is slim and elegant and nestled by a comforting graveyard with a handsome columbarium. It's in the center of exurbia but is protected by large trees. A jewel in the rapidly disappearing farm land. (Region: Tualatin River Valley)

Smyrna Cemetery

There are a lot of churches offering cemeteries in the lower Willamette Valley, but none are better planted or better maintained than this. The church is active; expect to see people when you visit. (Region: Central Prairies)

Walker Community Church Cemetery

Halfway up a steep hillside, the prim, white church dominates this stretch of the valley, but one doesn't notice the graveyard curling around the back of the building until you've climbed the drive. Like Smyrna and Tualatin Plains, this is a busy church with lots of comings and goings. A true community resource. (Region: Upper Willamette)

GUIDE TO OREGON CEMETERIES

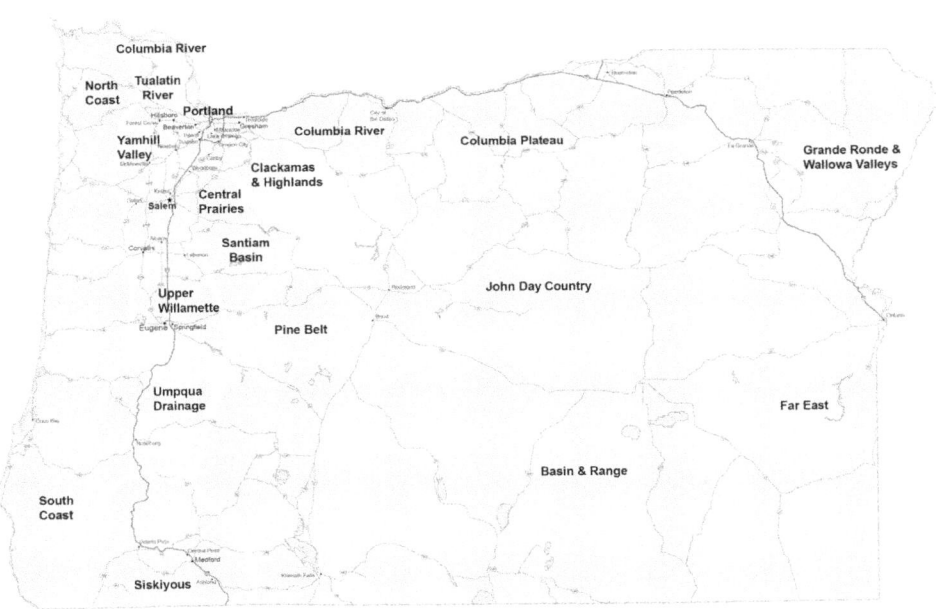

How To Use This Guide

Exactly what qualified a cemetery for inclusion in this book is, let's say, murky. Basically, it had to be an interesting cemetery in its own right, or have an interesting story associated with it.

Visiting cemeteries is not without incident, and cemetery keepers are occasionally spotted. I'm not inclined to strike up conversations with other visitors, though that has happened, but cemetery custodians are often more than willing to talk one's ear off. They are, I presume, used to talking to obliging listeners.

Many large lawn cemeteries are excluded, though there's no uniformity, but simply being big wasn't enough to guarantee a slot. In contrast, there are some tiny cemeteries that eat up a lot of print.

Not being included in the book does not mean that a cemetery isn't interesting. On some level, every cemetery is interesting, and there are many intensely interesting cemeteries in Oregon other than those displayed here. It doesn't hurt, if you've found a cemetery to visit, to see if there's anything else nearby. Often cemeteries come in clusters of which any single one might not be worth seeking out, but the cumulative effect tips the scale.

—How To Use This Guide—

For the purposes of this book and the convenience of the visitor, the state has been divided into eighteen regions. Some are geographically small, like the Portland Metropolitan area, but include many cemeteries; others, such as the Basin and Range, are enormous but sparsely populated. The cemeteries within each region are sorted by city name.

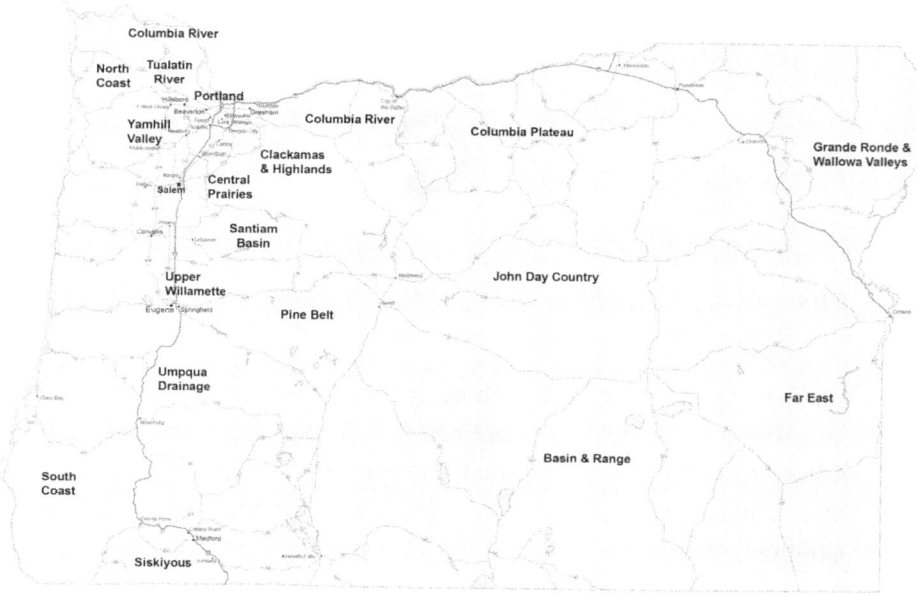

Each cemetery citation begins with directions. Finding cemeteries can be a challenge, and the directions should help eliminate that concern but are by no means foolproof. For more precise directions, I suggest you consult your own maps; visit the Google Maps page (link at www.ashlandcreek-press.com/books/madasmist.html); and visit the Dead Man Talking Flickr site (www.flickr.com/photos/deadmantalking), where each cemetery is geo-tagged and offers unequivocal directions and arial photos.

Most cemeteries are open to the public, and I know of none in this region that prohibits photography. There are occasional cemeteries posted with "no trespassing" signs, and I suggest you obey them.

Walking on the graves? It's a common-sense issue. The interred don't care, but the survivors might. Obviously, if someone has planted a flower garden over a grave, you aren't going to be marching through it, but if the lawn runs right up to the stone, there's no harm in standing in front of the stone to read it. For whatever reason a marker is erected over a grave, it's inevitably meant for the living, not the deceased. The people planted there want you to come visit. They don't even care if you're family or friend; they just want company. That's why they erected the stone. (Or the survivors wanted their enamored to be noticed.) Never forget that a graveyard is a park; you're supposed to come and enjoy it. It's also an art gallery, and you're supposed to come look at the works. Don't be shy. Respectful, yes, but comfortable. The denizens of the earth are expecting you, sooner if not later.

As mentioned earlier in the book, even when grammatical problems appear, I don't like to pepper the epitaphs with *sic*; epitaphs are presented as they are.

Two authors inform my exploration of cemeteries: Ralph Friedman and Lewis McArthur. McArthur is the author of *Oregon Geographical Names*. Friedman authored two travel guides to Oregon: *Oregon for the Curious* and *In Search of Western Oregon*. Ralph was an indefatigable cemetery sleuth and a sleuth of everything uniquely Oregon. I'd like to think I channel a touch of Ralph whenever I go into the field.

Basin & Range

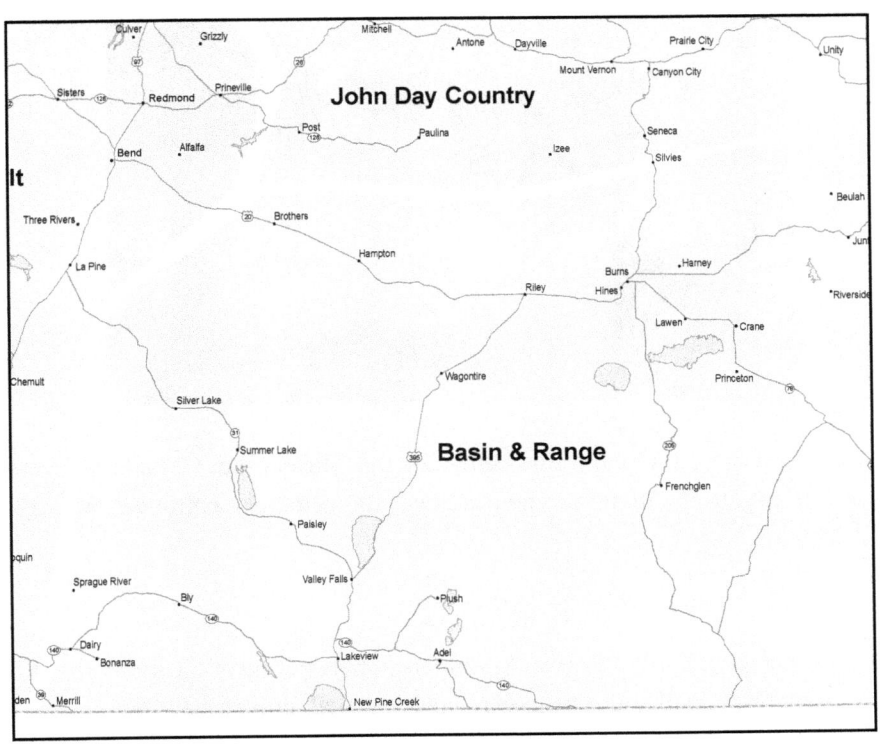

BEATTY

Brown Cemetery

From Highway 140 in downtown Beatty, take Godowa Springs Road north about 2.5 miles. Turn right on Sycan Road. At the fork, take Ferguson Road and keep bearing right at the subsequent intersection as the road turns to a one-lane track. At the crest of a ridge before the road drops down to the Sprague River, there is another fork; this time take the left-hand track to the cemetery.

Every source I find calls this cemetery the Masekesket Cemetery. Every source except the name on the arch over the cemetery entrance; that says "Brown."

Brown it is, then.

Nonetheless, it's still a Native-American cemetery, one of the many reasons to visit this small, out-of-the-way, and unusual graveyard. Getting there is half the fun. Except for power lines overhead, it's a good place for a cemetery, overlooking the river bottom and forested hills beyond. A cluster of statuary atop white pillars is very dramatic and surprising in a countryside not known for its wealth. Being small, there's not a lot of room here for self-expression, although the marker for Zetta John (1923–1959) in the shape of a four-foot-high arrowhead is distinctive.

An ominous epitaph is chiseled into Merlin Chocktoot's (1920–1941) granite: "Assassinated Dec. 6, 1941." "Murdered" shows up on tombstones infrequently, but this is the first time I've seen "assassinated."

Chief Schonchin Cemetery

North of Klamath Falls, get yourself to the Intersection of Highway 140 and Sprague River Road, then head west. The cemetery is east of Sprague River Road about a mile west of the junction.

Chief Schonchin, also called Old Schonchin to distinguish him from his brother, Schonchin John, was the titular chief of the Modocs during their war with the U.S. in 1872–73 (there was some debate as to his legitimacy). Unlike John, the Chief didn't participate in the war and has hence been a favorite of the Americans ever since.

This is Klamath Indian country, and they were historical enemies of the Modocs (Chief Schonchin was born at Tule Lake, California), but the two tribes were pushed together after the war, as often happened.

Aside from the memorial for Chief Schonchin, two other participants in the war are honored here with plaques. I didn't see headstones for either Schonchin or the others, so they could be buried elsewhere, but there's an implication they're laid to rest here.

The other two were a couple that went as interpreters to a council meeting between the Modocs and representatives from the U.S. government. Although it was supposedly an unarmed meeting between the two sides, the Modocs came armed and ambushed the council party (in fairness, two soldiers also smuggled in arms, but they were outdrawn), killing a number of them, though sparing the interpreters probably because the woman in the couple was a Modoc herself.

In any event, that couple, Frank Riddle and his wife, Winema, are honored today in this three-plus-acre cemetery under the ponderosas at the edge of a meadow. A cluster of pines greets the visitor at the cemetery gate.

You might note that the plaques for Schonchin and Winema were erected by the Daughters of the American Revolution in 1932, while Frank Riddle wasn't honored until 1985 by the Klamath County Historical Society.

DREWSEY

Drewsey Cemetery

As Drewsey Road heads north out of Drewsey, it meets Drewsey Market Road coming from the west. Take that, and the cemetery will appear on the north side of the road within a few blocks.

Wikipedia claims there were eighteen people in Drewsey at last count. When I passed by the grade school, it was out having its picture taken. I counted six students.

Drewsey is an excellent case in point of the power the post office used to wield in the days when people wrote letters. The original choice of the town name was, reputedly, Drusy; but the P.O. decided its spelling was better and hence that became the name of the town. Drewsey's greatest claim to fame, perhaps, is the name of an early saloon predating the founding of the town: the Gouge Eye Saloon. There is a faction that wished the town would've been named that too.

There are only two incorporated towns in Harney County, neither of them Drewsey. Despite that, Drewsey has a cemetery of some girth set on two levels along a hillside. There's not much in the way of cover, and the grasses are wild imports; still, the majestic setting and the delightful quirkiness of the place give it a distinctive charm. The era of gouging eyes out appears to have long passed.

The most distinctive feature of the cemetery is a plethora of animal profiles cut out of steel above the equally hand-cut steel word: "Unknown." Somebody went to a lot of trouble, and it was surely a labor of love.

Fort Rock

Fort Rock Cemetery

This cemetery is located on the right hand side of the road just prior to the entrance to Fort Rock Park.

Fort Rock is protected by a state park but should probably be a national monument, being the location where the arguably oldest shoes in the world were found by University of Oregon anthropologist Luther Cressman, also known as Margaret Mead's "student husband."

Fort Rock is a tuff ring, a circle of rocks pushed up by a volcanic explosion in an area with lots of water, which is somewhat hard to imagine given Fort Rock's current high desert location. Riddled with caves and originally an island, it was a popular dwelling place for Oregonians as early as 14,000 years ago. The human necessity to live near water drew people to this region in those moister times. Today it draws outdoor enthusiasts and tourists.

It also draws the dead. Or the would-be dead. There are hardly enough people in the region to warrant a cemetery, and most of the people from the area who die are probably buried elsewhere, as this is a lightly used cemetery. Conversely, the people buried here are often not those who live here but rather those who simply want to be buried in this romantic setting. It's a thoroughly western experience, an acre and a half of windswept sage and sand surrounded by barbed wire.

Despite its small size, there's enough eccentricity in this cemetery to warrant a detour, and its location makes it a must-see. Fort Rock is an iconic touch-point for the State of Oregon. In a very tangible sense, this is where our history begins.

HARNEY

Fort Harney Cemetery

A dozen miles east of Burns on Highway 20, take a left (north) on N. Harney Road until a road comes in from the west. Google gives the same name to both roads, but you should turn left rather than continue straight ahead. In a few hundred yards, the road will angle southwest, while a dirt road will continue straight on before bending to the northwest and the cemetery.

The substantial sepulchers for Catherine Rogers and Claire Luce are what make this cemetery stand out, but the historical association with an old fort, even if no graves from that period remain, makes the place special. It's a lonely place nestled under bluffs overlooking the vast Malheur marshlands. Vegetation lies tight to the ground, and the wind can blow you from the face of the earth, only to be found again in Idaho.

Fort Harney didn't last long, only from 1867 to 1880. In a typical campaign recounted in *The Deadliest Indian War in the West* by Gregory Michno, one Captain Perry caught up with a small encampment of Paiutes camped in the deep spring snow. Waiting till midnight to attack, Perry's men "gunned down" twelve men and twenty women and children "in the moon shadows. One woman and one child were captured, and it appeared that only two escaped." A couple of soldiers were promoted for their "gallantry."

LAKEVIEW

IOOF Cemetery

Located at the intersection of J Street and Highways 140 and 395 as they head north out of Lakeview; visible on the west side of the highways.

In 1869, a couple of sheep herders from a camp near what was to become Lakeview turned up missing. By the time they were found, they'd been out in the sun for a week and had well ripened. All their supplies were found with them and they appeared unharmed; it was evident they hadn't been waylaid by Indians or bandits. The presumption has been that they mistook poison hemlock for watercress and died eating it. Nobody saw any point in dragging the decomposing bodies home, so they were buried on the spot, which settled the problem of where to put the cemetery.

In time, the spot became the IOOF Cemetery and was expanded to eight or ten acres. Maintained today by the Lake County Cemetery Maintenance District (which maintains a number of other local cemeteries), it is similar to dozens of other municipal pioneer cemeteries in Oregon and includes a section set aside for military graves. A typical collection of older stones rests comfortably under a cottonwood canopy.

Unfortunately, old pioneer cemetery or not, aside from its general ambiance, it doesn't have its fair portion of compelling graphics or epitaphs. As seems to be a practice in these parts, at least one natural stone has been dragged—rolled in this case—from the hills to the cemetery. In this case it was for E. H. Smith (1873–1924), who, besides being a county judge for a dozen years, was the "founder of Lake County roads." How they got around before that is not mentioned.

If there's one feeling that permeates Lakeview, it's that it is a long way from the rest of Oregon. At 4,800 feet in elevation, Lakeview bills itself as Oregon's tallest town, small recompense for its isolation. A farm/ranch community supplying large spreads that have few employees, it lives by itself. The advantage to the tourist is that other tourists are few and far between compared to, say, Mount Hood—an advantage you might want to consider.

PAISLEY

Paisley Cemetery

A sign in the middle of Paisley points to the cemetery. If you miss the sign, find Main Street and follow it to its conclusion.

What's not to like about Paisley? Ask the foreign students who are enticed to this tiny desert community to boost enrollment enough to warrant keeping the school open. How would you like to be a high school student in a town of 427 people, 127 miles away from Bend, the nearest thing to a city? As it is, they still don't have enough students to field a football team. Halfway between Lake Albert and Summer Lake, on the edge of the Upper Chewaucan Marsh, the beginnings of the Fremont National Forest, vistas a summer long, a million stars lighting up the night sky—truly, what's not to like about Paisley?

And it has a cemetery, since 1881 (thanks to the IOOF, which no longer operates the place). On a butte on the edge of town, this is the place to visit in Paisley if you want vistas. As vast as the lakes of Lake County are, they're mere puddles, not deep enough to stick a boat in. It's dry lakes they have here, disappearing because there's little rain. The upside is that tombstones look as new today as they did a hundred years ago. If you want your pyramid to last, build it in a desert.

Apart from the view, the literature of the cemetery is lacking, as the denizens of Paisley are a taciturn bunch. Nothing flashy, nothing showy, nothing as ambitious as, say, Masekesket Cemetery (a.k.a. Brown), Paisley's three-acre cemetery is enlivened by a few small trees and shrubs and a wall of young ponderosa lining an interior drive. There's a tradition in this area of carving scenes and letters in relief onto natural stones, and there are samples of that here—but there's not a tradition of saying much.

An unusual aspect of Paisley Cemetery is the ratio of government markers to private ones. Veterans Affairs has long provided simple markers to veterans at no cost, hence they are common in almost all cemeteries, but at Paisley it seems that more than half of the newer markers are courtesy of the VA.

Silver Lake

Silver Lake Cemetery

On the northwest corner of the intersection of Pitcher Lane with Highway 31 east of the hamlet of Silver Lake.

With three to four meticulously tended, absolutely flat acres rimmed by a few trees, the cemetery has a good collection of natural stones with relief carving, a specialty of the region, but is best known as the resting place of forty-three people who lost their lives on Christmas Eve 1894 in a single-building fire.

If you take Pitcher Lane north, you'll eventually pass Fort Rock. The road is primarily dirt but is flat and well maintained. This is possibly the most dramatic way to view Fort Rock for the first time.

WESTSIDE

Westside Cemetery

On the north side of Dog Lake Road, between Andy Hill Road and Tunnel Hill Road, both of which intersect Highway 140 twelve or fifteen miles west of Lakeview.

The Westside Cemetery, while old enough to qualify as pioneer, has the appearance of a brand-new cemetery due largely to its careful maintenance and a border of young ponderosa and spruce defining the two acres. Someone has taken great care of late to upgrade the place, replacing lost stones with modest flat ones bearing, if known, the names of the interred. Mrs. Hubbard, Mrs. Whetstone, and Mrs. Morris all have red, square stone markers sans dates or first names. The cemetery boasts a new (1990) front wall and gate, and the care in upkeep is reflected in the care of tombstones. There's a goodly set of both graphics and epitaphs, amended by no end of curled lariats and old cowboy boots.

Sense of place is often present in cemeteries. There are no engravings of Haystack Rock in the cemeteries of Lake County, I can assure you, and I don't recall seeing any lariats on the coast. Westside goes beyond the norm, though, in having three natural rocks dragged to the cemetery from favorite spots in the area. Natural stones are not uncommon, but rarely is the origin of the rock pinpointed. In Westside's case, the provenance of the three stones is spelled out, including two from, I presume, brothers Levus (1898–1974) and Floyd (1899–1971) Reed, both of whose rocks are noted as having come from favorite hunting spots in Long Valley. The epitaphs as well are often regionalized as, for example, in the case of Robert Harmon (1957–1986), who specifies both a place name and a Westernism: "Powder River/ Let 'er buck," or of Kenneth Newton (1935–1995) with the sage (little bit of Western humor there) advice: "Stay in the buggy." Older epitaphs tend to settle for chapbook catch phrases; see Walter Nickle's (1830–1892) observation: "Thy trials ended/ Thy rest is won."

(A small aside here. You'll note Nickle's death date as 1892, while the founding date for the cemetery is given as 1898. Aside from error, there are possible reasons for that: the grave could have been moved to Westside from a different location after 1898, or the first interments preceded formal designation as a cemetery.)

Westside lies under Goose Lake, or would were the lake much higher, as it certainly has been in the past. The surroundings to the north of the lake are checkerboard flat and crisscrossed by irrigation canals as the road slices through productive farm land. If you approach Westside from the west along Highway 140, you'll get a lagniappe before arriving at Goose Lake Flats: Drews Valley, dominated by the Drews Valley Ranch. You'll pass the ranch-stead at the upper end of the valley. The ranch itself isn't overwhelming, but the serene beauty of the valley is overpowering: a bowl of large bands of cattle contentedly munching their lives away on luxuriant flatlands ringed by hunter's-green forested hills. It's the quintessential American West. A sign dating from 2004 at the head of the valley proclaims the ranch to be "permanently protected by a conservation easement," a blessing for which the state can be thankful.

Central Prairies

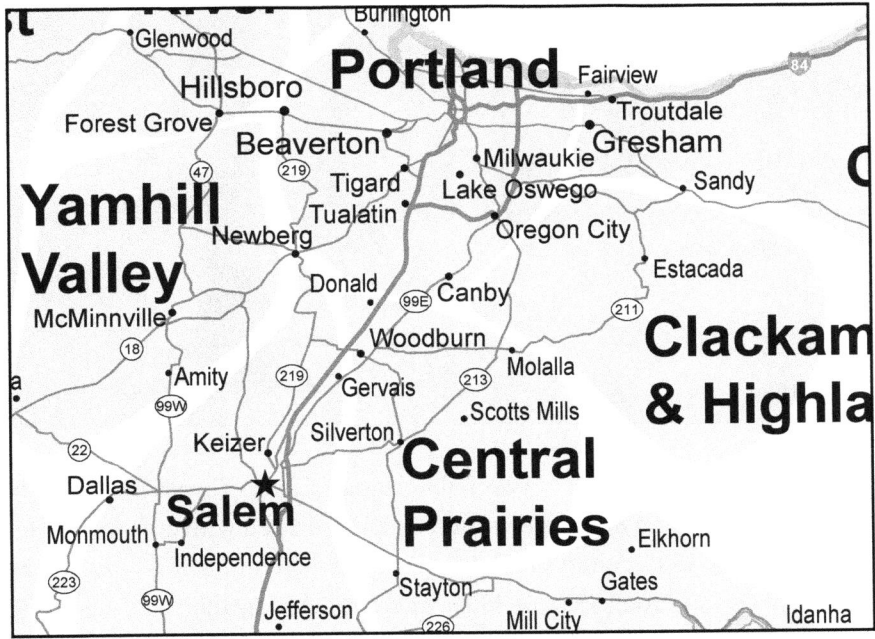

Aurora

Aurora Community Cemetery

Go west out of Aurora on Ehlen Road over the creek and up the hill. Oak Lane will appear on your left (south). Cemetery is at end of lane.

Aurora is arguably Oregon's best publicized example of what is a staple in Western history: the utopian community. Discouraged with creeping materialism at his 1845 colony in Bethel, Missouri, William Keil moved the largely German group west in 1855, where it held together until his death in 1877 (he's buried in the nearby Keil Cemetery), after which it succumbed again to creeping materialism. In the meantime, Aurora spawned one of the finest rural cemeteries in Oregon, whose very layout mimics the history of the town.

Covering perhaps three acres, there are two older sections with newer stones spreading out from the sides. Flat, new stones near the entrance area slope toward older sections fringed with tall firs. The entire cemetery is very well maintained and has one of the largest collections of mini-obelisks in the lower Willamette Valley. It has kept up with the Joneses by erecting a small columbarium at the entrance, and the landscaping has taken a downright serious turn the past few years.

The continuity of surnames since the founding of the colony is noticeable, and a descendant of the founder is responsible for one of the better modern epitaphs here. Leone Keil (1925–1991) inscribed on her stone: "Bend and say you love me/ And I will rest in peace."

For whatever reason, elegant fonts decorate the tombstones in Aurora Community, a tradition that carries on to this day, most notably in the adjoining natural stones of Alexander Cassaway (1924–1999), "teacher - seeker," and John Lester (1919–1999). Surely they were friends, and did they die on the same day? Together, perhaps?

In recent years, Aurora has been dominated by the antique market, though that, too, has had its day. Dwindling resources and competition from the Internet have both played their part. The town holds fast to its quaint, though.

Canby

Smyrna Cemetery

At the southeast corner of the intersection of Sconce and Canby-Marquam Roads, south of Canby.

Behind the Smyrna United Church of Christ is one of the best maintained and planted cemeteries in rural Oregon. The lawn is verdant under towering trees, the church gleaming, the iron fence coal-black, and even the children's play-yard is spiffy. Furthermore, it's out in the middle of the prairies and the lush nursery lands of the lower Willamette. This is the cemetery you want to compare with lawn cemeteries; this is what happens when you not only allow but encourage plantings. There are more than 300 people buried here, only three of whom are unknowns. One of those was a baby buried in the dead of night.

The church, long a focal point of the local community, remains a point of pride today. The local community is Yoder, once known as Yoderville—you can see why that name disappeared. According to Friedman, the Yoder store was begun in 1915 when an electric railroad ran lines through the area. The railroad folded, but the store remains, as does a picturesque lumber mill. The original mill was begun in the same year as the cemetery, but unlike the church, has burned down three times.

Smyrna is the most easterly of the four Yoder cemeteries (which include Hopewell, Zion Mennonite, and Rock Creek). The name "Yoder" is strongly associated with the Mennonite community, and it's my suspicion that the Yoders we're looking at are not all members of one enormous, fractured family, but are rather more like a gathering of Smiths: clusters of un- or not-closely related people who happen to have the same surname. "Yoder" is spelled "Joder" in Switzerland, where the original Yoders came from, and "Joder" is a familiarization of the formal name "Theodor(us)."

Two of the better headstones in the Smyrna Cemetery (the Mennonites not being ostentatious) belong to ladies with Yoder middle names. Leona Yoder Blatchford, "older twin sister to Rose," died in 1987 at the age of five months; her marker is faced with a metal plaque carrying a bas-relief sculpture of her head. It's both unique and unusual. Glenda Sano's maiden name was Yoder, which she proudly displayed on her tombstone, along with the advice: "Be generous."

In a nod to modernity, the cemetery boasts a level columbarium beneath a flagpole in the rear of the cemetery. In another sign of the times, a memorial bench has been placed there, carved with the words, "In loving memory of/ Paul Eyman/ Who never sat around much."

Zion Memorial Cemetery

From the Marquam Highway heading south out of Canby, take Township Road east. Cemetery is about a mile out.

—CENTRAL PRAIRIES—

Canby is a rock-solid working/farming town. From Canby south is nursery heaven. It may not be the heart of the Willamette Valley, but you can see it from here. It's the last town the Willamette sees before plunging over the falls at Oregon City, and the Canby Ferry is the only means across the river between the falls and I-5. Canby's biggest problem is its lack of a genuine town center. What should have been its heart got subverted by Highway 99E, itself overshadowed by I-5. It's a community of little frills, and Zion Memorial, the largest cemetery in the area, reflects its hometown. Zion Memorial continues to bustle with new mausolea and a "memorial garden," and looks to serve Canby for years to come.

GERVAIS

Gervais Masonic Cemetery

East of Gervais, on the south side of Mount Angel–Gervais Road a half-mile past its intersection with Highway 99E. Across the road from Sacred Heart Cemetery.

There may be some Masons buried here, but that's not what's going to strike you as you roll into the parking lot. It's the Russian three-barred (one slanting) crosses made out of one-inch hollow steel tubing painted white. They used to be made out of PVC pipe but upgraded at some point.

There's no designated driveway or parking spot in the cemetery, and the

Russian graves rim what passes for the parking lot. More and more rows of crosses are appearing deeper into the cemetery, and across the "parking lot" from the crosses is a burgeoning secular portion of the Russian graveyard. The core of the cemetery is covered with mature trees, but the edges are open and only beginning to be used. Despite its casual nature, it appears headed for a long life.

Mollala

Adams Cemetery

Find Freyer Park Road in the southeast quadrant of Molalla. Take that a half-mile to the intersection of Adams Cemetery Road, which goes south. Cemetery is at the end of the road.

For whatever reason—early morning sunlight, lee of the Cascades, or just plain soil—the east Willamette Valley has a distinct culture from that of the west. Given the paltry few miles between them and the similarities of their mega-cultures (Coke is available everywhere, no?) and history, one would expect the two to be mirror images, but they're not.

The towns and hamlets of the east side tend to be more working class than their tonier brethren across the way. Land here is more likely put to Christmas trees than vineyards; Molalla, hometown to Adams Cemetery, is a tough little burg more akin to Oakridge than Portland. Consequently, if you've prejudiced yourself by visiting downtown Molalla and the humble Molalla Memorial Cemetery, you won't be prepared for the Victorian patina of Adams.

On the edge of Dickey Prairie, once home to a colony of the eponymous Molalla Indians, the cemetery holds a gentle slope of land overlooking farm country. It is one of the gems of rural Oregon cemeteries (the east side equivalent of the Pike Cemetery), particularly since the installation of an octagonal gazebo in its middle to the tune of $50,000. The price tag started out at $25,000, but county codes doubled the cost, according to the groundskeeper.

The day I stopped by, the groundskeeper had at least three other men working the site. He said it took twenty-four man-hours (there being no women on his crew) to completely mow and monitor the cemetery. He does this once a week in the early spring, later dropping to once every other week, and finally to occasional upkeep as the dry period extends itself.

The cemetery expanded a couple times recently and now encompasses better than seven acres, at least three or more of which are available for future use. Unless Molalla experiences an unprecedented building boom—something there's little reason to expect—they have land for many years to come. Most of the cemetery is treeless, save for a grove of old oaks near the original burials. One suspects the grove was the traditional gathering spot for graveside services now given over to the gazebo.

Jane Doe is buried next to that grove. Her epitaph reads, "She died a tragic death and was unclaimed. As long as a stranger cares, she will always be remembered. She's in God's care."

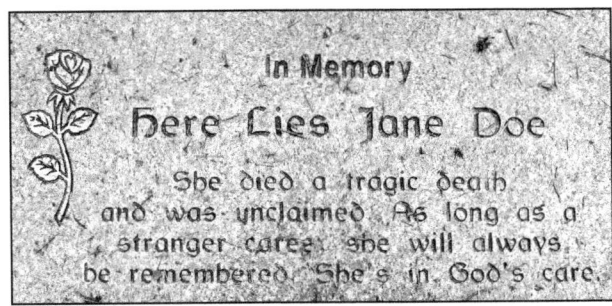

But it's Donna "A Whisper Away" Friton who holds the honors for bowing out in style. She's the one who insists that "A lady knows when to say goodbye."

—CENTRAL PRAIRIES—

MOUNT ANGEL

Mount Angel Cemetery

On the north side of Marquam Road, a half-block east of its intersection with Highway 214 on the north side of Mount Angel.

Mount Angel had a couple of other names before Benedictine priest Father Odermatt arrived in 1863 to name it after the town where he'd done his training: Engleberg, Germany. Nothing's been the same since. Soon there was a monastery, then Oktoberfest, possibly the worst time to visit Mount Angel. (I don't know because I've always been too afraid to attend. Otherwise, though, I come often.)

Surprisingly, the cemetery is tiny. It can't be more than an acre set among backyards and surrounded by a padlocked chain-link fence. Not very friendly, but I guess they know what they're doing. What you'll see inside the gate is the finest collection of iron crosses in the region, truly an outstanding representation. There are not many epitaphs here, but the visuals are top drawer.

Mount Angel Abbey Cemetery

Behind the first building you come to when driving up the road to the abbey.

The cemetery is the least of the reasons to visit Mount Angel; the greater draws are the cathedral, the Alvar Aalto library, and the sublime views of the heart of the world (am I overstating the case for the Willamette Valley?).

If not its main attraction, arguably its most fun is a secreted Old Believers museum stuck in an incongruous, white, slightly odiferous house out behind the cathedral and down the hill a bit. The displays were assembled by Brother Ambrose, a Benedictine monk turned Old Believer (I didn't know you could do that). In colorful costumes, tidbits, icons, pictures, and memorabilia, the history of the Old Believers, their peregrinations over the face of the globe, and their obscure debate with religion back home (largely hinging on whether the depiction of a particular saint should be made with two fingers raised or three fingers raised) are laid out upstairs and downstairs in a labyrinth of tiny rooms.

Mount Calvary Cemetery

On the north edge of Mount Angel as you leave town on Highway 214; east side of road.

Mount Angel is a cemetery lover's dream; there are a slug of cemeteries within close proximity. If you're planning on dying here, though, you'd be better off if you were Catholic. There's the minuscule, unkempt Simmons Cemetery further down Highway 214, and even further out in the country is Trinity Lutheran, but you'll have to go all the way over to the Miller Cemetery to die if you're secular or Jewish or whatever. If you are Catholic, though, Mount Calvary is where you'll probably be buried; it's the only sizable, active public cemetery in town. Both Mount Angel Abbey and the Benedictine Sisters of Saint Mary have cemeteries for members only.

Mount Calvary, perhaps seven acres in size, doesn't distinguish itself as much as one would hope, save for a curious array of sunken sepulchers at the entrance. It's a type of vault that was popular in the late 1930s and

1940s in this area, and they're commonly scattered here and there among the tombstones. Concrete bunkers large enough to carry a casket and slightly arched, they look as if they're either sinking into the ground or bobbing up, either of which is a bit unsettling.

One end displays a tilted "lectern" holding the actual marker, made either of metal or a type of black glass that was popular around the same period. That style of glass was used on regular headstones as well, though they're often now cracked, whether from aging or vandalism, I don't know. A few of these randomly found provide a visual rhythm to a cemetery, but at Mount Calvary they're a movement unto themselves. There must be a couple hundred of them lined up in perfectly neat rows, a sight unlike any other in the region.

Those crypts are part of an older cemetery core, surrounded, as is common, by flat-stoned, newer sections; the whole shebang is surrounded by a neatly trimmed arbor vitae hedge. At least two sections are devoted entirely to babies, and a new committal shelter has been erected on the open ground.

New Era

Saint Patrick's Historic Cemetery

Off Highway 99E, a couple miles north of Canby. Cemetery is a few hundred yards up the road on the east side.

This three-acre cemetery is divided roughly into thirds, with an older rear section including uprights, a newer lawn cemetery in front, and an unused side strip. There was a church on the property until 1942, and a distinguishing feature is a clutch of handmade iron crosses, common to parts of the Midwest but rare out here. The only comparable collection in the state is at Mount Angel Cemetery, and that's behind lock and key.

This Catholic cemetery greets you with a stone dedicated to "the loving memory of all precious babies lost through abortion." Of note is the liberal use of an unusual red, weeping stone that was often cut quite deeply by the local artisan(s). The United States Geological Survey lists this as the New Era Cemetery. When you're done with the cemetery, continue on out New Era Road, paying special attention to the collection of Victorian buildings at the Herman Anthony Farm on your left.

Saint Louis

Saint Louis Cemetery

Cemetery is behind Saint Louis Church, which is on Manning Road at the intersection of Manning and Saint Louis Roads. Saint Louis Road runs through the center of Gervais.

People who write about the pastoral crossroads of Saint Louis like to point out that it was named after the French king and not the Missouri burg, a distinction that eludes the average soul. The cemetery is off the road but plainly visible over the fields. On a slight rise backed by trees, its sparseness wears the grace of age, and the approach down the long open drive gives the visitor time to appreciate the sobriety of the setting. It's not heavily used, but a few thoughtful people find it now and again, and it's well cared for.

The Saint Louis Cemetery is unusual, if not unique, in the layout of its graves. Common practice, particularly in pioneer and church cemeteries, is to orient bodies east-west; Saint Louis, for the most part, follows that pattern, save for a few rows along the north edge where the bodies are laid out north-south. The contrariness of it is puzzling.

The church itself is the graveyard for Marie Dorion, an Iowa Métis married to a Canadian Métis, Pierre. Marie came to Oregon with the 1811 Astoria Overland Party, stopping to give birth along the way and then catching up a few miles down the road. The first time her husband laid a hand on her, she cold-cocked him with a club, convincing him to forgo the habit. Posted in southern Idaho in 1814, Marie set out to warn Pierre, who was away at the time, that Indians were about to attack. She found Pierre, all right, already slaughtered by the Indians. By the time she got back to the settlement, everyone there had been slaughtered, too, forcing her to spend a winter with her two young sons in the Blue Mountain wilderness, surviving by killing and smoking her horses. She ended up living in that area, marrying a couple other times, before moving to French Prairie in 1840. For that they buried her under the church steeple.

There is a tantalizing, modern marker that connects back to the Louis and Clark Expedition, this for a child of seven who died in 1957: "Our Darling," Linda Charboneau. Charboneau was the Métis "country husband" of Sacagewea. Oregon didn't have founding fathers so much as founding mothers.

Saint Louis is toward the southern end of French Prairie, the greatest of the Willamette Valley prairies, which, by the way, were not naturally occurring prairies of the Midwestern sort but were maintained via annual field burning until the Americans usurped the land and stopped the practice. If you continue on Manning Road to the north, it becomes Arbor Grove Road, which is one of the more delightful ways to traverse the prairie. It bobs and weaves along Case Creek through one continuous nursery to McKay Road.

SALEM

Chemawa Indian School Cemetery

From Highway 99E, turn west on Blossom Drive NE, which is just north of I-5 and at the southern end of the school grounds. Follow it over the tracks where it turns and becomes Indian School Road. Cemetery is on the west side of the road.

Chemawa has been a flash point between Native American and American cultures since 1880. The oldest of four national Native American schools, it serves the Northwest and Alaska. Its history is checkered at best, beginning as a coercive institution designed to mold Native Americans into the American culture, whereas by now it does its best to retain and instill native customs in its students. Chemawa became a vocational institution to provide Native Americans with marketable skills, gaining accreditation as a four-year high school in 1927. Currently it looks more like the campus of a community college than it does a residential high school and is orienting its program toward college admissions. In 1992 its 86 acres, including the cemetery, were placed on the National Registry of Historic Places.

The original 1880 building burned down in 1885, and the new institution was built in its present location. One year later, the first grave was dug, followed by 200 more. Unfortunately, during the 1960s in an attempt to clean the place up, it was bulldozed and most of the headstones and many of the graves were lost. The extant markers are, primarily, steel plates arranged by chronological order of death, level with the ground. Aside from a few trees, the healthiest crop is poison oak. Despite its rough history, Chemawa has become an important institution in modern history of Northwest tribes, and it is largely at their insistence that the school remains.

City View Cemetery

At the west end of South Hoyt Street, south of downtown Salem. Take Commercial south until it crosses Hoyt and turn west.

Contiguous with Salem Pioneer, this cemetery is not as old but certainly as interesting. Worth a repeat visit, City View boasts the largest collection of Civil War stones I've seen outside of a similar memorial at River View in Portland. Surrounding a flagpole, the Civil War stones are matched by stones for soldiers in subsequent wars, such as the one "given to Capital Post #9 in honor of my father, Oliver C. Fursman, and other veterans of World War I," by Kathleen Beaufait in 1999.

Salem has had its share of interesting characters, some of whom, naturally enough, died here. Salem Pioneer has the bulk of the best old stones—though there are plenty of older ones here as well—but when it comes to the newer stuff, City View is the mother lode. For some reason, the citizens of Salem are an unusually verbose lot, and City View presents some of the longest tombstone essays around.

Lee Mission Cemetery

On the south side of D Street in downtown Salem, due west of the State Hospital.

An 1838 founding date, five years prior to the first wagon train, gives an indication of the early nature of this famous cemetery on the National

Registry of Historic Places. It's chock full of old and interesting markers commemorating many of the first settlers of modern Oregon, such as George W. Smith, who was "on the Oregon Trail at age 5."

A number of graves bear small plaques presented by the Multnomah Chapter of the D.A.R. (Daughters of the American Revolution) in 1931, which read: "To honor one of the patriots who on May 2, 1843 founded the provisional government at Champoeg, Oreg."

Jason Lee, after whom the cemetery is named, was the first Protestant (Methodist) minister in the territory and took part in the founding of the mission, Willamette University, and the City of Salem. Both he and his two wives are buried here, and his first wife's slab implies an interesting tale:

> *Beneath this sod*
> *The first ever broken in Oregon*
> *For the reception of a*
> *White mother and child*
> *Lies the remains of*
> *Anna Maria Pittman*
> *First Wife of*
> *Rev. Jason Lee*
> *And their infant son*
> *She sailed from New York in July 1836*
> *Landed in Oregon June 1837*
> *Was married July 15, 1837*
> *And Died*
> *June 26, 1838*

Salem Pioneer Cemetery

Drive south on Commercial (near the river) from downtown Salem, and the cemetery will appear on your right.

Friedman backs this cemetery's claim as *the* state cemetery by noting, in *In Search of Western Oregon*, that "probably more veterans of the 1843 'Divide' meeting lie here than in any other cemetery." You can read his account of some of the more illustrious: Tabitha Brown, Virgil Pringle, Charles Bennett, Rev. David Leslie, Asahel Bush, Ruben Patrick Boise, John Pollard Gaines, and the Hon. Sam'l R. Thurston, among others.

Among the many interesting stones are those of the Rev. John Daniel Boon (*sic*) and that of Mr. Gaines, who was not only governor of Oregon but a congressman from Kentucky and a veteran of the Mexican War of 1846.

The Ford family mausoleum with pink granite pillars and a blue door is unusually handsome. This is a long, large cemetery with lots of reading material. Be prepared to spend some time.

At 16.5 acres, Salem Pioneer is little more than half the size of Portland's Lone Fir, but Lone Fir doesn't have City View next door. Nonetheless, the 8,000 or so souls buried here make for interesting reading. And while you're here, drive around Salem and take River Road out to Independence for a gentle way out of town.

Silverton

Miller Cemetery

Three miles northeast of Silverton on the east side of Highway 213; associated with a pioneer church. (Highway 213 between Oregon City and Silverton is a busy highway, and the cemetery entrance is blind. Be careful.)

With six or more acres, Miller is a surprisingly large rural cemetery containing a collection of old and new stones and accompanying a pioneer church "built with a unique sloped floor." It was added to the National Registry of Historic Places in 1978. The church, locked when I visited, is notable for being set on stone pilings, unique to the area.

It's a gorgeous setting for a church and graveyard overlooking the rich farmlands of the Abiqua drainage. The land was donated by Richard Miller as a cemetery in 1860, and the first grave belongs to a friend of his who died in 1852. The poet Edwin Markham's dad, Samuel, is buried here, of which Sam's marker makes considerable hay.

Silverton Cemetery

On the south side of Highway 213 as it exits Silverton toward Salem, next to a fire station.

Spared much of the ravages of modernization, a revitalized Silverton is one of the best preserved towns in the valley, with an enviable collection of Victorian and craftsmen homes. Driving in from the north on Highway 213 always gives me a thrill. It is only appropriate that the Oregon Gardens chose Silverton as its home, for Silverton nestles among some of the most charming countryside in all the Willamette Valley, which means, by definition, in all the world. Nearby, as well, are Mount Angel, the prairie country, the lower valley's only original covered bridge, Silver Falls Park, and the beguiling Waldo Hills. Moderately sized, maybe four acres or so, the cemetery's most curious feature is a square "foundation" of black stones in one corner that surrounds a number of graves. One wonders if it's the remains of a walled plot or truly is the remnants of an old foundation. Regardless, it adds character where it can well be used.

Homer Davenport, arguably the most famous and powerful Oregonian you never heard of, is buried in the Silverton Cemetery, where his grave is marked by an oversized gray stone "erected by his friends to the memory of Oregon's world-renowned cartoonist."

During his prime, the late 1890s and the beginnings of the twentieth century, Davenport's Populist pen scuttled some politicians while floating others, notably Teddy Roosevelt. Pushed into cartooning by his parents, Davenport was discovered by W. R. Hearst (who paid for his funeral, by the way) and given a princely salary. From then on he consorted with the rich and famous and spent his days longing to return to Silverton, which he only accomplished in death.

Silverton's most unusual marker—H. Davenport's notwithstanding—is the pitch black steel "lectern" surmounted by a hand-carved 4x4 wooden cross for Evanell Black (1911–1982).

One stone here approaches a quiet fear I've carried with me for some time—tombstone sponsors: "This headstone brought to you in part by the caring people at Miracle-Gro," or "Keeping your loved ones green forever with Monsanto." You get the picture. Headstones with little golden arches carved into them. A Nike swoosh.

The closest we come to that so far are the stones erected and so marked by the Woodmen of the World, a quasi-fraternal insurance organization, or the insignias of fraternal orders engraved on people's markers. This stone is a "transitional" headstone. It has three corporate logos engraved into its face, all three subdivisions of a company out of Hubbard. Seeing as it's all in the family, the logos can't probably be called sponsor's logos, but they're the next best thing.

What about the company that offers a low-cost life insurance package that covers the cost of a stone, provided it carries the company's logo? What about a stoneworks that offers discounts if its logo can be displayed on your stone? What about someone offering to pay part of the cost of a stone for the privilege of putting an ad on the back?

As Ester Lyon (1914–2002) put it: "Well, I'm only curious."

Woodburn

Belle Passi Cemetery

On the south side of Belle Passi Road, which runs east from Highway 99E, south of Woodburn.

This fine pioneer cemetery is graced by a gilded, life-size statue of a soldier attired circa 1865, erected in 1911, dedicated to the "memory of our comrades." The planting of the flags on Memorial Day is a major occasion at this highly active cemetery. Plantings are especially nice with a succession of daffodils, peonies, and Asiatic lilies providing seasonal displays, presided over by a full-time gardener—unheard of in the pioneer cemetery business—with a five-bay maintenance shed. Five bays, I kid you not. A new mausoleum has been built across the road, and there are new flat-stone sections at the edges of the uprights. All told, the cemetery controls twenty-eight acres, of which about ten are in play.

Belle Passi, taking its name—under a variety of spellings—from an extinct community at this location, is the pioneer cemetery of record for Woodburn, one of the lower valley's older and more important centers. Heading west, Belle Passi Road ends at Boones Ferry Road. As Boones Ferry passes through Woodburn, it becomes Settlemeier Avenue, a main street through the town's finest residential neighborhood, which includes the stalwart Settlemeier house. One can only imagine the stately funeral processions out this graceful promenade to the elegant cemetery.

Woodburn has always been an agricultural center and continues so today, although today the farmers tend to be Mexican immigrants, and downtown Woodburn is a buzz of Mexican entrepreneurship harboring the best

Mexican food this side of Madras. There are Mexican graves in Belle Passi but little of the exuberance associated with traditional Mexican grave sites; for that one has to go to Hilltop Cemetery outside Independence.

Clackamas & the Highlands

Beavercreek

Beavercreek Memorial Cemetery

From the intersection in downtown Beavercreek, take Kambath Road due south and the cemetery is a half-mile or so on your left.

"Beavercreek" is alternately spelled as one word or two, but the cemetery sign spells it thusly, so I do as well. Beyond Beavercreek, one can still imagine an earlier Oregon, but from Beavercreek to Portland, there's no question but that the modern world is here. Currently, though, the cemetery is genteel and quiet and still in active use. Its uniqueness lies in being the only Welsh cemetery in the state. The cemetery is nicely maintained under a good canopy of trees, and nearby is Bryn Seion Welsh Congregational Church. You might wonder about the epitaph for Thomas Kasner (1940-1993). His stone is engraved with the image of an electrical insulator under which is written: "In search of the elusive insulator."

Carus

Moehnke Cemetery

East from Carus, the cemetery is on Carus Road before it intersects with Lower Highland Road.

I was alerted to this seventy-two-person cemetery (pronounced *mink*) by a friendly lady working in the Beavercreek Store. It functions largely as a family cemetery for a limited number of families, four of whom have contributed wrought-iron benches backing up to a chain-link fence. It got its name by being "deeded to the Church Corp. of the Ohio Senate on Jan. 23. 1897, for the sum of $10 by Michael and Catherine Moehnke." Carus Road is a delightful drive in itself, but if there's one reason to drive out to this little-known cemetery—it's to see the graceful, handmade stone for Marshall "Don" Higgins: an ingenious use of stained glass.

CARVER

Logan–Pleasant View Cemetery

Go over the bridge at Carver from Highway 224 and turn left on South Springwater Road. Stay on it until it begins to ascend into the highlands past Baker Ferry Road. Sign for the cemetery will be on your right.

One has to admire the way the "eastsiders" maintain their cemeteries. Going east from Portland, the land is hilly and broken. Small valleys offer limited farming opportunities, the logging has disappeared, and the hills aren't big enough to attract tourists. The geography does, however, attract loyal residents protective of their privacy. They're proud of who they are and don't care if you never find out about them. Exactly the reason you should.

Despite its name, this delightful cemetery is really closer to Carver than Logan. Oregon has a number of cemeteries that require driving through a farmer's front yard to get to, and this is one of those.

With a broad hilltop view, the cemetery is in spiffy condition, and a corner shed has two plaques devoted to the people responsible: "Thanks, Dorothy Johnson, for initiating the restoration of this cemetery," and "In memory of

Roy Hattan for his dedication to this cemetery."

DAMASCUS

Damascus Pioneer Cemetery

Slightly to the south off Highway 212.

Turn to the left as you come through the main gate of this well-maintained pioneer cemetery and look for the portrait of Captain Jack with his jaunty Union cap embossed in a white bronze (lead) marker.

Captain Jack fought with Company A of the Maryland Infantry from 1861-1865 and was buried here in 1903. His real name was Hugh Miller, and there's no explanation for the "Captain Jack" nor date of birth. (One might note that the leader of the Modocs in the Southern Oregon Indian Wars was also known as Captain Jack.)

Relatively large for a pioneer cemetery, perhaps four or more acres, this one probably dates prior to 1855, though it was deeded as a cemetery in 1876, and the cemetery association began in 1895. It's stuffed to the farthest corners and is far more fun than the average rural cemetery. Its popularity is attested to not only by diverse plantings (exemplified by the Olson grave's redwood surround) but by arguably the best cemetery sign in the region. In the spirit of the times, it has tucked a small columbarium into what looks for all the world like a maintenance shed, which may be why no one has used it yet. It's faith that counts.

EAGLE CREEK

Forrester Cemetery

On the north side of Highway 211 at the intersection of Howlett Road, a mile or so from where 211 meets 224 on the way to Estacada.

This is one of the more delightful cemeteries in this area for two reasons: One, it has a preponderance of upright stones, including new ones; and two, it's flanked on two sides by a commercial berry patch. That it's presided over by a grand tree and has great views doesn't hurt. Eagle Creek is famous for its berries, and it's only appropriate that the dead are accompanied by the sweet smell of ripening fruit. In *In Search of Western Oregon*, Friedman relates that there's an Olympic medalist, Rick Sanders, buried here who was killed while hitchhiking in Yugoslavia. I didn't see him, but I did run across the sweetest photo I've ever seen encased in ceramic—of the Gibson boys, who died twenty-two years apart; the last, Russell, died in 1999. Russell's brother, Kori, died at age eleven in 1977. In the photo they can't have been but four and six. They wear irrepressible grins and rubber mud boots.

Foster Cemetery

Easiest way to find this is to ask at the feed store or at the Foster Farm at the intersection of Highway 211 and Eagle Creek Road. It's up a gated driveway about 600 yards up Highway 211 from the feed store on the same side of the road. If you reach the elementary school, you've gone too far.

The first two graves in this cemetery, now marked by new stones engraved "Came over on wagon train," belong to two nine-year-old girls, Nancy Black and Mary Conditt, who died on September 7, 1853, after consuming too many peaches on a hot autumn afternoon. The cemetery is on a bluff above the original Foster place, now an historical site.

GEORGE

George Cemetery

To find the George Cemetery, find the road to Eagle Fern Park—Wildcat Mountain Road—a couple of miles before Estacada on Highway 224 and follow it to its intersection with Howlett Road and turning right. Howlett becomes Eagle Fern Road, goes past the park and eventually to the cemetery, a few miles after it has climbed out of Eagle Creek Valley.

George is the easternmost cemetery in the Estacada Cemetery Maintenance District, about five miles due east of town as the eagle flies. The community of George lies on a flat, high above Eagle Creek. Not far after George, the Cascades start in earnest.

In many ways Estacada is a mountain town, but unlike, say, Oakridge (a mountain town totally dependent on timber), Estacada has an agricultural base as well. And a middling amount of tourism as Estacada is an entrance to the mountains, not to mention the draw of the fabled Clackamas River, fabled in part by being extolled by Robert Louis Stevenson on his way to the South Pacific, from where he would never return.

The George Cemetery is distinguished by a short tower holding the school bell from what was once the George School, which stands a few hundred yards from the cemetery. At its base, a plaque commemorates thirteen

George families and makes special mention of Nedra Chaney (1995), who "loved the land and its people." All Estacada cemeteries are smartly maintained.

Mulino

Clarkes Pioneer Cemetery

At the very southern end of Beavercreek Road, past the intersection with Unger Road. Cemetery occupies a small hillock on the west side of the road.

The crossroads of Clarkes has also been known as Clarke, Clarkes Corners, and, according to McArthur, the Ringo Settlement. This small cemetery covering the crest of a tiny hill contains several hundred graves yet feels like an intimate family plot. In *Oregon Geographical Names*, McArthur writes that about the same year the cemetery was founded, 1870, one "'Friday' Jones bought some property there for '1 yoke of oxen, a shotgun and $200.'" Six years later he sold out to Irving Clarke and the name stuck. Where the Ringos fit into this is not explained.

Pleasant Home

Pleasant Home Pioneer Cemetery

Behind the church at the intersection of Bluff and Revenue Roads between Sandy and Gresham.

Pleasant Home is in the center of an ellipse of land bordered by Highway 26, the Sandy River, and Gresham. It's no more than a crossroads with a church, the Pleasant Home United Methodist Church (a United Methodist Historical Site graced by a collection of heritage roses), behind which lies this modest, two-acre cemetery. Many of its once upright stones have been laid flat and encased in cement, as is popular, so the cemetery doesn't have the stature of many other pioneer cemeteries. But that shouldn't stop you from visiting it; not only is the surrounding nursery business well worth the diversion, but visible from the graveyard is a small, private, circular garden that is one of the most beautiful garden structures I've ever seen. It is an astonishing find.

SANDY

Cliffside Cemetery

On the west side of Ten Eyeck Road about 2.25 miles north of Highway 26 as it departs Sandy's east side.

The name is somewhat misleading; this cemetery doesn't hang on the edge of a cliff as, say, Meridian Cemetery does. In fact, it covers two or three acres of perfectly level ground. The cliff referred to is the one separating it from the town of Sandy. The cliff is best appreciated from the lookout on Bluff Road east of Sandy. The view is inspiring, but a trip down Ten Eyeck Road will convince you that it's no mean cliff, either. While through the trees, the view disappears and the road is a drift of hairpins with little room to spare, should you meet someone going the other way—which you will—I don't need to tell you to drive cautiously; you'll figure that out for yourself.

In *In Search of Western Oregon*, Friedman claims that the earliest grave dates to 1874. The entrance sign has 1890 above it, but some sources claim 1890 as the address—though, if so, it's not in agreement with its neighbors. The 1978 Oregon Department of Transportation survey has no date listed, and the USGS doesn't know it exists. I'll stick with Friedman; presumably he looked. There aren't a lot of old graves here, and the new ones, of which there are plenty, are primarily flat. What makes Cliffside special is the large number of homemade or self-designed headstones.

SPRINGWATER

Springwater Cemetery

Holman Road intersects Highway 211 two or three miles south of town. Turn west onto Holman, and Metzger Park Road will be the next road you encounter. Take it south. Shortly, the road will bend to the west (right) and the drive to the cemetery is past the curve on the right (west again). The cemetery can be seen from the road.

The town is blessed with a citizenry willing to pay for the upkeep of its cemeteries even in tight financial times. They are to be commended. They maintain nine cemeteries, not all of which are equal. Arguably, the three finest are Forrester, George, and Springwater. Arguably, Springwater is the finest of the three if for location alone.

Not only is Springwater far enough off a minor road to provide solitude, it's a manicured peninsula extending over a deeply cut, wooded valley with a gurgling stream, seen but not heard at its bottom. Walking to the edge of the cemetery and peering through the trunks, one can glimpse pasture land beyond the forest verge, and the land plunges steeply to a thickly bushed ravine. The peninsula harbors the pioneer part of this still-active cemetery and is studded with uprights and obelisks. It is serene. It is why people are still using it. Moving toward the road, the stones begin to lie down in low-maintenance fashion.

There was a gravedigger there the day I stopped by; he didn't know how far back the stones went, but I saw one from 1862. The proliferation of recent stones provides better than average reading for a rural cemetery. It has more than its share of pathos.

Columbia Plateau

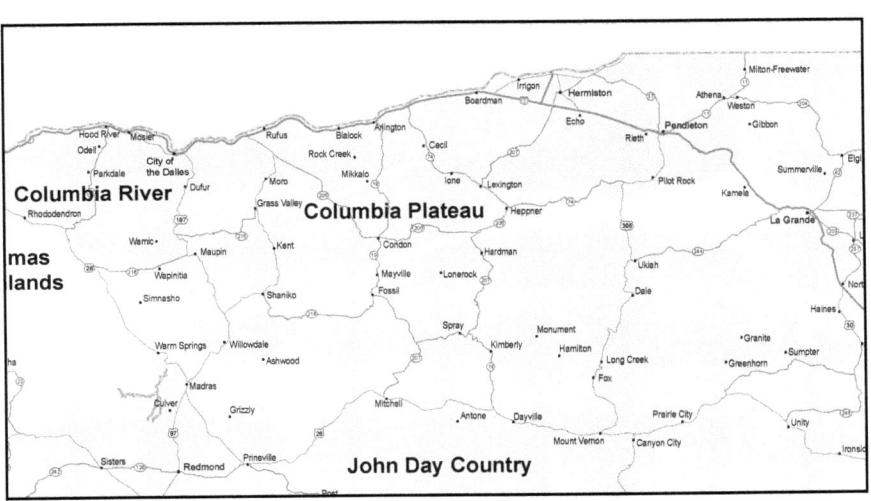

ANTELOPE

Antelope Cemetery

Head northeast on Union Street out of Antelope. Three or four blocks out of town the road bends east (to the right) and becomes Bennett Road. There is no sign at the road, but the drive is paved as far as the cemetery.

An acre-and-a-half under the sun and wind, Antelope Cemetery is as Oregon as it gets. At the bottom of a run of barren hills, it rests on flat land with an unobstructed 360-degree view of the magnificent Oregon outback. Take that, Australia!

This was one of a couple of cemeteries that have no exterior fencing; some individual plots had their own fencing, but the cemetery is open. If its cemetery is any indication, Antelope is not dead yet. "Thriving" is not a word you might use, but Antelope and the cemetery both evidence some sort of maintenance.

BAKEOVEN

Bakeoven Cemetery

About a third of the way from Shaniko to Maupin on Bakeoven Road, you'll see Hinton Road, a dirt road. Take it. The cemetery is 3.5 miles along.

As typical a Wild West pioneer cemetery as one can find, I wouldn't call this half-acre cemetery abandoned, but a headstone dated 1925 might be its most recent. It certainly hasn't been abandoned by the critters that make enormous holes all over the place.

The story is that Bakeoven got its name when a German baker hauling supplies to set up a bakery in the gold fields of Canyon City was waylaid by Native Americans who took his horses, stranding him there. Resourceful fellow that he was, he set up his bakery on the spot and sold bread to miners on their way to the fields.

The only problem with the story is that there's not timber enough to fire a donut kettle, much less a bake oven, within forty miles of the place, and I doubt there was any more in those days. The current owner of the Bakeoven Ranch told me that he and archaeologists have searched unsuccessfully for the site of the supposed oven, which leads one to suspect that the name "Bakeoven" derived from the summer daytime temperatures.

Condon

Condon Cemetery

The north boundary of Condon is Old Cottonwood Road on the west, which becomes Condon Airport Road on the east. Turn east on Airport Road, and the cemetery will appear shortly on the north side (Saint Joseph Cemetery is across the road).

You gotta like Condon for its visions of grandeur. Seven-hundred and fifty-nine people don't take being the capital of Gilliam County lightly. And well they shouldn't.

McArthur, in *Oregon Geographical Names,* calls Condon an "important trading center," though even by 1974 it was dwindling fast. When you go, you'll likely have the place to yourself.

The cemetery tells stories of Condon's rich past. It says, not only was Condon prosperous enough to have both an Odd Fellows *and* a Masonic section, but that it was important enough to warrant a much rarer Knights of Pythias Cemetery, which is sandwiched between the other two, and there is no clear way to tell where one begins and the other ends.

As being on Airport Road would suggest, the topography is dead level (pun intended), giving one a clear view of the distant hills and an intimate experience with the wind. But that's not all; across the road is Saint Joseph Catholic Cemetery.

None of the four cemeteries is being maintained any longer by its parental organization; instead, they've all become wards of the state, which in this case is the South Gilliam County Cemetery District, to whom we doff our hats.

These cemeteries may not be as cute or as well located as the nearby Fossil cemeteries, but they make up for it by being up-to-date with an open-air mausoleum holding forty-eight caskets and ten cremains. That and a couple tin sheds maintain the semi-industrial feel of the landscape.

Driving high above the Columbia can be hypnotic as the land rolls and breaks toward the irresistible river. A landscape once majestically stationary is now decked with rows of wind generators many stories tall slowly grinding out power. Their patient turning only adds to the hypnotic effect. The roads are measured by handmade memorial crosses.

DUFUR

Star #23 Rebekah Lodge Cemetery (IOOF Cemetery)

On the west side of Highway 197 a mile or so north of the Dufur turnoff. No sign, but cemetery is visible from road.

Dufur, named after an early farmer, nestles into a hollow in the center of a treeless massif and once boasted the world's largest apple orchard, which eventually failed, giving way to wheat. Only recently are orchards creeping back up the gorge toward Dufur. In its apple heyday, Dufur was a railroad terminus and a much larger and livelier town. Its current size reflects a more reasonable reality.

The cemetery, the largest one around at four to five acres, doesn't get a lot of use, though it's still being maintained. Like most cemeteries in the neighborhood, the views are stupendous. The black locusts rimming the cemetery are the only trees for miles around, leaving an unobstructed panorama. If there's any drawback to the cemetery, it's proximity to the highway, which is a tad noisier than I'd prefer. Its visibility and prominent location make it an easy choice for a traveler's rest stop.

The cemetery has a fair collection of old stones presided over by three carved faux stumps, which in themselves aren't unusual, except that this time only one is a Woodmen of the World monument.

Another of the trio is from Women of Woodcraft, the female counterpart to Woodmen of the World. Their monuments aren't uncommon, but faux stumps are usually reserved for men. The third marker is strictly an IOOF affair, which is more unusual. Look for the steel profile of a conestoga wagon erected in honor of pioneer John Hanna.

EAST MAUPIN

Buzan Cemetery

Bakeoven Road heads east out of Maupin on the east side of the river. Buzan Cemetery is seven miles east of Maupin on the south side of Bakeoven Road and is visible from the road.

An open acre alongside a little-used road between nowhere and the other side of it. This place has eternity written all over it. It's the freshly painted white gate that sets the tone. A 2003 date shows that the cemetery is still in use, but barely.

ECHO

Echo Memorial Cemetery (Siphon Cemetery)

Take the Echo exit off I-84 outside Hermiston and head toward Echo a couple miles from the highway. Cemetery drive is the last road heading east before one gets into Echo. There is a sign.

The wayside community of Echo has one of the all-time great pioneer cemeteries in Oregon. An historic little town that likes to think it's pushing 700 people, and despite being but a mile from I-5 with big signs on the highway proclaiming it a National Historic Site, Echo doesn't get a tenth of the recognition it should. It's worth it to pull off and visit the cemetery.

Well cared for, the cemetery is an incongruous island of green in a semi-desert, brown-earth world. Irrigation provides what farming there is in the area. Echo owes its existence and whilom fortune to being at the spot where the Oregon Trail left the Umatilla River and headed overland to the Columbia. It was a resting spot for the next push. Even today, the Old Pendleton River Road, which follows the Umatilla from Pendleton west to Echo, is a rugged, poorly maintained blacktop that one is happy to quit at the end of the trail.

With all that, the Echo Cemetery still might not have exceeded the norm were it not for one man, Joseph Cunha, an Azorian Portuguese who made it to America as a young man by stowing away on a Boston-bound ship.

He struck it rich in Echo with ranching, construction, and other business ventures, not unlike a lot of other people in the West; but unlike others, he memorialized his family in death in grandiose fashion.

Instead of mere stones, he had four sculptures commissioned, one for his wife and each of his children.

The sculptures portray people life-sized, with those for the children on separate pedestals while the figure on the wife's memorial is clinging to a massive stone cross. Below the cross is a photo-ceramic of Rita Cunha (1878-1923), flanked by other Cunhas. The Cunha Farmstead is now an historical site, but the cemetery is where the family lives on.

In the past few years the cemetery has upgraded itself considerably with new fencing and parking. They're prepared for much more business, touristy or otherwise.

Mission

Old Agency Cemetery

Head west from the intersection of Mission Road and Highway 331 east of Pendleton 10 miles or so. As Mission Road bends to the right, the drive to the cemetery will be on the left at the beginning of the curve.

Raw and exposed, as is typical for Native American cemeteries, yet despite being supplanted by the newer agency cemetery down the road a piece, this three-quarter acre cemetery still attracts its share of new customers.

It's anything but abandoned and well warrants a stop-by. Behind the agency cemetery is another half-acre cemetery with as yet only two graves in it. What differentiates the one plot from the other is unexplained.

OLEX

Olex Cemetery

Olex is a whilom community where Highway 19 crosses Rock Creek. On the east side of the creek, Upper Rock Creek Road departs from the highway and follows the creek south. Take that road. The cemetery is on the east side, a half-mile along. It's not directly on the road but is quite visible from it.

The size of the cemetery, even if not more than an acre, is far bigger than it needs to be and speaks to the community that was once here. When wind generators die, they don't need cemeteries. Neither do combines, I suppose, but farmers do.

There's a grand starkness here reminding one of the austerity of Nebraska, except that one knows that tens of miles away, rather than hundreds, a whole other world awaits. An austerity sliced through by breathtakingly deep gorges that lead back to fiercely tangled mountains. This is not country for the faint of heart.

Pendleton

Olney Cemetery

Heading south out of Pendleton on Highway 395, as soon as you pass under I-84, Tutuilla Creek Road enters from the east. Take that; the cemetery will appear immediately upon your right (south).

It's not surprising that Pendleton, which has worked overtime presenting itself as a quintessential western town with the woolen mill and roundup and all, should have a stately and well-cared for cemetery. It's big at twenty or more acres rolling over steep hills dotted with mature black locusts, the signature tree of Eastern Oregon cemeteries.

"Stately" is the operative principle here. While there's a great collection of Woodmen of the World stumps and a couple spectacular modern markers, there's not a lot of room given to homemade expressions. It reminds me of Fir Grove in Cottage Grove in that both have similar layouts and both make concessions toward modern times with up-to-date landscaping and provisions for the growing trend of cremation.

And it has a pet cemetery called "Treehaven," though I haven't found any pet stones yet.

WAMIC

Lone Pine Cemetery

Head east from Wamic on State 48. Take Smock Road south. Take a right at the next intersection, and you'll see the cemetery at the top of a hill on your left.

In this quintessential rural cemetery are brand-new graves as well as rows of stone stumps weathering into the ground. A plot chart shows many unknown graves. Situated on a bump in the middle of Smock Prairie, the cemetery has a sweeping 360-degree view encompassing the majestic Cascades, Mount Hood, and the forbidding, dry interior. There's a touching grave on which a father has installed a homemade weathervane for his son. If you're lucky, the cows will come and visit you. R. A. Gerity (1928-1998) is here, with advice spot-welded onto a steel plate: "Listen to the wild.../ It's calling you."

Wamic and neighboring Tygh Valley are among my favorite Oregon towns. If you continue on past the cemetery, you'll eventually come to a little-seen, dramatic crossing of the White River, illuminated with swaths of colored sandstone. It's only a short drive, but the road is terribly maintained; drive slowly.

Pratt Pioneer Cemetery

Downtown Wamic. The lane to cemetery is just past the creek when heading toward Mount Hood. There is a sign.

A nine-grave cemetery in the heart of the hamlet of Wamic (everyone has to learn how to pronounce it on his or her own; try *wah´-mick*). In true peasant style, the *n* in "pioneer" is written backwards. Wamic was Prattville until 1880 when the post office operating under that name closed. It reopened in 1884 as Wamic, named after another local family, the Womacs. (Spelling is not of great import in Oregon.)

Columbia River

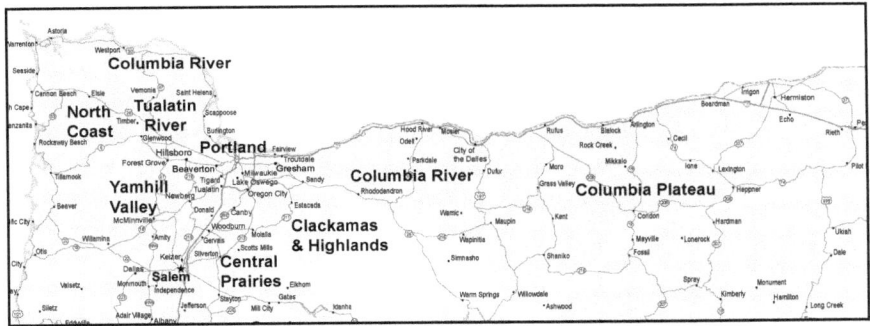

ARLINGTON

Arlington Masonic Cemetery

Take Main Street in downtown Arlington to its end, and there you'll be.

Arlington cleaves to a cut in the high, dry fortress-like cliffs lining the Columbia River before it gouges its way through the Cascade Mountains. One can imagine the rain not falling for years here (although one would be wrong), and the only businesses seem to be a couple of motels and a grain elevator. It's not a place where one would expect to find a first-class, exceptionally well-maintained cemetery. After all, who's to die out here?

Apparently, at least in erstwhile times, quite a number, and their descendants have gone the extra mile to make sure they are well cared for and honored. I don't know when the Masons abandoned this cemetery, but the North Gilliam County Cemetery Maintenance District has picked up the ball and spares no expense growing a sea-green lawn worthy of an English vicarage. In particular, one might note a quartet of Woodmen of the World stumps; quite a catch for such a small-town cemetery.

CORBETT

Mountain View Corbett

Turn south on Evans Road in downtown Corbett. Stay on Evans until Smith Road meets it from the right (west). The driveway for Mountain View is past this intersection.

Mountain View Corbett is the jewel in Metro's crown of fourteen pioneer cemeteries. Lone Fir has the cachet, publicity, and famous names, but Corbett has the beauty, community, and Mount Hood.

For most people, Corbett is a spot of congestion on the way to Crown Point along the scenic Historic Columbia Highway, but for the residents, Corbett is a highly individualistic and artistic community nestled onto the flanks of Oregon's highest mountain, and the cemetery reflects their association not with the river but with the mountain. The mountain is their icon and their guardian. Providing, of course, it doesn't blow (the mountain, not the wind).

Surrounded by steeply sided nursery lands and forested knobs while loomed over by the white point of Mount Hood, this small, two-acre graveyard has fantasy views unparalleled in the lower valley.

Without a doubt, there are many cemeteries that can boast views of Oregon's signature peak—there are five cemeteries in the lower valley alone named "Mountain View"; even Metro lists another Mountain View Cemetery, Mountain View Stark, in its stable—but none nestles as up close and friendly as does Corbett. The other cemeteries only borrow views of the mountain; Corbett owns hers.

DIXIE

Mountain View Cemetery

From the extreme west end of Skyline Boulevard, take Dixie Mountain Road west. Cemetery is on the south side of the road about a mile-and-a-half down. There is a sign. If you get to Pottratz Road, you've gone too far.

At the top of the mountain, beside the cemetery, you'll find the incongruous Dixie Mountain Grange, far, far from any field. The Tualatin Mountains, of which Dixie Mountain is one, aren't much, but they're enough to bend the course of the Columbia—the same Columbia that sliced right through the Cascades—north for a considerable stretch before resuming its march to the sea.

Mountain View Cemetery is small, sparse, and a tad austere. It adjoins an overgrown noble fir Christmas tree lot where all the trees have been topped at some point, leaving a gnarly forest behind. Coming or going from the North Plains side allows one to catch the intimate Shadybrook Cemetery, which one passes on the way.

—COLUMBIA RIVER—

HOOD RIVER

Idlewild Cemetery

Heading out of Hood River on the Hood River-Odell Road, this is the first of two Hood River cemeteries you'll run across beyond the city limits sign.

It's the "with it" cemetery in town, with an outdoor mausoleum, columbarium, and—hang onto your hats—a pet cemetery (one grave: Yoyo Seavert [1989–2003]) complete with its own columbarium. It also has a "Walk of Honor" with "Veterans Scattered Ashes," ending at a basalt memorial column.

Until the outdoor recreation boom of the past couple decades, and in particular the recent rise of windsurfing, Hood River was a prosperous farming community that happened to be in a spectacular location. Except for the disturbing incidents of World War II, the town has led a charmed life, and the inner-city neighborhoods reflect that charm. Its recent boom, fortunately, came too late to suffer the ravages of 1950s and 1960s urban renewal bulldozing, and a good deal of the original core architecture has been retained, except that now the storefronts are filled with fancy emporiums and upscale eateries. The town is ripe with new building that, for the most part, compliments the old.

KNAPPA JUNCTION

Prairie Cemetery

From Old Highway 30, Knappa Dock Road slices off to the north. Take it. Cemetery is on the west side of road less than a mile up.

Prairie is somewhat unexpected. It's good sized for a rural cemetery—two open acres and a couple more in reserve—properly cared for, and while short on epitaphs, is long on personalizations.

The unquestioned centerpiece is the totem cross in full Coastal regalia, deep carving and bold colors, over the grave of Karan White (1942–1973). Another stone boasts membership in the Chinook Indian Tribe; this was their territory.

The other noticeable phenomenon is a large collection of occupational images, including, as one would expect on the river, a slew of fishing boats; unlike the ones on the coast, many of these are gill netters. Boats with poles exist here, but they're in the minority. The felled and limbed tree trunk (death, north-woods style) is a popular image here, one of which is found on the marker for WWII POW Clarence Barendse, which has an unusual engraving of Clarence on the front side. The appearance of POW medals on tombstones also gives one pause for thought. The real merit of Prairie Cemetery (where's the prairie?) is that it gives meaning to the river hamlets slowing traffic on Highway 30. Down here is where the river got working.

Mosier

Mosier Cemetery

At the intersection of State and Davenport Roads in Mosier. Third Avenue in Mosier becomes State Road. Cemetery is barely out of town.

If Mosier were in Europe instead of Oregon, it would be a separate little kingdom à la Liechtenstein. Except without the people. Or the castles. But it does have cherry orchards, and frankly, who needs castles? Roughly a third of the way from Hood River to The Dalles, Mosier is usually bypassed on I-84 at seventy miles an hour with nary a thought. Truth to tell, there's not a tourist infrastructure here as there is in Hood River—just a gas station, convenience store, school, post office, and the like. Also unlike Hood River, there is no flat land in Mosier; the town, the homes, the orchards, and the cemetery all cling to slopes dying to plunge into Mosier Creek. Every headstone has a view.

What a view it is. Surrounded by cherry trees, the landscape is filled with fir forests rambling over mountains, interspersed with neat-as-a-pin orchards and the occasional roof hidden away among the trees. At blossom time, the effect is ethereal. It seems improbable that one could farm such a steep grade or find land closer to heaven.

The Mosier Cemetery proper is hardly more than three or four mostly uncovered acres backed by few gnarly oaks, and it seems likely that many, if not most, Mosierians chose to get buried elsewhere. Nonetheless, this is an active and well-maintained cemetery, with enough interesting graves to make it worth a quick stop.

Mosier is also a good example of a "cemetery dialect." Large, urban cemeteries are designed and operated by professionals who are trained and are current with industry standards that tend to blend out local idiosyncrasies—but small local cemeteries (at least in Oregon), which have often grown out of land-claim donations, tend to be designed and maintained by people who have a restricted cemetery experience, usually confined to their immediate surroundings. In those cases, what's normal and proper (if there is such a thing) is often unknown. Sometimes local customs arise that are limited to one cemetery alone, and traditions whose origins are obscure are nevertheless followed by a number of the inhabitants (hence the "dialect"). In Mosier, it's the "cross in the ground."

It is common, though not universal, for people to build curbs around their plots, although many cemeteries have none at all. Mosier is a mix, but those that are curbed tend to be at least six feet square and infilled with a variety of materials—pebbles, crushed rock, or bark mulch. None of that is unusual, but what is out of the ordinary is that a number of these plots have a cross within them, outlined by two-by-fours on the edge that are infilled with differently colored materials. If you collect cross images, it raises the value of this cemetery considerably. (The handmade, erect cross over Charlotte Seymour's [1946–2002] grave is worth searching out.)

"Mosier Cemetery" doesn't come up in some Internet databases, but the IOOF Mosier Cemetery does. Presumably they are one in the same, and the cemetery probably was turned over to whoever now controls it in the 1950s, when the Odd Fellows abandoned so many of their cemeteries. It's a story oft repeated in Oregon.

PINE GROVE

Jackson Family Cemetery

From Highway 35 south of Hood River about four miles, take Fir Mountain Road to the east. Cemetery is about 1.5 miles and has a sign.

The Jackson Family Cemetery is just that: a one-family cemetery at a bend in a back road—a handful of graves under tall firs. The cemetery will probably still be used yet, but it's a low-key operation. Don't let that stop you from visiting, though, because if the cemetery is modest, the neighboring countryside is fairy-tale beautiful, and otherwise you'll most likely never see it.

The valley has four major sections: essentially the upper and lower valleys and Dee Flats. The gorge of Hood River is deep and only breached by bridges in two places, one down by the Columbia. Smack dab between the valleys and Dee Flats, Middle Mountain sticks up. All these areas make their living growing fruit, and they all market together, but their physical separation makes each area a recognizable unit. The southern half of the Lower Hood River Valley—which is the upper half of the lower half (got it?)—centers (if you could use that word) around Odell.

Highway 35 stays exclusively on the east-south side of Hood River and cuts through the middle of the valley as one would expect. But for the full valley experience, take East Side Road instead. The road goes up and down and twists around sharp turns through a land you thought existed only in mythology. When East Side Road turns back toward the highway, continue with Wells Road, which continues to creep along the eastern valley edge. Eventually, it will meet up with Fir Mountain Road, which heads off into the mountains. This road turns left heading up the mountain, and the cemetery appears on the outside curve of the corner under a crop of fir trees surrounded by open fields. This is as far off the main road as you can get in this neck of the woods without heading into the forest proper.

—COLUMBIA RIVER—

RAINIER

Knights of Pythias Cemetery

Highway 30 in downtown Rainier is B Street. Go south from B Street up the hill to F Street. Turn east on F and follow it as far as it will go. It will eventually become Neer City Road. Cemetery is on the west side.

The Knights of Pythias are a fraternal order begun in 1864. If diminished, like all their brethren, they still exist. Fraternal orders run the gamut from insurance organizations (Woodmen of the World, for example) to secret societies (Yale's Skull and Bones) to benevolent societies we usually associate with "fraternal orders" (Masons, Odd Fellows). Mainline orders tend to be quasi-religious, vaguely militaristic, and overtly patriotic. For a while they were interested in cemeteries.

This smallish cemetery of a couple acres holds on by its fingernails to a steep hillside overlooking the dogged town of Rainier. If not the fingernails of the dead preventing the cemetery from sliding down to town, it's the roots of several large old elms and maples that grace this cemetery protected by a water tank. It's a pleasant enough cemetery, smartly maintained, and with a hawser fence; pity it's not used much anymore. I noted a 1987 stone, but that was a rarity.

Appropriately for a fraternal order cemetery (Pythias, by the way, was a character in a Greek legend), there are at least four Woodmen of the World tombstones here, three of the decorative variety.

SCAPPOOSE

Columbia Memorial Gardens

Take Highway 30 north out of Scappoose about a mile. There's a lot of traffic and not much warning for the cemetery entrance, so beware.

The towns of Scappoose and St. Helens occupy the banks of the Columbia River below the Tualatin Mountains. You may never have heard of the Tualatin Mountains, yet they're enough to bend the Columbia River north after it tears straight west through the Cascades. The Missoula Floods did their part in scouring out the eastern flanks of the Tualatins, leading to precipitous drives over what pass for passes. What remains is a narrow strip of land sandwiched between the water and the hills, through which Highway 30 travels and along which are many of the local cemeteries. Convenient in the old days, but death-defying now.

The lower Columbia was a heavily populated countryside with a number of tribes vying for supremacy until wiped out by disease in the early 1800s. Since then, it's been home to small river communities. Columbia Memorial carries a St. Helens address, but is closer to Scappoose. It's the biggest cemetery around and gets by far the most local traffic.

Saint Wenceslaus Cemetery

Behind Saint Wenceslaus Church at the southwest corner of SW Jenny Lane.

King, a.k.a. Saint, Wenceslaus was a Bohemian Duke of a thousand years ago who was canonized as a martyr for the cause. His name is now attached to the church fronting this cemetery, which, you won't be surprised to know, is filled with Bohemians as well as a number of Italians, resulting in a graveyard with considerably more flair than its neighbors.

Being a Catholic cemetery, and Eastern and Southern European Catholic at that, there's a goodly collection of other crosses here that merit a stop in themselves. This could be a much more decorative and pleasant cemetery were someone to take the care to do a few plantings, but as it is, it's another "backyard cemetery" surrounded on three sides by the rear ends of new, undistinguished housing.

SHILOH BASIN

Kobel (Goble) Cemetery

Cemetery is on Whitney Road, a quarter mile north of Clark Road.

There is some confusion as to name. The USGS lists it as "Goble," as in the former river port down the hill. The Heritage Trail Press Oregon Cemetery Survey site has the correct name of "Kobel," but misspells the town as "Gobel." As John Crawford, Sexton for the Rainier Cemetery District, explained to me, "Kobel Cemetery is named for the original family whose homestead is right across the road from the cemetery. They donated the land, according to Mr. Crawford [no relation] who has the berry farm [across the road]."

The Kobel Cemetery does have a view, and its remoteness in the dense Coast Range above the Columbia River will undoubtedly assure its privacy for years to come. On the other hand, the small cemetery is tree- and shrubless and can only be described using the word "windswept." You may not want this for your final resting place, but you may want to come up and consider what happened to the people drawn to this hardscrabble spot.

John Crawford, who maintains this and nine other local cemeteries for the district (and does a bang-up job), claims this as one of his and his wife's favorites.

SVENSEN

Svensen Pioneer Cemetery (Forest Hill Cemetery)

Svensen is about eight miles east of Astoria on Highway 30. Take a left (south) on Svensen Market Road until it intersects with Old Highway 30. Take Old Highway 30 east to its intersection with Simonson Loop Road heading south. Take that road. Sign to cemetery will appear shortly.

Of all the Finnish cemeteries, this is the jewel. Not more than an acre in size, decorated with a few small shrubs, it's set within surrounding woods that don't let you appreciate its comforting and enclosing nature until you're inside the picket fence fronting it. The picket fence alone is a signal of extra care; the couple of benches strategically placed bolster that impression. The deal is sealed by the tidy kiosk inside the gate, holding jugs, glass jars, plastic pots, and other decorating paraphernalia. The top shelf holds a photo of all twenty-one people who help maintain the place.

THE DALLES

IOOF/GAR [Grand Army of the Republic] Cemetery

Cherry Heights Road intersects with West 6th Street (Highway 30) on the west end of The Dalles, where the new mega-stores and drive-ins are. Take it south, and after three blocks the cemetery will appear on your left. You'll pass Saint Peter's Cemetery on your right shortly before getting to the IOOF/GAR Cemetery.

In French, a *dalle funèbre* is a large, flat stone covering a tomb. Otherwise, *dalles* can be whatever stones you'd like them to be. One theory has it that the French use the word to describe a stone with which they line their gutters, and that the meaning has more to do with the gorge-like effect of constricted stone passages. My *Petit Robert* cites a French idiom, *"se rincer la dalle"* meaning "to drink," so perhaps the town did take its name more from the gorge than the rocks.

While many fraternal order cemeteries have been converted to municipal or community ownership and a few have been abandoned, some fraternal order cemeteries are still going great guns. This is, obviously, the major cemetery in town (at what must be more than twenty acres) and comes equipped with caretakers and a mausoleum. As in many amalgamated cemeteries, it's impossible to know where the IOOF and the GAR cemeteries divide.

The Dalles IOOF has also assumed control of nearby Sunset Cemetery, making them the only fraternal order I know of that has actually expanded its holdings in modern times. The local Masonic Cemetery, in contrast, was "vacated" some fifteen years ago.

A smattering of interesting graphics can be found here, and the cemetery is large enough to have something for everyone. There's an occasional Native American interment or Native American reference, more than you'll find in your average Portland cemetery. It has a tremendous view—but then again, every place in The Dalles has a tremendous view.

Saint Peter's Cemetery

See directions for IOOF/GAR Cemetery.

You know what I like about Catholic cemeteries: That they stand up so tall. They bristle. They shout their presence. Nothing shy about them.

Saint Peter's is not big—a few acres behind a church set back from the road—and, as Catholic cemeteries go, it's quite demure. Nonetheless, all those crosses thrusting immodestly out of the cold stone are impressive.

Like many Catholic cemeteries that give the visitor unexpected surprises, Saint Peter's does not disappoint. Upon entering the cemetery—it slants slightly from left to right—against the left edge, down where the real graves start, there is a small but definite Native American grouping that, once again, demonstrates the Catholics' ability to be catholic as well. The Indian graves may have crosses, but they have native spiritual references too. And a couple of haunting photographs.

The cemetery also has a tree-stump tombstone of the Woodmen of the World genre, but this one is from their sister organization, Women of Woodcraft, and, while one sees their headstones from time to time, one less often sees them assume the stump form.

Sunset-IOOF Cemetery

Find Dry Hollow Road on the east end of downtown The Dalles. Follow Dry Hollow as it heads into the country until it separates into Dry Hollow to the right and 3 Mile Road to the left. Take 3 Mile. Cemetery will appear on the right.

Sunset has one huge plus going for it: the drive through the intense cherry orchards. This place doesn't have the charm of Hood River Valley, but it sure has the trees!

Beyond that, Sunset is a curiosity, an enigma, and an eye-opener. It's a curiosity in that, at hardly more than three or four acres, it's the smallest "memorial park" style cemetery I've seen, and smaller than any I would have imagined. In fact, it seems too small to be profitably run as a lawn cemetery. One wonders how it got here. Lawn cemeteries by definition don't have upright stones and tend to be divided into sections called "gardens," usually presided over by a piece of non-denominational Christian statuary. Sunset is only large enough to have a single garden, but it follows form, as the center of the field is dominated by a statue of Christ.

Then there's that name: Sunset. That's how the cemetery is listed by all my sources—except by the sign at the entrance, which is identical to the sign at the IOOF/GAR cemetery in town. The name "Sunset" has entirely disappeared. Evidently, the IOOF has assumed responsibility for both cemeteries, establishing that, indeed, the cemetery was too small to be profitably run.

In my experience, all other IOOF and Masonic cemeteries have been handed over to someone else or are disappearing or hanging on by a thread. In The Dalles, however, the IOOF is prospering—or, at the very least, they're doing a noble job of maintaining the town's most important cemeteries. (They aren't responsible for the dissolute pioneer cemetery, below.) What is certain is that no IOOF chapter ever began a cemetery such as this, and the questions of who did start it and what happened to it and how it came into IOOF hands remain enigmas.

What's interesting is how well the IOOF is doing compared to the Masons. The Masons still exist in The Dalles, I'm told, but their cemetery no longer does. The Mason I talked to said the cemetery was "vacated about fifteen years ago." He pointed to a row of new houses and said, "Right there is where the cemetery used to be." He allowed that he didn't know where the old bones had gone.

In Sunset, I can report, there's a memorial stone there dedicated in 1984 to the "Early Pioneers from Masonic Cemetery," implying that their remains have found safekeeping in the hands of fellow fraternalists.

In the final judgment, Sunset is like every other lawn cemetery: There's stuff there, but it's hard to find, and you have to scrunch over to read it. The place is worth a visit primarily for that drift through the cherry orchards.

The Dalles Pioneer Cemetery

Find Jefferson Street in downtown The Dalles and take it south until it starts up the hill and comes to a Y; the cemetery will be dead ahead.

It's hard to overestimate the importance of The Dalles pre–white man and what damage The Dalles Dam did to its historical significance when it flooded Celilo Falls, the ancient fishing grounds. The falls were the site of one of the world's great salmon fisheries and a perch at the entrance to the magnificent and terrifying gorge that divides the world of the rain forest from the world of the high desert. Its unique location and abundant fisheries made it a central marketplace that hosted an annual trade fair that brought Native Americans from all over the Columbia Plateau and as far south as California. In its day, The Dalles was one of the most international spots in the West.

Now the fishery is gone, but The Dalles is still on the cusp between two worlds at the entrance to one of America's greatest natural wonders. There's a lot to recommend the place.

The pioneer cemetery is not one of them. It does have a sturdy, no-nonsense entrance sign: two uprights and a crossbar welded together of five-inch pipe painted battleship gray with the words "pioneer cemetery" stenciled in packing-crate lettering on an equally gray, suspended sheet of metal, which at first glance could mistakenly be read as "prison cemetery." It's that compelling. And sturdy.

A small sign at the entrance gives an abbreviated history of the cemetery, which hints at intriguing information. Yet once one gets past the utilitarian entrance arch and the informative sign, one finds a few desultory acres of unkempt oak woods with a stone here, a stone there, and a few fenced private plots overrun with weeds. As has been suggested, there's nothing more forlorn than a ruin of a ruin. By all means stop by—one should visit The Dalles now and again, anyway—but save most of your time for Saint Peter's and the IOOF/GAR cemeteries.

Far East

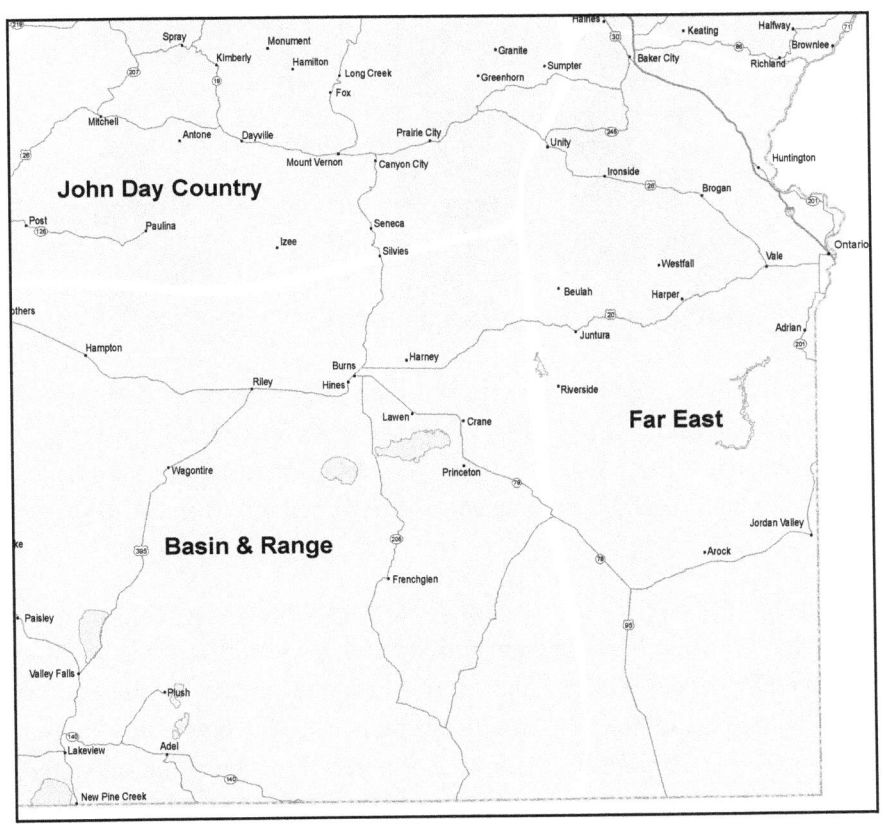

—Far East—

Baker City

Chinese Cemetery

Head east on Baker-Copperfield Highway (7) to where it passes under I-84. Cemetery will be visible on right; look for the pagoda.

Across the road from the truckers and the cowboy angels, a collection of depressions in the ground marks where the bones of Chinese were dug up and repatriated to China. An 1890 stone prayer house still stands, and someone has recently completed a small pagoda with a triangular footprint.

Footpaths are graveled, and a single stone bears witness to seventeen named and fifty unnamed Chinese once buried here. A separate stone honors Lee Chue (1882–1938), whose name is not included on the common stone. Burials here ceased in 1940. There are no names of women, which could either mean none were buried here (not unlikely, as few Chinese women made it to the mining camps) or that they were ignored in the repatriation process (also not unlikely).

This is not an impressive site and it's in a degraded situation. Nonetheless, it's an important remnant of Oregon's history.

John Whealan Grave

Go to the north end of College Street, and where the street bends west (right), there is a curb-cut leading toward a field behind the buildings. The Whealan obelisk is visible from the curb-cut.

Mr. Whealan (1840–1889) was from County Galway, Ireland, and probably came to America fleeing the Irish potato famine of 1845–1849. His is the sole marker in this "cemetery."

His epitaph speaks for itself:

> *The days has come when*
> *All thy conflicts*
> *Have vanised from thy*
> *Path*
> *Thy lonely child who*
> *Mourns for thee*
> *Hopes thourt free from*
> *Pain or smart*
> *Resting thy head on*
> *The Sacred Heart*

Mount Hope Cemetery

South of town, on the east side of South Bridge Street east of Highway 30.

Baker City, known for a time as simply "Baker," has one of the best old-time downtowns left in Oregon. It is an archetypical Western town. Mount Hope is its primary cemetery, half modeled after the Garden Cemetery variety. It's big and fairly treeless, leaving good views of the surrounding hills.

I wouldn't say that Baker City has attracted a particularly creative bunch, but their cemetery reflects better times. For what it's worth, it has an extensive collection of Woodmen of the World headstones, approaching Lone Fir in number.

—Far East—

COPPERFIELD

Copperfield-Homestead Cemetery

From Copperfield—which is where the highway crosses the Snake River from Oregon to Idaho—stay on the Oregon side of the river and drive up Homestead Road (a dirt road), which parallels the river heading north. Take the cutoff to the airport, which starts at the same point as does a runway for a private airport. Cemetery is on the west side of the runway.

This is pretty much the end of the road on the Oregon side of the river. It goes upriver a few miles farther on the Idaho side before petering out there, too. This river, the Snake, and its mother river, the Columbia, have the unnerving habit of going *downhill* into the mountains, which is a tad counterintuitive. It makes for some spectacular gorges; this one is known as Hell's Canyon. It may not be as colorful as the Grand, but it's deeper, and as the name implies, no walk in the park. There are no froufrou tourist attractions rimming Hell's Canyon, only a clear view of God.

The runway along which the cemetery lies is incongruously well paved in contrast with the humble approach road. It is, after all, a fairly select spot. The cemetery is tiny and would hardly be worth the drive were not the location so great. Not more than an acre in size and surrounded by hogwire, it's not well maintained; still, you'd think more people might have taken advantage of its remoteness. When I visited, iris were pushing up under the flowering lilacs.

HAINES

Haines Cemetery

On the east side of Highway 30 a mile or so north of Haines proper.

Haines is not much more than a lump in the highway before getting to Baker City, on a highway (30) that most people no longer use, thanks to I-84. Yet Haines has an above-average cemetery, well maintained and surrounded by cypress trees visible from quite a distance. Even more surprising, it harbors one of the better collections of Woodmen of the World faux stump headstones in the state, especially for a small town. I found three in very good condition.

You might also note the modern marker of John Marcum (1980–2001), which has a cavity carved out of its top surface, inside of which nestles a sculpture of three mountains. *Wow*, I thought when I saw it, *a unique monument*. Must have cost a fortune. I even thought the mountains were carved to mimic the real mountains in the background. By the time I'd seen a half-dozen nearly identical markers, I stopped thinking the mountains reflected any real mountains, but I still thought they cost a pretty penny. Those aside, it's three to four mostly open acres with a smashing view of the mountains. The folks in Haines can be proud.

Halfway

Pine Haven Cemetery

At the southwest corner of the intersection of East Record Street and Slaughterhouse Road on the east side of Halfway.

Founded in 1880, this cemetery comprises a few well-maintained acres with a scattering of trees and a heck of a view. Its most distinguishing characteristic is a quantity of natural-rock headstones with distinctive fonts. Aside from being the butt of infinite local jokes (Halfway to where?), Halfway made recent national fame by selling its name to become Half.com for a year or so as a publicity stunt for a company with that name. Since then, they've floated back to their native obscurity under the lee wall of the Wallowas.

Ontario

Evergreen Cemetery

Adjacent to Treasure Valley Community College in the SW quadrant of Ontario.

The most noticeable thing about the cemetery is its shape, which is a regular rectangle but one block wide by six long and flat as a baking griddle, relieved by only a few small trees. It takes a lot of hoofing to visit it all.

Ontario, named for the somewhat more familiar Canadian province, is the largest town in Malheur County, at roughly 10,000 people. It's found in the very farthest northeast corner of the county, where most of the rest of the county's 30,000 people live. The population density of the county is about three people per square mile. Below three people per square mile is still considered "frontier"—out here, three people per mile is considered crowded. It's enough to know that the county name means "bad luck" in French.

The cemetery faithfully records the historical demographics of Ontario:

white Americans, Japanese, Mexicans, and a smattering of Basques. The Americans and the Mexicans came because of the agriculture; the Japanese were brought to the Minidoka War Relocation Center in Southern Idaho in the 1940s, many of them farmers whose land was stripped from them when they were sent to our concentration camps and who decided to stick around and start over again after the war. The Basques came to herd sheep.

Fairview Cemetery

Cemetery is on the west side of Highway 95, just north of its intersection with Highway 201.

A geo-political orphan, this cemetery functions as the main cemetery for Weiser, Idaho, yet is located across the river in Oregon. Not too large, it's bordered by pines and is as flat as Kansas. Its location near the interchange makes it feel as if any day it could be turned into a gas station or a mini-mart. Nonetheless, it has some interesting stones, including one of the all-time best epitaphs: "Quin" Meyers (1980–1999); "Where the sidewalk ends.../ True life begins./ 'What the hell...?'"

SPARTA

Sparta Cemetery

From Highway 86 at Richland, take Sparta Lane (a dirt road) about ten miles to where Sparta Butte Road takes off north. The cemetery is behind the log house in the NW quadrant of the intersection.

Sparta is the only cemetery I've encountered with a formal Notice of Discontinuance affixed to its entrance. Others have been as surely abandoned, but never so notified. "Abandoned" is not quite the right word; it's still a cemetery, and it's still tended to, albeit in a truncated manner.

The cemetery belongs to the log house below it. The people who own it, Leland and Crystal Sadlowsky, do what maintenance is done, as Ms. Sadlowsky's father, Almon McKnight, is buried there. Other nearby graves for

Minnie and Frank MacKey are even more impressively maintained with a border of rocks around each grave and the ground kept clean and growth free. Ms. Sadlowsky grew up in Sparta, but, according to Leland when I spoke with him in 2010, she moved away some 67 years prior. They currently live in Washington and summer in Sparta, which is officially listed as a ghost town, implying that few or none over-winter anymore.

The oldest building in town, a rustic fieldstone ex-store built in 1872, has apparently been converted to a summer residence, though you can't tell by the outside. The exterior hasn't changed in a century and a quarter, and no landscaping competes with the wild grasses, but the interior is completely refinished. Were I to have a lust to live in any particular building, this might be it.

Grande Ronde & Wallowa Valleys

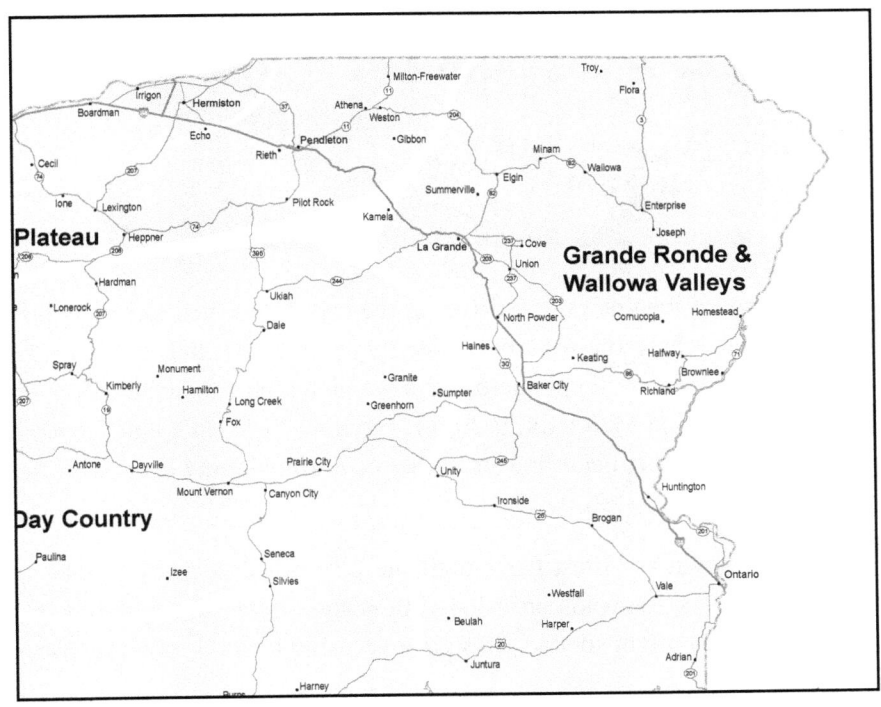

Cove

Cove Cemetery

Take French Street (which becomes Mill Creek Road) southeast from the intersection in the middle of Cove to the first drive on the right (south) one half-mile out of town. There is a sign.

Cove Cemetery begins on the drive up the hill. If you're heading uphill, you'll notice, where the road bends sharply to the left, that dug into the road bank under a young ponderosa is a wooden tablet dedicated to "Fred of Cove," who died March 24, 1929, and remains "beloved by all," evident by the stones and artificial flowers at the memorial seventy-six years after the fact.

Cove was known as Forest Cove until the post office decided in 1868 to shorten the name to avoid confusion with Forest Grove. If you stop by the hot springs, you might spot an old sign advertising it as Forest Cove Warm Springs.

Story has it that it was once in line to be the county seat, but a split in votes between Cove and Forest Cove lost them the opportunity.

The cove for which the town is named is a bite out of the side of the sky-swept Grande Ronde Valley, where it lies up close under the Wallowa wall of the joyfully named Mount Fanny. Some six hundred people snuggle in this nest of Victorian cottages and nondescripts.

Its white cement-block library boasts a neon sign (open Tuesdays and Thursdays), and Cove houses Oregon's most spectacular country church—belonging now to the Episcopalians who maintain camp quarters there—one with wooden flying buttresses and a charming parsonage with peaks over all the windows.

The main intersection—well, the only one, really—is dominated by the grade school, high school, and a one-stop-fits-all car wash, gas station, Laundromat, and convenience store.

Cove Cemetery is a "luncher": a good place to plan a picnic lunch. Aside from the grand arch (matched by one at the entrance to Lower Cove Cemetery), there's plenty of evidence that the cemetery is a point of considerable community pride, most noticeably a bevy of massive stone benches recently scattered around the grounds and a number of groundskeeper buildings.

Also unusual in a rural cemetery are two half-high personal mausoleums, one of which is new. Top design award goes to a brass trio of cross (with a sword haft), anchor, and heart on the cemetery's west side.

It's not an overly literary four acres, nor does it have a plethora of unique stones, but its management and care and tall trees and commanding views make it unusually comfortable.

A motif running through a number of graves is mention of war duty. Despite the usually short duration of such engagements, they were of enough significance to be the only memory recorded on their stones; oldest being that for John Smith (1839–1912), who fought under the command of Colonel Grigsby at the Battle of Nashville in the Civil War.

More unusual is the marker for Grace Byrnes (1921–), who is apparently not only not dead yet but wants to be remembered as having been a B-17 inspector at Douglas Aircraft from 1941–1945 during WW II.

Joseph

Old Chief Joseph Grave Site

Take Highway 82 south out of Joseph; the cemetery is on the right just before the highway reaches the lake.

Old Chief Joseph was father to the Chief Joseph of "I will fight no more forever" fame. He and a handful of others are buried in a small graveyard at the foot of Wallowa Lake. The setting and view of the majestic spires of the Wallowa Mountains are a stark contrast to the minimal memorial. A simple, handmade stone pillar holds a bronze plaque with an embossed likeness of the chief. People leave offerings at its base: bundles of sage, fragments of bone, pebbles, pens, a horseshoe, an MGD beer bottle cap. Amulets dangle from a flanking bush: feathers, scraps of cloth, a spirit catcher.

Old Chief Joseph does not occupy the site alone. He is joined by three members of the McFarland Family and Martha (1875–1947) and Frank (1859–1939) McCully. There are a few pebbles at the base of their stone but no trinkets, no sage bundles, no beer caps. The epitaph reads: "Frank David McCully/ the Father of Wallowa County/ was buried in this Indian Cemetery because of long friendship with Chief Joseph and his People."

La Grande

Grandview Cemetery

At the end of Foothill Road, which is what 20th Street becomes on its southward journey after crossing Gekeler Street.

La Grande has lumped all its cemeteries under Hillcrest Cemetery management, and they do a bang-up job. This cemetery has eight to ten acres and a goodly collection of graphics and epitaphs, led by a small but finely detailed sculpture of a fireman in full regalia.

La Grande was named after the Grande Ronde Valley, a pancake-flat bowl flanked by some powerful uplifts. The scenery is majestic.

Hillcrest–Hillcrest East

On 12th Street behind Eastern Oregon State College; Hillcrest East is across the road.

This well-maintained, well-used cemetery is the flagship of the La Grande Cemetery District. The larger of the two cemeteries, Hillcrest at fifteen acres, was once a Masonic cemetery; and Hillcrest East, a more modest four acres, used to be Calvary Cemetery and still sports a large crucifix dedicated to the Rev. P. J. Driscoll (1872–1920) "by his parishioners."

A small chunk of Hillcrest has been reserved for an orderly alignment of modern military uprights, somewhat like the displays at River View and Salem Pioneer, yet these honor current veterans, not long departed ones. Most recent military stones in Oregon cemeteries are of the flat-earth variety, so it's especially nice to see ranks of white monuments.

Hillcrest is not a grand cemetery and has none of the pretensions of an Echo, but under a canopy of locust trees it captures a large view of the surrounding countryside and is a more than adequate final stop. Should you chose to get off here, you'll be accompanied by at least two wonderful names: one is Bozo Grubich (1865–1940), and the other is Sierra Skye Carlson, October 27, 1986. Her stone reads, much like the John Denver song: "And the wind will/ Whisper her name to me."

Meacham

Meacham Cemetery

Take Meacham exit from I-84, halfway between Pendleton and La Grande. The road parallels the interstate heading northwest. After a half-mile, Ross Road enters from the west under a bridge carrying interstate traffic. Take that road, which forks after it goes under the viaduct. Bend right, and the sign for the cemetery will appear on your right.

This tiny, scraggly cemetery has only a handful of markers and is close to a freeway, yet it's one of the more curious cemeteries in the state. Despite its remote location, the cemetery is in active use, and the majority of the few graves are recent, but its distinguishing characteristic is that every grave, instead of being marked by a stone or plaque of some sort, is located by a section of PVC drain pipe to which is attached a wooden board with the deceased's vitals. Two babies' graves are surrounded by white picket fences, and one grave is marked "In honor Chinese labor." This cemetery may be small, but you'll never see anything else like it.

NORTH POWDER

North Powder Cemetery

On the west side of Highway 237 as it enters North Powder from the north.

Although you may have never heard of it, North Powder is a venerable community by Oregon standards. Its name was translated from Chinook and describes the powdery dust alongside the river. It's a still-active and well-run cemetery of several acres that dogleg to the left toward the rear. Its collection of new material is good, if limited, but it excels in older stones, including a couple of unusual Woodmen of the World markers.

Summerville Cemetery

Imbler is a crossroads community on Highway 82 north of La Grande. Summerville Road meets Highway 82 at the north end of Imbler. Take that west. After a bit, the road will bend northwest and the cemetery will appear on the east side.

With twelve acres of well-tended land on a slight rise in the middle of the spectacular Grande Ronde Valley, this cemetery's majestic location somewhat overwhelms it. It has a good collection of older stones and plenty of new, including a larger than usual collection of good epitaphs. Those cowboys get to talking. What distinguishes this cemetery is a centrally located bungalow that looks for all the world like somebody's home but turns out to be, upon closer inspection, a chapel and cemetery office. Imbler is not far south of Elgin, around which there are a few other interesting graveyards.

UNION

Union Cemetery

At the east end of E. Fulton Street in Union.

Union has one heck of a cemetery, especially given the size of the place.

The secret, according to the sexton, is the $100,000 annual budget that, he told me, was due to increase as neighboring wind farms came online. In any event, it's big, at twenty-five acres, of which only a dozen or so are currently in use. Part of its land, in fact, is rented out as horse pasture.

Aside from a sterling collection of Victorian and modern markers, the cemetery maintains an on-grounds office and is building a cenotaph memorial-cum-columbarium on the high side of the cemetery, both of which pale in comparison with a minuscule chapel containing two pews that hold three people each, at best. It's a converted tool shed and may not get much use, but it certainly is charming. The sexton doesn't know its age but says that it's built entirely with square nails. He also claims that the original foundation was of field stone and was only one-thirty-second of an inch off level on one corner, and that only because a ground squirrel burrowed under it.

Like most cemetery workers, the sexton was willing to talk all day, and one of his stories concerned a statue of a young lady that was carved in Italy and always sports a bouquet of red plastic flowers, replaced annually by an unknown party. "I spent two nights sleeping in the chapel trying to catch whoever puts up the new flowers, but I never did," he said.

Wallowa

Bramlet Cemetery

West of Wallowa on Highway 82 coming into town, take Promise Road north. Take a left on Bramlet Lane. The cemetery is a few hundred yards along.

A one-acre cemetery on flat ground watched over by one lone tree, with sweeping views of the Wallowa wall, this cemetery is actively accepting new residents but is definitely a neighborhood cemetery sans amenities.

Wallowa Cemetery

Take Highway 82, the main drag through the hamlet of Wallowa. Heading east through town, when the highway bends south, continue straight on what becomes Troy Road (also known as Whiskey Creek Road). Cemetery is about a mile along.

This has, arguably, the best location of the Wallowa Valley cemeteries, being backed by a barren hillside and looking out toward the Wollowa Wall. Consequently, it has (again arguably) the best "feel" of the local graveyards and has inspired some of the better monuments around. It also has one private mausoleum, unusual in any part of Oregon.

John Day Country

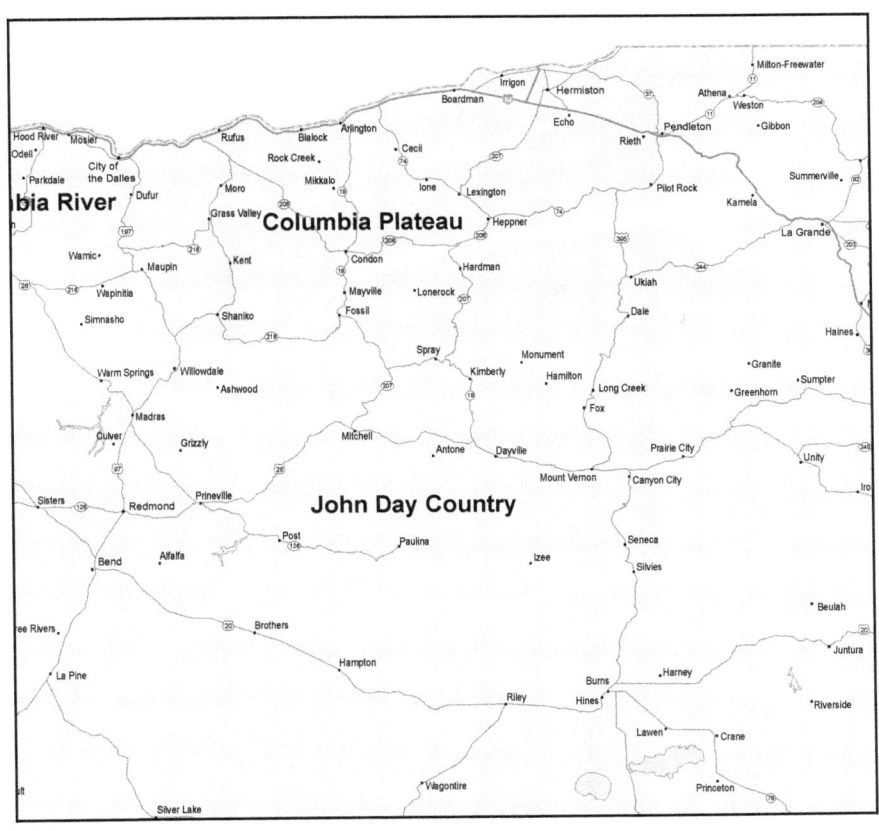

CANYON CITY

Canyon City Cemetery

Take Main Street east up the hill and follow the second cemetery sign (the first leads to Saint Andrew). This cemetery shares a parking lot with tiny Boot Hill Cemetery (see below).

Canyon City is one of the fabled cities in Western history, not to mention Oregon's. Gold was discovered here in 1862, and for the next few decades it was a wide open town. If there was any law, it didn't show up on Friday nights. Besides miners, the town attracted gunslingers, card sharks, saloon keepers, "ladies of the night" (see also Boot Hill, below), and a number of Chinese miners.

Not more than a five-iron wide, Canyon City is a couple miles long, trailing up a narrow canyon at the foot of the gold fields. Two fires destroyed most of the old buildings, but there are enough left to give the town character, and its rambling streets were not so much laid out as grown. There's no other town in the state remotely like it, and anyone with a yen for seeing the "Old West" should come see it before the tourists hit.

The Canyon City Cemetery, seemingly, serves as the primary cemetery for John Day, the town at the bottom of the canyon. John Day, the mountain man who lent his moniker to the town, never saw his namesake. While John Day sports a modest cemetery of its own (Rest Lawn), Canyon City has the space, upkeep, stones, and view. When I visited, it also had deer, perhaps a dozen, that drifted slightly in front of my own peregrinations: grand dame, yearlings, children, and a young buck that all lined up behind the matriarch when she finally led them out of the grounds.

While ODOT gives a date for the cemetery as 1880s, I ran across a grave for James Daulby, "Born in Baltimore MD./ Killed by Indians in/ Grant Co. Or. during the/ Raid of the Bannock/ and Piute tribes/ in June 1878/ Age 23 years." And Boot Hill next door claims a date of 1863 for persons buried there because they were unworthy of the common graveyard, implying that Canyon City Cemetery already existed.

It's hard to imagine that people weren't dying in Canyon City within a year after the 1862 strike, so one can probably assume that the cemetery, graves marked or not, dates back to roughly that age. The community has long recognized the importance of its cemetery and, consequently, it's well maintained, without evidence of the vandalism common in some pioneer cemeteries.

I found many markers that reflected the community and its history, ones that moaned "Old West." Any cemetery adjoining one called Boot Hill is aiming for romance, and Canyon City is happy to assume the image. Its mining persona is well represented by a modern, hand-carved wooden slap marker for "Milt 1914–1982." The West is fond of its first-name-only markers, usually wooden. We know Milt was a miner because a pick and shovel have been carved into the marker's face.

Boot Hill Cemetery

Shares a parking lot with the Canyon City Cemetery.

Boot Hill is explained via two postings at the cemetery site. The wood-burned, sturdy sign is accredited to an "Old Timer" who tells of the four graves belonging to two horse thieves and a couple "ladies of the night." A more recent three-page report under plastic elaborates and corrects (we presume) much of what is burned into the larger sign.

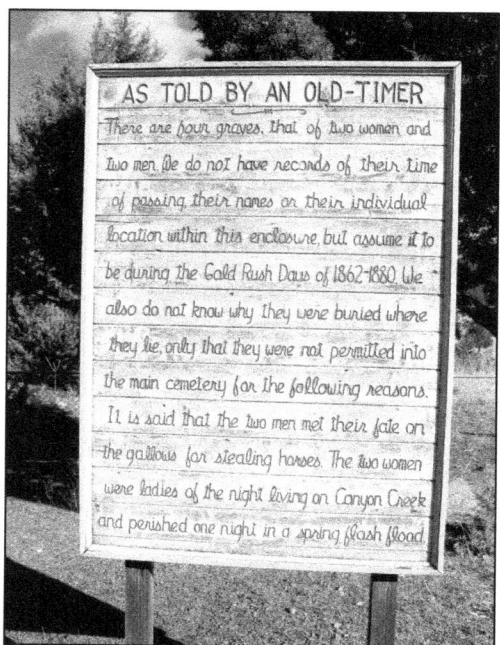

According to that document, all four graves belong to murderers who were hanged on separate occasions. The Old Timer, it appears, was only passing rumors and had no solid information.

Fossil

IOOF #110 Cemetery

Head south out of Fossil on Highway 218, a.k.a. Washington Street. The drive to the cemetery heads east off the highway on the outskirts of town.

Fossil, Oregon (population 470) is connected to the Ochocos mountains, not as grand as the Cascades but with steep and broken land that repels most casual visitors. The vistas here are broad and sublime. To the north lies the high wheat country of the Columbia Plateau, but Fossil ultimately turns its face to the fossil beds and painted hills of the John Day Country, so that's where I place her cemeteries.

The intense concentration of 470 people in the middle of the sage brush means that Fossil is not only the urban center of Wheeler County but also its county seat. But don't count this town out. It has, after all, both Odd Fellows and Masonic cemeteries. Often these two cemeteries cluster together, but here each claims its own hilltop on opposite ends of town.

The IOOF Cemetery (Lodge #110) is much the larger of the two and is well organized along a ridge into long rows of curbed plots. I was there late on a perfect autumn day, shooting pictures as the limpid afternoon sun cast a golden patina over everything and shadows stretched and fell into dark pools. This cemetery is well maintained and quite active. You're in good company if you're buried here.

Mount Vernon

Moon Creek Cemetery

Moon Creek Lane (or "Road"—both seem to be used) heads north from Highway 26 about five miles west of Mount Vernon. You'll cross the river then reach a T, with Moon Creek Road continuing to the west. Cemetery is about two miles from there on the north side of the road.

Moon Creek Cemetery is as evocative a name as you'll find, and its site fits the name. The John Day river cuts an impressive swath through the center of Eastern Oregon, much of it an awesome gorge, but a relatively tame section from a western terminus, where the highway snakes through an improbable cleft in a mountain wall to Prairie City in the east, is a green, rich, bucolic oasis in an endless sea of rugged mountains. Moon Creek Cemetery has an exquisite view of the western end of that valley.

The cemetery, hardly more than an acre, is accompanied by teenage trees shading a well-watered, mowed lawn. It is an actively used cemetery, as I imagine it will be into the foreseeable future. All in all, a delightful place to be buried—so much so that, were I buried there, I'd want business cards printed up saying so. Putting it on the north side of the John Day across the river from the highway was a capital idea. It's hard to imagine anything will disturb this peace or view for a long time.

Spray

Haystack Cemetery

Find this five or six miles (at milepost 36.2) up Highway 207 from where it takes off from the John Day River east of Spray. There is a sign at the highway.

Location is everything. What this cemetery lacks in quantity of graves, it more than makes up for in view down a long fade toward the John Day River.

It would be hard to over-dramatize Spray's location. The drive up Highway 19 from Fossil to Dayville in the depths of the John Day Canyon is as awe-inspiring a drive as one can have in this state, and this state is stuffed with awe-inspiring drives. This one's a swooner.

Halfway between Fossil and Dayville there is Spray. There are farms scattered along the river, there are ranches in the highlands, and there's a considerable amount of back-country adventuring possible here. This is the heart of the John Day Country; hold your ear to the ground and you can hear it beat.

North Coast

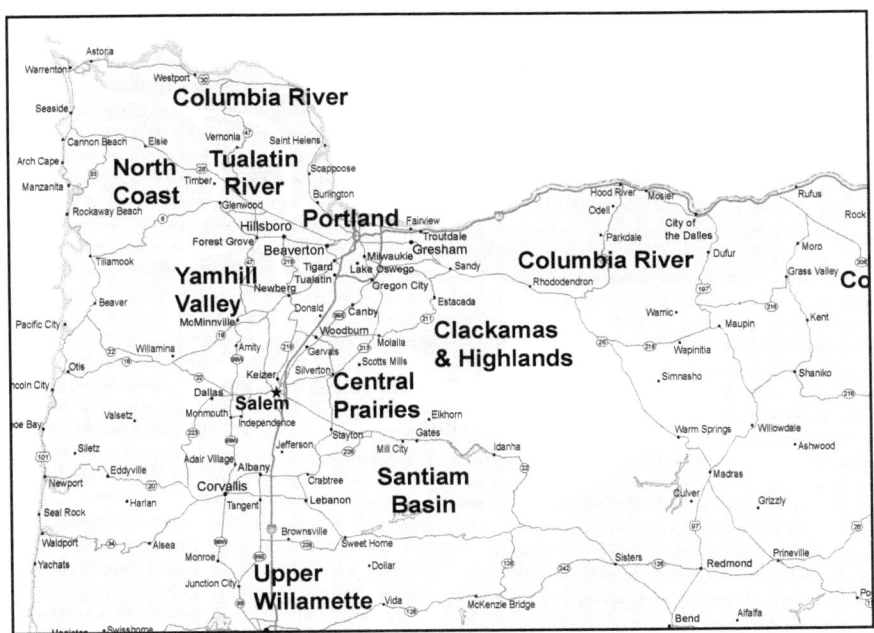

ALSEA

Alsea Cemetery

On the north side of Highway 34 about a mile west of Alsea proper. There is a sign at the highway and the cemetery is visible from the road.

I wouldn't call Alsea a secret place, as most Oregonians know of it, but it's not an oft-visited place, due to the narrow twisting road that connects it to Waldport on the coast and to Corvallis in the Willamette Valley. Most of the road is serpentine, but driving though some sections, like rounding Mary's Peak, are downright tortuous.

That's its first virtue. Its second virtue is that not only is it a pretzel, it's a skinny pretzel. There's not a lot of room for cars to pass each other, so bridges and hairpins must be navigated with caution. The third virtue, a corollary of the first two, is that because of its skinny nature and secession of tight turns, very few trucks use the highway. For that matter, few people use it, period. Much of the time, particularly during the week, you'll have it to yourself.

Which brings us to its fourth virtue: beauty. Not only are the turns tight, but the neighboring slopes are precipitous. There are places along the route called Little Switzerland, which provides some hint as to the terrain. It's secluded, it's verdant, and it harkens back to a lost era. There are places more remote in the Coast Range, but this is a painless way to get a sense of isolation. In winter, the road gets even hairier and the isolation more palpable.

Alsea, the hamlet, hardly more than a drop in the road with a population hovering in the teens, has a brand-new sidewalk in front of its school, with faux brick walkways—the only sidewalk in town. Alsea is the center of the farming, artist, and outback community of Alsea Valley and provides services to the even more remote Lobster Valley. Even with those people thrown into the pot, there's not a lot of company back here. Strangely, though, there's enough folk to maintain, and maintain well, this relatively huge rural cemetery of twenty acres, not all of which is cleared. It's old for the Coast Range and the largest I've yet run across this deep in the mountains. Alsea has always had its own magic.

As one would expect, there are stones with etchings of log trucks and loggers and one with a metal detector, and there's a particularly nice wooden slab marker, maybe three inches thick and a couple feet wide, hand-carved on top to look (roughly) like mountains, and accompanied by other logging paraphernalia.

The caretaker pointed out the white-bronze marker for Thomas Phillips (1826–1924), tall and square with decorative panels bolted to all sides. According to him, this marker was used as a drop point during prohibition for transferring booze and money, one panel being unbolted and rebolted over and over again so often that the original nuts wore away and have been replaced by mismatching ones. I've heard the same story told about many a cemetery, which either means it was a common practice, or that it's an urban myth (see Crystal Lake Cemetery in Corvallis, in the Upper Willamette section).

ASTORIA

Greenwood Cemetery

A couple miles south of Astoria on the west side of Hwy 202, slightly past the bridge over the Wallooskee River. There is a sign.

Greenwood may not be the cemetery of choice for most Astorians, that honor probably going to Ocean View in Warrenton, but it's still a fair-sized cemetery reaching up the slope of a hill overlooking Youngs River, with land left to fill.

The most noticeable feature of this cemetery is a larger-than-life-size statue of (presumably) the Chinook Chief Concomly, for the pedestal carries a dedication to "deceased members of Concomly Tribe No. 7." The good chief has an ornamental braid down his back, reaching to the ground, and in his hands he holds a hatchet and a knife. There's a cherub on a pedestal further up the hill, but it pales in comparison with Concomly. As a bonus, there are three Woodmen of the World concrete tree stumps here.

BIRKENFELD

Fishhawk Cemetery

Fishhawk Road enters Highway 202 from the north approximately four miles west of Mist at the crossroads of Birkenfeld. Take it. You will shortly cross over a small bridge, and a few hundred yards later Fishhawk Road will bend to the left; take the left-hand dirt road and follow it to the end.

In a place where one would expect a primitive, forest-bound cemetery, instead one finds a neat and tidy two-acre cemetery with two large stone crosses worthy of River View. Half the cemetery is planted with scattered evergreens—cedar, cypress, and holly—including a few young Douglas firs that will eventually overwhelm the place if something's not done about them. It's not a lush or abundant cemetery with rows of personalized stones—it's small, but if you lived in the neighborhood, this wouldn't be a bad place to settle down for the millennia.

ELSIE

Elsie Cemetery

It's easiest to find this cemetery by heading east on Highway 26 toward Portland from the coast. About a mile east of Elsie, Red Bluff Road intersects from the north. The cemetery road heads south just thirty yards east of the Red Bluff intersection.

The Elsie Cemetery is somewhat of an anomaly, as not many cemeteries exist in the middle of the Coast Range, but Elsie is about as middle as one can get. Few live around here, yet traffic on Highway 26 can be nerve-wracking and downright dangerous.

A gently crested acre of mostly open ground surrounded by the coastal rain forest, the Elsie Cemetery would be a perfect place for a picnic, were not the traffic noises from nearby Highway 26 so intrusive.

An opening in the trees offers a glimpse of deeply mantled hillsides, and the air smells of the ocean. It's kept well clipped and is an active cemetery despite there being almost no nearby residents. Perhaps people from elsewhere chose this romantic spot. Or maybe it just fills up from accidents on Highway 26.

The crowning jewel of the cemetery is a handmade, wrought-iron bed frame surrounding the grave of Christie Marie Miller (11-29-66). At one time there was a row of crude crosses in what looked like a pet cemetery off to one side—at least I hope Tuffy Malone, Edna Ferber, Chester A. Riley, and "Blackie" aren't really buried there—marked with hand-painted crosses and signs, which have since disappeared.

The cemetery only goes back to 1887, and there are not a lot of old markers here. Some have, likely, moldered to the ground. Noticeable is a regulation government stone for David Wilson, who died in 1897. David was a First Sergeant in the Second Oregon Mounted Volunteers who fought in the Indian Wars. Such fighter graves are found scattered among the rural cemeteries of the state.

MANZANITA

American Legion Cemetery

Turn south (toward the ocean) on Necarney City Road, about a mile south of the Manzanita turnoff on Highway 101. A few blocks down, Cemetery Road meets Necarney City Road from the right.

The ratio of American Legion cemeteries to the population of cemeteries in Oregon is (at current count) 1/610. Why Manzanita should be so blessed is unaccounted for. It is a two- to three-acre park with an acre addendum, surrounded by a low chain-link fence, as if that is going to keep out the rain forest.

The lack of other fencing suggests a tentative standoff between the guardians of the memories and the forces of nature, which would as soon eliminate the place.

What a pity that would be, as there are innumerable treasures within its small confines, making a lengthy stop well deserved. An abundance of natural stone markers in varying sizes is capped by a several-ton split monster marking the grave of ex-Adidas chair Paul Strasser (1947–1993), still being bedecked with new baby shoes.

Manzanita has been spared the ravages that have hit many Oregon coastal towns. It is one of the few coastal communities where the new architecture is on a par with the old, and the downtown, what there is of it, hasn't been marred by fast-food joints or tacky bars.

Swarms of teenagers don't clog the streets; nor, for that matter, do swarms of tourists. It's a delightful place to spend a couple days walking the rustic streets. Dogs nearly outnumber people here, and everyone has to take theirs for a daily walk on the beach. The mountains behind Manzanita are some of the more rugged on the coast, and the scenery is bulked up to match.

MIST

Mist Cemetery

Follow Highway 47 east from its junction with Highway 202 in downtown Mist and you will soon see the cemetery and associated church on your right.

There might not be a trail of crossroads more romantically named than that of Jewell, Vesper, and Mist (interrupted by the less euphonious Birkenfeld) along a thirteen-mile stretch of a backcountry two-lane in the bosom of the Coast Range. Vesper and Mist share the banks of the Nehalem River, which curls a virtually complete circle through the knuckle of Oregon on its way to reach the sea. At 118 miles in length and draining nearly 1,000 square miles, it's the largest of the Coast Range rivers other than those issuing from the Cascades: the Umpqua and the Rogue.

A major difference between the Coast Range and the Cascades is that the Coast Range is occupied. The Cascades—with the exception of the late, lamented timber town of Oakridge and a few vacation/tourist spots—are pretty much a blank slate (albeit with a hide of fir trees). The Coast Range, on the other hand, is riddled with tiny valleys just large enough for a few cows or goats and their herders. Few tourists ever depart from the cross-range highways, and Portlanders flood through the gaps toward Seaside and Manzanita without ever knowing that a world of small farms and lumber outfits lies hidden behind the precipitous hills and perpetual fog and, well, mist. The Nehalem River is spotted, especially in its upper reaches, with these verdant holdings. Mist—named, naturally, for the moisture laden air prevalent here—occupies the heart of this agricultural micro-world.

There used to be more people living in these valleys, but paved roads and the Internet have driven many into the big cities. Jewell and Vesper don't rightly exist anymore, but Mist hangs on as a presence. Maybe the cemetery has something to do with it.

More or less in the center of Mist, it runs along the road behind a white fence and is properly called a churchyard, thanks to a simple, white pioneer church poised on the edge of a small cliff at the east end of the cemetery. The church, which looks as if it's still in use, is pretty basic, sans steeple, but has the right touch for this unpretentious fairyland. The one-acre churchyard matches the church in simplicity, touched up with a few rhododendrons and small evergreens. Like the neighborhood, it's not crowded. It's most distinguished set of markers is a row of four low, handmade, cement crosses toward the west end, the fanciest of which (Lottie Titus, 1919–1990) is faced with crushed rock.

NEWPORT

Eureka Cemetery

Find NE Third Street as it parallels Highway 20 coming into Newport from Corvallis. Take Third Street east. Shortly after it leaves the city grid, the cemetery will appear on the left side of the road.

A fifteen-acre, uphill park around a wooded gully, Eureka Cemetery is Newport's answer to the garden cemetery movement and is evidently the cemetery of choice for current Newportians. It has grown by increments, each addition marked off by natural boulders. The original, central "Bensell Addition" (I'm somewhat confused as to how an original donation can be termed an "addition") allows uprights under its canopy of trees, while the newer sections follow contemporary lawn cemetery practices.

When it comes to natural boulders, the one for Joseph Palmer (1970–2003) stands out, being several feet high and engraved with a pictograph. The other new monument that is unavoidable is a white granite obelisk capped with gold and mounted on a black granite pedestal polished to a mirror-image shine. It commemorates the birth and death of Leland Borges on June 19, 1990, and the life of his mother, Donna Borges (1952–2004), who "died unexpectedly." New obelisks are almost unheard of, though they are beginning to make a minor comeback. Wouldn't the Egyptians be surprised?

I was met by Gary, the affable sexton, when I peeked into the small office building to see what they had to offer. Gary was willing to give me the rundown of the entire central coast. In the office, he showed me Eureka's license from the Oregon Mortuary and Cemetery Board. "There, look there at that number." He beamed as he indicated Number 00001. "When the state decided they could make money by licensing cemeteries, we were the first one they thought of," he said.

Gary also pointed out the enigmatic epitaph for Kay Shineflug (1939–1998): "Excuse me...."

SILETZ

Paul Washington Indian Cemetery

At the east end of Siletz heading out Logsden Road, the last drive to the north is Park Way and goes to the headquarters of the Confederated Tribes of Siletz. The cemetery is located on the tribal grounds; keep driving around to the rear of the main building.

Originally named the Siletz Cemetery but renamed for a Native American Pfc. who was killed in France during WWI in 1918, the cemetery's sponsor, the Confederated Tribes of Siletz, has prospered recently thanks to gaming casinos. As recently as the 1960s, the cemetery was mostly brush; in those days, the town was gritty and run-down. Now, the graveyard brush is all gone; instead, great ancient trees spread their limbs protectively over a verdant lawnscape cosseted by lush shrubbery and floral plantings.

The undergrowth tangle of rain forest has given way to one of the most beautiful cemeteries in the state; if you're lucky enough to come on or shortly after Memorial Day, you'll see it transform from "one of the most" to "the most" beautiful cemetery in the state. If you've had any experience at all with Native American burial grounds, where so often the destruction wrought upon the people is reflected, the opulent serenity and the hyper-manicured and decorated graves are a wonderment here.

In contrast to the meticulously maintained lawn, individual plots and associated decorations—which can border on the fantastic—are scrupulously cleaned of the slighted suggestion of vegetation; the grave sites themselves, instead of leveled with the ground, are mounded to a foot or so high with dirt. Come Memorial Day, the burial mounds fairly disappear beneath blankets of real or artificial flowers. And that's the mere beginning. Anything and everything else can be used to embellish the grave of a loved one, but it's never hit-and-miss nor randomly thrown together.

Everything is arranged with the utmost care. I've seen other cemeteries gussied up for celebrations, but never with such attention to detail and taste. (My favorite display was a four-foot, eight-inch-wide pitch blackboard with yellow dashes down the center of a miniature highway where dozens of toy cars and trucks filled the lanes.) The cemetery in full flower is simply gorgeous.

The trees harbor a scattering of old stones now joined by many more modern ones. The cemetery is very active, and sometimes several graves group together in orchestrated arrangements of plantings, arches, benches, ephemera, etc.

TAFT

Taft Cemetery

Heading south on Highway 101 in Taft, turn left of SE Fortieth Street (opposite the Inn at Spanish Head). The cemetery is at the end of the street.

Simply put, this cemetery offers an enormously awesome panorama. Other cemeteries promise an ocean view, but this one delivers and delivers and delivers. If you squint hard, you might see Hawaii. There are no trees, no bushes, no hummocks, no dunes, nothing between you and an endless expanse of sky and sea. The hill upon which the cemetery climbs is high enough that Highway 101 and the Inn at Spanish Head shrink beneath one's feet. Pray to God that the wind doesn't blow; when it does, you'll know why all the trees sweep toward the mountains and bare their teeth to the gale. Try visiting on a nice day.

Be prepared to spend some time, as the grave markers keep pace with the prospect. Large, small, extravagant, or modest, each is more delightful than the last.

Once you're able to tear yourself away from the view, you'll first be struck by two "altars" built to commemorate the Fletchers: one for Herbert (1901–1991) and Stella (1900–1989), and one for, presumably, a grandchild, Colleen (1955–1992). Colleen was a sergeant in the U.S. Air Force during Vietnam and is memorialized on her monument with a photo-ceramic of her in military headgear.

The Fletchers' extravagances might catch the eye first, but the more one pokes around the ground, the more one will find, including a large number of handmade markers: a hand-cast and painted coastal scene complete with pelican, a blue mosaic sunset guarded by broken bricks, a simple wooden cross carved with the deceased's name, a three-part marker honoring two male friends from Wisconsin, handmade and painted tiles surrounded by crushed white rock and blue boards, and the ubiquitous PVC pipe cross.

TILLAMOOK

Tillamook IOOF Cemetery

South of Highway 6 (First Street) on the east end of Tillamook, between it and Third Street.

Bless the Odd Fellows' hearts for pouring out so many cemeteries. This one is quite typical, giving rest to many prominent early Tillamookers without a lot of attention to aesthetics. Give them credit, though, for having erected a mausoleum on a low corner near the entrance, an unusual nod to modernity in fraternal cemeteries.

Other than the slope at the front, this is a flat, open, six-acre cemetery adorned with one cedar and one rhododendron and the largest collection of white bronze markers I've encountered. There must be nearly fifty, and this collection is phenomenal. None is particularly large, but their sheer number is astounding.

There are two coastal valleys large enough to have an agricultural significance: the Coquille River Valley and the Tillamook Bowl, a nearly round, flat valley at the end of five rivers. Tillamook is smaller and more concentrated than its southern competitor, but its tenacious devotion to its industry has made its cheese a national brand.

Not only is the Tillamook Basin smaller than the Coquille Valley, but the mountains surrounding it are steeper, tougher, and climb right out of the valley floor. The valleys behind these hills are too small to have notable farming, and few people live outside the basin proper.

TOLEDO

Toledo Cemetery

Cemetery is at the east side of NE Arcadia Drive, about a half-mile south of where it intersects with Highway 20 outside Toledo.

Alas, the mill in downtown Toledo is not steel. Perhaps it would smell better that way. As it is, only the persistent odor saves this place from being perfect. Toledo does have its arts community, probably an economic spillover from Newport, but until the air quality improves, it's safe from gentrification.

If cemeteries are an indication of community, though, then Toledo ranks high, as this modestly sized two-acre cemetery, while built on a veritable roller-coaster landscape, is richly planted under big old trees. The hills are steep enough to warrant caution when the grass is wet, but there is lots of personalization here, so a hike through the place repays the effort.

The extreme nature of the turbulent landscape, coupled with mature plants, creates many a small outdoor "room," giving the prospective lot-selector a wide choice of locations.

WARRENTON

Clatsop Plains Cemetery

At the intersection of Clatsop Avenue and Highway 101 south of Warrenton, behind church. At the entrance to Camp Rilea.

A sign at the entrance reads: "Established in 1850 on land donated by Robert Wilson & Irwin Morrison as a 'common burying place for all persons wishing to bury in same, free of expense.'"

On rolling links land like that of nearby Gearhart Golf Course and fronting a military base, this has a haunted feel unlike the average cemetery. It has long since stopped receiving new graves, though there's plenty of vacant land left. A number of Gearharts are buried here, by the way, as well as a family of early settlers from Australia.

Not to forget Solomon and Helen Smith: "Oregon's first school teachers: Solomon Howard Smith of New Hampshire—pioneer, missionary, millwright, farmer, merchant, state senator and his wife Helen, born Celiast, princess-daughter of Coboway, Chief of the Clatsops."

That brief epitaph doesn't begin to fill in the picture of Celiast, who was originally married off by her father to a French trapper, as were her two sisters. It turned out that her French husband was already married to a woman in Quebec, and when that family moved to Fort Vancouver, Celiast and her three children were abandoned.

Despite its proximity to Highway 101 and being backed by a military camp, this remains one of the "purest" pioneer cemeteries in the state.

Fort Stevens Cemetery

From Hammond take Pacific Drive/Fort Stevens Highway 104 west to Seventh; turn left (south) to Russell Street; take Russell to where it dead-ends at the cemetery gate.

Also known as Soldiers or Military Cemetery, it is tucked away in an unlikely place, but once you get there, it's a world apart. Smartly fenced, well maintained, and enclosed, servicemen and their families can still be buried here under the mature trees. There is a section reserved for children of the servicemen, and the few civilians buried in the cemetery are buried here with the children. Stones marked "unknown" honor bodies that washed up from the sea. Owing to the slope of the land, burials here are north-south, rather than the traditional east-west alignment. The cemetery was moved to this location in 1905; the iron fencing dates to 1913. Fort Stevens, as the outermost place on the Oregon shore of the Columbia, is well worth a visit in its own right, but do take the time to find this precise and peaceful cemetery. It's not Arlington, but it has its own measured dignity.

Ocean View Cemetery

Delaura Beach Road runs between SW Ridge Road and Alt. Highway 101 south of Warrenton. The cemetery is on the north side of the road in about the middle.

Conceivably, one could see the ocean from here. At one time it was probably easier. There's a veterans memorial mound in the middle of the cemetery with a flight of steps to the top, but I didn't see the ocean from there either.

The lack of an ocean view is not the most noticeable feature of Ocean View; it's the size. It's huge. Okay, huge is relative. It's no River View (see Portland region), regardless of how big the ocean is. But for a town the size of Warrenton, Ocean View is a monster. Evidently, a lot of Astorians choose Ocean View as their final resting spot.

Ocean View, like Greenwood overlooking Youngs River, is a design descendant of Père Lachaise Cemetery in Paris, only with more panache. Here half the people are Finnish and the other half pure Scandinavian. The war memorial is small but pleasant with a cluster of old military stones at its base. Most of the cemetery is given over to solid, respectable stones found everywhere until recently, when tombstones went through the roof. So to speak.

The roof of Ocean View is in the very back. Bless them, they still permit uprights, and the back-left section is an explosion of personalization. Everybody has something carved onto his or her stone. I've never been to any cemetery where the ratio of personalized stones to generic was as high as at Ocean View.

The range of designs is amazing. I had to stop photographing because I was getting dizzy, but before I did, I recorded designs of a school bus; a dump truck; a steam engine; a cluster of cows; a swimmer (with the notation underneath, "The miracle of swimming"); the Los Angeles Lakers' logo; numerous boats of various kinds including a paddle wheeler, a Viking ship, and several fishing boats often pictured in front of the Astoria Bridge; an Army personnel carrier; and a bundle of shakes. The gamut runs large here.

—North Coast—

Yachats

Carson Cemetery

Take Yachats River Road east out of Yachats. After 4.8 miles, Carson Creek Road enters from the north (left). Take that. The cemetery is up the first drive to the right (east).

Highway 101 is an ocean-side carnival ride, almost without letup, from California to the Washington border. Any time of the year, the traffic can be maddening, but in summer it's insane. Tacky gift shops, smoked salmon shacks, and seaside resorts mixed with auto-glass places, outlet shopping malls, and used boat centers line the highway for miles on end, broken here and there by jutting headlands. Four thousand cafes serving indifferent clam chowder. It's awesome.

Whereas a turn inland down almost any road may take you to a sparsely settled valley dripping with moss and drained by fast-running streams. A few cows in stream bottoms constitute a farm. People here drive pickups and wear mud boots. They live unseen by the conveyor belt of people lurching past the mouth of their valley—people not even aware the valley is there, not aware that people live in the hills behind the mist.

Yachats River Road reaches into one such valley. Yachats, named for a now-extinct Native American tribe and charming in its intimate location, will always draw its share of visitors, but the river road behind it will continue to be a local pathway only for two lesser, if quintessential, attractions. One is a covered bridge crossing the Yachats about six or seven miles from town. Turn left at the T; the bridge is another mile or two upriver. By this point, the road is down to a one-lane dirt road, so drive carefully.

The other attraction, reached before the covered bridge, is the Carson Cemetery. As mentioned, it's off Carson Creek Road, but Carson Creek Road is used by hardly anyone—even less than the Yachats River Road—so the chance of accidentally running across the cemetery are practically nil. There is a sign for Carson Creek Road that runs north off Yachats River Road, but I missed it on the ride up and didn't see it till coming back, after stopping for directions. Once you're on Carson Creek Road, the cemetery is the first drive to the right.

At the entrance to the cemetery, a sign explains that contributions to its upkeep can be sent in the cemetery's name to the Yachats Lions Club and that the caretaker is one Sam Morgan. The plot thickens when one notices that a new and unusual stone marks the grave of one Sam Morgan (1938–1999).

Yet someone is keeping the brush at bay and providing plastic flowers in what looks for all the world like a Hobbits' graveyard. It climbs a steep hillside through an uncleared forest, and it doesn't look as if there's room for whole bodies at most grave sites. At least not whole *human* bodies. While the underbrush has been replaced by rhododendrons and boxwoods, the forest floor is still a tangle of roots that would surely give any gravedigger fits. The majority of the graves have either handmade markers, funeral home tags, or none at all. The cement, hand-lettered stone for James Ingram is typical. He was "born 1821 Tenn." and "died 188[?]/ near here." S. Traves has his name—no dates, nothing else—held up by a curved length of rebar. Zanta Clarno's (1888–1950) "A Saintly Lady" on metal plating set in black stone is an exception.

One feels that, were it not for the caretakers, this cemetery could well have been lost by now. Instead, it remains a cemetery unique in my experience for having been built into the existing forest rather than the forest having been cleared for the cemetery. A picnic bench and a couple plastic chairs off to one side leave no doubt that social occasions occur here from time to time. A white, quasi-birdhouse containing a glass-covered copy of Longfellow's "God's Acre" centers a sunny spot in this ethereal cemetery:

>
> ### GOD'S ACRE
> *I like that ancient Saxon phrase, which calls*
> *The burial-ground God's-Acre! It is just;*
> *It consecrates each grave within its walls,*
> *And breathes a benison o'er the sleeping dust.*
> *God's-Acre! Yes, that blessed name imparts*

Comfort to those, who in the grave have sown
The seed that they had garnered in their hearts,
Their bread of life, alas! no more their own.
Into its furrows shall we all be cast,
In the sure faith, that we shall rise again
At the great harvest, when the archangel's blast
Shall winnow, like a fan, the chaff and grain.
Then shall the good stand in immortal bloom,
In the fair gardens of that second birth;
And each bright blossom mingle its perfume
With that of flowers, which never bloomed on earth.
With thy rude ploughshare, Death, turn up the sod,
And spread the furrow for the seed we sow;
This is the field and Acre of our God,
This is the place where human harvests grow!

Pull up one of the lawn chairs and sit here in the evening. Make no sound and slow your breathing to a sigh. Wrap a blanket around your shoulders and wait for the little ones to come out. I'm sure they will. It's that kind of place.

Pine Belt

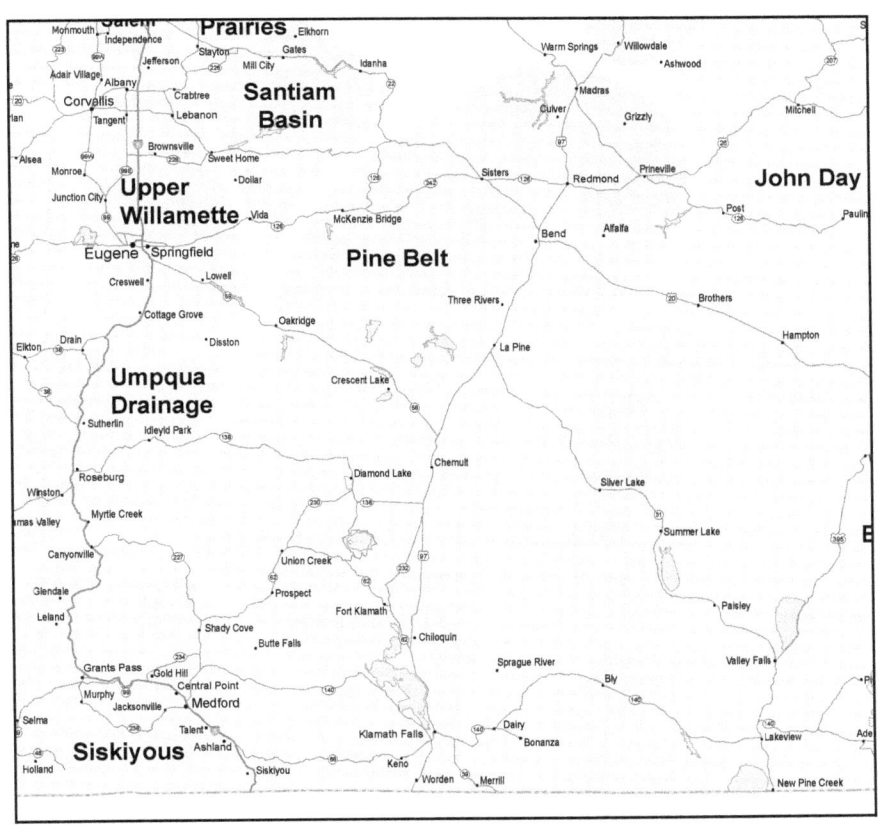

—Pine Belt—

BEND

Pilot Butte–Greenwood Cemetery

Located on the eastern side of Bend, south of Highway 20. Entrance to the cemetery is off NE Bear Creek Road.

This is a large double cemetery, and I couldn't tell offhand where one started and the other stopped. It's a many-acred, well-planted, and well-maintained example of a garden cemetery. There's much here to read and digest, and it's worth carving out time to spend here.

Bend, more or less smack in the center of the state (an honor that actually goes to Post), sits in the pine belt between the high desert and the Cascades and has central access to the vast outdoors of Oregon, save for the coast. (Can't have everything.)

CHILOQUIN

Friendship Cemetery

At the east end of East Schonchin Street in Chiloquin.

In *In Search of Western Oregon*, Friedman characterizes Chiloquin as "a poor-looking, dismal town…bitter cold in winter, stultifying in summer," and also notes that Chiloquin is "HQ of the reborn Klamath tribe."

"Chiloquin" is one spelling of an Indian chief's name, and better than half the current residents are Native American. Schonchin, after whom the cemetery's street is named, was another chief and has a cemetery named after him near Beatty.

The cemetery, named "Friendship" but listed in ODOT as "Friends" cemetery, comprises a couple of hardscrabble, sandy acres creeping up a hillside being reclaimed by 10,000 ponderosa starts.

The cemetery is still used, but it's pretty rough and tumble. The best indication of its Native American connections is in the engraving on Fanny Jackson's (1884–1970) stone of a woman harvesting food thigh-deep in a float of water-lilies.

My favorite headstone is that for Ora Summers (1901–1979), which has a photo of Ora in his old age in a cowboy hat, wearing a slightly concerned expression. It also has a photo of Ora's beloved horse, War Paint. One can only hope that War Paint wasn't buried with Ora.

—Pine Belt—

Madras

Milo Gard Cemetery

Fir Lane crosses Highway 26 three miles or so north of Madras. Head west on Fir Lane. Cemetery is less than a mile away, on the north side of the road.

Named after one of its residents, Milo Gard rests on the Agency Plains, better known to Oregonians as that flat place where Madras (pronounced *mad'*- [as in "mad as a Hatter"] *ras*) is. They don't raise cotton there and they don't make cloth, but they do farm. Geographically, the region is not part of the Pine Belt as I've described it, but it's not a part of any other region and is part of the economic and demographic axis that includes the Pine Belt.

Milo Gard is a sprightly cemetery of little more than an acre rimmed by trees with a few more inside the fence. It's dead flat and has dead spectacular views of the Cascades from the Three Sisters to Mount Hood and beyond. My visit was accompanied by squawking crows and a killdeer feigning, "Follow me, follow me, not my children."

SISTERS

Camp Polk Cemetery

Road to the cemetery is 3.5 miles up Camp Polk Road from the northeast corner of Sisters. There is a sign.

Named after a long since abandoned army post, unwatered and wild, Camp Polk Cemetery is the epic, homegrown backwoods Oregon experience. Though pretty much untended, it's still in heavy use. If nothing else, it's romantic. There's a grand collection of hand-carved and hand-poured markers here; a perennial favorite is that of Robert Krug (1849–1919): "Murdered by A. J. Weston" (reputedly for his "valuables").

Some plots are sectioned off with chain, some are surrounded by wrought iron fencing, and none is laid out in accord with anything else. Some have handmade benches and fire pits, and there's a pack's worth of hand-carved coyotes.

The cemetery sits atop a knoll surrounded by a wildlife refuge and is covered with scrub pines and boulders oozing out of the ground. Graves are squeezed in wherever the soil permits and there are, seemingly, no rules. I have no idea who runs the place or to whom one would petition for a plot. Occasionally one runs across "reserved" signs.

Portland Metro

GRESHAM

Forest Lawn Cemetery

Take SW Walters Drive south from Powell Boulevard in Gresham; drive past the Gresham and White Birch Cemeteries, over Johnson Creek, and the cemetery will be on your left.

This cemetery is more than twice what I thought it was, despite having stopped by on several occasions. As the name implies, Forest Lawn is a lawn cemetery barring uprights, except, it turns out, in a back corner of the back half where, by God, a little forest of uprights has grown, several of which are quite interesting. A second, smaller mausoleum also anchors the back lot, along with a half-dozen freestanding columbaria grouped together. The main mausoleum, though not large, is quite nice.

An added bonus is that to get to the cemetery one has to first go past the minuscule pioneer cemeteries of White Birch and Gresham.

Gresham-Escobar Pioneer Cemeteries
White Birch Cemetery

SW Walters Drive, south of Powell Boulevard and behind the West Gresham Elementary School. The cemeteries are one in the same; they simply have two names.

Escobar was named for Frank Escobar, and Forest Lawn across Johnson Creek bought the cemetery from Escobar's estate in 1947 for $5. Even at that price it didn't prove profitable, and ten years later it was turned over to Metro. It's combined with and is indistinguishable from Gresham Pioneer Cemetery. Truth to tell, not many get buried in this double cemetery.

Four cemeteries straddle Johnson Creek here where it almost touches Powell Boulevard—three pioneer cemeteries on the north side of the creek and the modern Forest Lawn on the other. The Springwater Trail runs between the pioneer cemeteries and the creek, and a steady stream of joggers and strollers flows by. Gresham Pioneer and Escobar occupy the east side of the road, and White Birch sits on the west. Gresham Pioneer is about two acres, whereas Escobar is only half an acre—the downhill side—but there is no delineation between the two, and they are effectively treated as one. There's still room to be buried here, and some people occasionally are.

Saint Joseph Cemetery

Powell Boulevard and 198th Avenue. North side of road.

When Mount Calvary took over Saint Mary's Cemetery in downtown Portland, they moved the remains to their place on the hill. I don't know why they assumed control of St. Joe's, but they left this 1.7 acre cemetery in place. Despite the heavy traffic outside its door, the cemetery boasts two fairly new wooden benches and arbors as well as a new iron fence, and the grass is maintained by a volunteer force. In response, the place has been used as recently as 2000. It's surrounded by condominiums but has a lot of vacant land left, and I once read that the cemetery has a nineteen-year-old resident ghost. A bulletin board contains a plot map, last updated in 1976; but no one's moved, as far as I can tell.

—Portland Metro—

Lake Oswego

Oswego Pioneer Cemetery

On the west side of Stafford Road as it leaves Lake Oswego, prior to the golf course (if you're coming from town).

At five acres and with only modest additions of new graves, Oswego Pioneer is obviously not the destination of large blocks of Lake O'ers, which is a pity because it's a nice little cemetery with a variety of plantings and more than a dozen stone memorial benches—the largest collection I've encountered anywhere. There are cemeteries with more extensive graphics, ones where the inhabitants wax more poetic, but none has more places to sit. Most of the benches are in a newer section on the northern border of the cemetery, where it adjoins Sacred Heart Cemetery. Not only are the stones newer, but the grass is greener. Many of the older stones are laid within concrete curbing, but the newer ones follow more conventional practices. This little cemetery's claim to fame—even though the benches are nice—has to be two-time Nobel winner Linus Pauling.

OREGON CITY

McLoughlin Grave

East side of the McLoughlin House at the northwest corner of Seventh and Center Streets in Oregon City at the top of the hill.

Chief Factor John McLoughlin of the Hudson's Bay Company stands out as one of the great men in Oregon history for the aid he gave, against company wishes and British interests, to the early pioneers as they straggled in from the trail. Looked upon with suspicion by the British, he was equally shunned by the Americans because he was, well, British. In the end he threw his lot in with the Americans and moved to Oregon City, then the major town in the territory, where he and his wife, Marguerite, finished their days. Their graves, surrounded by an iron fence alongside their Oregon City home, have been moved there from their original location, and the original stones have been reset in brick. As a cemetery, this may not topple your wall, but it's an important place.

Mountain View Cemetery

Find Mollala Avenue leaving Oregon City toward the southeast, and take Hilda Street east (there is a light). Cemetery at end of street.

Mountain View Oregon City ("Mountain View" may be the most popular cemetery name in Oregon) is an all-purpose cemetery, containing within itself pioneer fraternal order cemeteries all the way up to modern mausolea and "garden features," from oak-covered crumbling monuments to state-of-the-art personalizations. It easily covers twenty-five or more acres, and while pound for pound it doesn't compare with other, more intense, cemeteries, it has more than enough detail to warrant anyone's visit. There are a couple Woodmen of the World stones in the older section, and if you head to the farthest reaches of the new sections, you'll find a scattering of personalizations.

Besides, it's in Oregon City, the bypassed capital of early Oregon. For most modern Oregonians, Oregon City gets dismissed as "that town up by the falls"—Canemah writ large—yet the falls were one of the most important gathering spots in the territory prior to the arrival of the Euro-Americans. Oregon City feels older than most Oregon towns, which, frankly, is part of its charm.

Portland

Columbia Pioneer Cemetery (Columbia Masonic Cemetery)

At the juncture of NE Sandy Boulevard and Killingsworth Street in Portland. There is, however, no parking on Sandy. You have to go east of the cemetery to 100th Avenue and turn south on that, then west again on Wygant Street to 99th Avenue, where you turn back north into a dead-end that ends at the cemetery. A little loop-de-loop.

Portland has a lot of cemeteries that have been swallowed up by growth, this two-and-a-half-acre former Masonic cemetery among them. Who in their right mind would put a cemetery at the corner of Sandy and Killingsworth? No one. Which, of course, no one did. In 1877, it was far from any neighborhood. If it's noteworthy, it's because it has a remarkable number of obelisks for a cemetery of this time and stature, implying that at one time it had more stature than it currently exhibits.

Like some other Portland cemeteries, this one gets considerable foot traffic, and there are a couple of well worn tracks through it. Despite its proximity to traffic, it remains in use, with at least one newly dug grave in 2004.

Columbian Cemetery (Love Cemetery)

At the junction of I-5 and Columbia Boulevard. Approach from Columbia Boulevard. Entrance to the cemetery is east of where Columbia Boulevard passes under I-5. The entrance is minimal and the traffic can be fast; vision is limited. Be careful!

The manager of the website for the Columbian Cemetery (www.columbiancemetery.org), Celine Chamberlin, —was able to fill me in on current operations at the graveyard, one of the more heavily vandalized and threatened cemeteries in the county. Celine's mother, Glenora Chamberlin, runs the cemetery as a volunteer via a nonprofit organization—Families of Historic Columbian Cemetery—of which she is president.

The cemetery has made a remarkable comeback from the brink of doom, thanks primarily to the efforts of Dave Foland, the Families of Historic Columbia Cemetery, and a donated lawn mower. Dave's not only mowing the grass, he's trimming the trees, clearing out the brush and debris, and beginning to set the toppled stones upright once more. It's a volunteer labor of love, and transformation of the Columbian is dramatic.

And none too soon for, despite being in continual use, the five-acre cemetery is constantly threatened by neighborhood development; it's in a perilous location. As it is, there is little parking available, and at times traffic can be heavy on Columbia Boulevard. The rear northeast section holds an erstwhile baby plot distinguished by regular rows of box hedges, which also includes the very handsome upright and amazingly unvandalized stele of G. W. Schaeffer, who died in 1857 at the age of 31 years, 2 months, and 6 days.

Columbian Cemetery was originally known as the Love Cemetery, not because of early day hippies but after Captain Lewis Love, on whose land claim it was located. His stone, a big heavy one, has been toppled. Lewis was an interesting and resourceful immigrant of 1849 who dictated his memoirs to his granddaughter in 1899. Thanks to the Center for Columbia River History (www.ccrh.org), we can get a glimpse of his life on the claim, which was not always easy:

"In the spring I moved in a little log house joining my farm on Columbia Slough and soon after we all took the Mountain or Camp Fever, and also ran out of provisions, yet we had good friends. The year before we moved there, there was a good crop of potatoes raised on the place, and that year there was a few volunteer potatoes came up. Our friends, the wood rats, would dig them up and bring them in a pile them up in the log cabin and we would steal them from the rats and make our soup of them. This was our living for some time."

Love made his first money rafting logs from his place on the Columbia slough to Portland. At the time, there were fourteen houses in town: "There came a high water the next summer, and I had in about 300,000 ft. and started them for Portland. We kept close around Gattens Point and went out into the Willamette opposite Sauvies Island. Before starting I went to Vancouver and got four old government tents, put up masts on the rafts and stayed them with lines and stretched these tents up for sails. In a little over four hours we landed in Portland. Soon after this there was quite a number of other fools in the same business."

The Columbian has had its glory days and is another example of how unfortunate growth often swamps cemeteries. Surely it's haunted. Surely it's worth saving. Currently, the place looks the best I've seen it, and consequently, it's seeing a resurgence of use.

Gethsemani Catholic Cemetery

At 11666 SE Stevens Road, a few blocks from Sunnyside Road close to I-205; past a roundabout fronting the New Hope mega-church.

Gethsemani has a scattering of trees, which will someday grow, but in the meantime it's pretty much a six- or seven-acre open field, as all stones are supine. There is a mausoleum at the top of the hill and a few thick crosses marking the quadrants and one memorial announcing, "The peaceful resting place of Vietnamese Catholics." Most of the markers are in Vietnamese, many of them are embellished with the image of the deceased, either under glass or laser etched.

All of these stones are found toward the top of the hill. Begun in 1959, it's one of the newer cemeteries in the region and one of the very few that has been able to strictly maintain a no-upright policy. I don't recall seeing any exemptions. It's a subtle cemetery, but rewarding.

Havurah Shalom Cemetery

Take the Sylvan exit from Highway 26 and head south toward Scholls Ferry Road. Immediately south of the viaduct over Highway 26, at the intersection of Humphrey and Hewell, is the driveway for Sylvan Hill Church. Take that drive and go around to the parking lot behind the church. At the far end of the lot, there is a gate through the hedge. Behind the gate is Jones Pioneer and within Jones Pioneer, in the back right-hand corner, is Havurah Shalom.

This hidden cemetery within a hidden cemetery is a small but very bright jewel. Havurah Shalom feels like a community of very bright, very conscious, very loving friends. There are more pebbles placed per grave (a common Jewish custom) here on average than in any other Jewish cemetery

I've visited. As telling is that more stones here describe the interred as "activist" than I've seen elsewhere. You won't find that amongst the Odd Fellows.

The cemetery it shares ground with, Jones, is protected by stately old trees, but Havurah Shalom is under the open air, strengthening its jewel-like nature: Out of the gloom comes this place of light. One can see heaven from here.

A mere handful of graves near a shelter of boxwood hedges corral the best, pound-for-pound epitaphs I've run across. Restrained, simple, elegant. This is a cemetery chosen with care. Few find it that aren't directed here. The solitude is profound.

Arguably, the most important person to have been laid to rest here is Benjamin Deutsch (1912–1994). Benjamin has to be ranked as one of the most important persons to be buried in Oregon; as his headstone reads, he "Pioneered the introduction/ of pastrami into the/ United States & Jewish culture."

Jones Pioneer Cemetery

See directions for Havurah Shalom Cemetery.

Jones is one of the "hidden" cemeteries that Metro manages, and being secluded is one of its attractions. Jones has all the earmarks of a rescued cemetery, once forgotten but now returned to the fold. Underneath a park-like setting of large old trees, a handful of stones scatter themselves about as if none was too friendly with the other. Families cluster together, but there's a lot of spare room under the canopy.

There are, though, new graves, with a few clever souls having found their way to this sanctuary behind Sylvan Hill Church. You have to drive around to the back of the church to a parking lot and then drive to the farthest end of the parking lot before it's evident there's a cemetery beyond. One step through the gate, though, and you enter into a world apart, which you're likely to have all to yourself.

The entrance sign says the cemetery was established in 1872, but other sources credit the father of one Nathan Jones having been buried here in 1854. With cemeteries, there's often more than one "founding" date, the result, I suspect, of the date of the first burial often preceding the date of the decision to use the place as a cemetery.

Kesser Israel Cemetery

Take 65th Avenue east from SE Flavel. Cemetery driveway is in crook of street where it makes a little jog a few blocks down from Flavel.

Kesser shares space with the equally well hidden Shaarie Torah, separated by a chain-link fence and a padlocked gate. By far the smallest and perhaps the most unusual of Portland's Jewish cemeteries, probably not a fifth of the fairly small cemetery has yet been used.

It has a number of interesting stones, many with photos dating back to the 1930s. My favorite stone has to be that of Edith Porter (2000), which reads: "I have three wonderful sons, it's too bad you couldn't keep me a little longer."

Lincoln Memorial Park

Take Foster Road east from I-205 to 110th Street. Turn south on 110th Street, which soon becomes 112th. Keep going past the entrance to Willamette National; Lincoln Memorial will be on your right.

A large cemetery rambling up Mount Scott on the edge of Portland, this cemetery could be dismissed as a lesser cousin to River View, which would be a mistake, as it has more burial options than River View, including a couple of nice, hard-landscaped gardens as columbaria in a style suddenly becoming fashionable, one of which shelters under trees at the new entrance.

There's also a beautiful memorial garden with private plots and a stunning view north to Mount Tabor, downtown, and the Cascades. The garden is joined by Portland's most refined new private mausoleum, reputedly built at a cost of a quarter of a million dollars.

Older sections lower on the hill could use a little attention, but as one rises on the slope, things get better and better, until one arrives at the handsome new office and funeral home at the top.

Lincoln Memorial has succumbed to the flat-stone menace in much of their newer grounds, but they have plenty of uprights to make for a proper cemetery experience, plus they've done a better job than anyone else in the region of both expanding in new directions and fitting their new ventures "seamlessly" into the old.

The Portland Chinese Cemetery is at the top of the hill, and Lincoln Park has installed a new Asian Garden. There are large public mausoleums as well as the scattered private few, which command expansive views over Portland.

With a plethora of roads here, finding things can take some sleuthing, but your efforts will be rewarded. There are a number of cemeteries in the region which can be considered children of Père Lachaise, but this is one of the best and brightest.

Furthermore, it's across the road from Willamette National Cemetery, the government's interpretation of Père Lachaise as unhindered park. Together they make up Portland's largest cemetery space.

Lone Fir Cemetery

On Portland's eastside at SE 26th and SE Morrison, in the heart of populist Portland.

Lone Fir Cemetery Founders

The Mother Lode. The premier (and largest, at 30.5 acres) pioneer cemetery in the state. The cemetery by which the other pioneer cemeteries are judged. It may have had a lone fir at one time, but it's since been joined by a considerable forest.

For quirky epitaphs, Lone Fir is the virgin spring, the tone being set by the original owners of the land, James (1805–1887) and Elizabeth (1806–1889) Stephens, whose remarkable stone reads: "Here we lie by consent, after 57 years 2 months and 2 days sojourning through life awaiting nature's immutable laws to return us back to the elements of the universe, of which we were first composed."

It was the death of James Stephen's father, Emmon, in 1846 that was the actual beginning of the cemetery. He was joined in 1854 by victims of a steamship accident, at which time it was formally dedicated as a cemetery.

Metro also lists 25,000 burials in Lone Fir and 10,000 unknowns. It's somewhat unclear if the 25,000 includes the 10,000, and at current writing there is a process in gear to build a memorial at Lone Fir to the unknown deceased Chinese who remain after the majority of the men's bones were shipped back to China, leaving the woman and children behind. As to the rest of the cemetery, one would expect many unknowns to make sales of new plots a tad iffy. It has a few individual mausoleums and a slug of interesting stones, old and new.

You might start with the flagpole centering on the fallen firefighters. Or you can look nearby for the monument to the Grand Army of the Republic and a plaque with the Gettysburg Address. Lately there's been a healthy infiltration of Russian immigrant graves, distinguished by colorful plantings of genuine, live flowers creating a patchwork of color among the somber greens.

The cemetery gets the greatest usage of any Portland cemetery, not by number of burials but by number of people using the cemetery as a park (something Willamette National, for instance, discourages). Lone Fir has a steady stream of visitors: musicians, readers, artists, picnickers, lovers, drinkers, diners, thinkers, mourners, and curiosity seekers. If you choose only one cemetery to visit in Oregon, this should be it.

Marks Friedman Grave

In a parking strip on the southwest corner of SE Main and SE 34th Avenue.

The smallest accessible cemetery in the county: a tombstone lying flat in the ground. Which brings into question just how many bodies does one require before it becomes a cemetery? Not to mention the question of just where, vis-à-vis the tombstone, is the body? Under the sidewalk or under the street? This gravesite is only two blocks away from bustling Hawthorne Boulevard.

Mount Calvary Catholic Cemetery

333 SW Skyline Boulevard, straddling the junction of Burnside, Skyline, and Barnes Roads.

The Irish do themselves proud when it comes to burying people, at least here in Portland's Mount Calvary Cemetery, where there are so many Irish you'd think you were in Boston. Newer sections of this seventy-acre cemetery, unfortunately, are given over to flat stones, but the older, upright sections (including a few family mausoleums) under a canopy of mature trees are some of the best in the Portland area.

Mount Calvary was begun by the Archdiocese of Portland because its eastside cemetery, Saint Mary's, was full. Begun in 1858, Saint Mary's was located where Central Catholic High is now, across Stark Street from Lone Fir Cemetery. Remains were removed from Saint Mary's between 1930 and 1937, largely to Mount Calvary, which also maintains Saint Joseph Cemetery in Gresham.

A contingent of fifty-seven Civil War veterans, including one Confederate, rests here across the dale from the Sisters of Mercy of Portland (begun in 1898 by the Reverend Mother Joseph Lynch), laid out in neat rows, with the latest entry from 1996. It also houses the remains of the first Portland police officer killed in the line of duty, Thomas O'Connor, in 1867.

Multnomah Park Pioneer Cemetery

Southwest corner of the intersection of SE 82nd Avenue and SE Holgate.

This is in an uncomfortable location on busy 82nd Avenue, but once you're inside, it's an island of calm and a not bad source of interesting reads.

Powell Grove Cemetery

In the southeast corner of the intersection of 122 Avenue and NE Sandy Boulevard.

Another contestant in the worst-location-for-a-cemetery contest. No bigger than an acre, a number of trees have been cut down due to age and disease. In 1999 Donald Stueckle (1929–1999) was buried there, joined by his wife, Wilma (1928–2001) in 2001; and recently someone has planted a bunch of pansies on a mound of clippings. Chuck Palahniuk writes in *Fugitives and Refugees* that "road widening has crowded [Powell Grove], and scores of graves have been misplaced." They're rumored to be under the parking lot of the old Michael's store. Drive carefully.

River View Cemetery

At 300 SW Taylors Ferry Road, although another pleasant access is via the carriage house entrance at the west end of the Sellwood Bridge.

Three years of planning and planting created the major domo of Portland cemeteries, where since 1882 (thirty-one years prior to Forest Lawn in L.A.) the *crème de la crème* Portlandaise has been buried. Neither as quirky nor as endearing as Portland's cemetery queen, Lone Fir, River View is unrivaled locally in opulence or beauty, and it's not surprising that many of Portland's early heavy hitters are buried here: Terwilligers, Failings, Corbetts, Pittocks, Ladds, etc., with today's home run hitter, the Pamplins, having recently built a handsome private mausoleum. Some quarters have speculated that the era of expansive private funeral memorial was over, but, instead, one sees a resurgence in tapophilic art.

One of the more sought-after grave sites in the cemetery, although nothing to look at, is that of Virgil Earp (1843–1905), Wyatt's brother—a close brush with fame for Portland. After that, the list of notables disintegrates, unless you're into finding tombs with Portland street names. Sports fans might look for the grave of Oakland Raider great Lyle Alzado (1949–1992), though Red Sox pitcher Carl Mays (1891–1971) holds a unique record: He threw the pitch that killed Ray Chapman, the only fatality of major league baseball.

The greatest unsung hero is, likely, Leah Hing (1907–2001). While still in high school, she formed a Chinese all-girl band which toured vaudeville, after which she became the first Chinese-American woman to take flying lessons and the second to earn her license. During World War II, Leah contributed as an instrument mechanic at the Portland Air Base, but after the war, regardless of her accomplishments, she ended up as a hat checker at the Aero Club.

A large cemetery that takes days to thoroughly cover, River View has newer sections of lawn cemetery, but not all new sections are exclusively flat-stoned. The Taylors Ferry entrance (across the road from the unrelated River View Abby and Mausoleum) opens to a two-part memorial where 165 veterans of the Spanish-American War are honored.

Many cemeteries sport flagstaffs (frequently a gift from the local American Legion post) commemorating veterans, but the rings and rows of white stones in this display go a step beyond, approached in dignity only by a similar memorial at City View in Salem.

In the main area, the river has long since been lost to view with the growth of the commanding trees, although a new lobe sweeping down from high on the hillside offers new unimpeded views, in the center of which is a sleek columbarium. Graves get younger as one ascends the hill.

When you get near the top, where River View blends in with Greenwood Hills, take a rest on Timory Hyde's (1975–1997) bench. Along the seat's stone edges, words are crammed together in a Joycean stream of babble two lines high, all the way around the bench. A sample from one side reads:

frogsguitardidjeridumotorcyclessunflowersthingsthatbouncedeepbellyla

The seating surface is blank, inviting you to rest a spell. Discreetly inscribed in small lettering in one corner are the words "bite me," which Timory's mother told me she had to fight hard for permission to write. You don't have to sit there, but it sounds as if Timory would smile.

Rose City Cemetery

Main entrance to Rose City is off SE 57th Avenue at Fremont.

Some cemeteries are less than they appear; this one is more. From the outset it looks like a flat, rectangular, well-packed cemetery—which it is—organized into neat rows, and for the most part devoid of literature on the markers. One entire side of the cemetery is given over to loculi and niches for aboveground interments. Ostentation is toned down on this side of the river compared to the monuments at River View, except for a cluster of low-rise sepulchers in the center of the cemetery devoted primarily to Gypsy graves, indicated by Frank Ellis's (1905–1966) tomb, emblazoned with the proclamation: "King of the Gypsies." Nearby other Gypsy names abound: Ephrem, George, Ristick, Stevens, and more Ellises; often their stones are detailed with glass cameos. There are a number of prominent Greek and Russian graves as well, and toward the rear is a separate and unique Japanese cemetery. While the graves may be shy on literature, many have photo-ceramics of the dearly departed.

The cemetery goes on seemingly forever toward the rear; and like many other cemeteries, it's at the fringes where the newest and most interesting graves tend to lie, including that for Jack (1913–2000) and Thelma (1920–) Dempsey. Aside from the fact that there are at least two other Jack Dempseys buried in the lower Willamette Valley, this Jack's headstone is remarkable in having some of the more elaborate laser etchings in the valley. Above Thelma's name is a typical Oregon scene of river, forest, and mountains; but Jack's side carries the tools of his trade: printing presses and type boxes. Keep an eye on this area; it's where the future lives.

Shaarie Torah Cemetery

At SE 66th Avenue and Tenino Street.

As noted elsewhere, Portland's Jewish cemeteries are often hidden from public view, and this entrance is at 66th and Tenino, in a place where no roads go past; you can't see it from anywhere. Let this be an urban adventure for you.

Skyline Memorial Gardens

Driving west out the ever delightful Skyline Drive, and it can't be missed.

Skyline is big. Skyline has fantastic views of the Tualatin Valley. Skyline is acres of green sward interrupted by occasional "memorial courts" sprouting columns or statuary. Skyline has no messy upright stones to interfere with mowing the sward (although some uprights are allowed in flower beds bordering gardens). Skyline is very hard to read. One feels aimless wandering around the park looking for something beyond the generic. I did find one enigmatic epitaph, that of Frank (1935–) and Carmen Kay (1948–1998) Hoffman: "I'll love you forever. I'll like you for always."

Sunnyside Chimes Memorial Garden (Little Chapel of the Chimes)

Across the road from Gethsemani Catholic Cemetery on SE Stevens Road near the intersection of Sunnyside and I-205.

This cemetery appears to have begun as Little Chapel of the Chimes but morphed into what you see above. In some way, Sunnyside is a large columbarium. It does have a field for old-fashioned burials but seems to be pushing cremation. On the same hill as Gethsemani Catholic Cemetery, Sunnyside uses the lower half, the bottom of which is landscaped into several different "gardens," either with freestanding columbaria or naturalized area where memorial boulders and plaques can be placed, as well as a scatter garden higher on the hill. A stream runs through part of the property, and the top of the property is dominated by a full-body mausoleum.

Visit Sunnyside not for the epitaphs (you'd do better across the street at Gethsemani) but to see the future of the burial business. This cemetery is among the youngest in the region and will likely point the way ahead. When the talking video headstones appear, they will probably appear here first.

Wilhelm's Portland Mausoleum

At 6705 SE 14th Avenue, in the Sellwood-Moreland neighborhood.

If there's any place in Oregon that deserves the name "necropolis," this mausoleum is it. It goes on forever, with ten or eleven (depending on how one counts) labyrinth floors of corpses and ashes.

A combination of towering sprawling wings, built in Victorian, Art Deco, and Spanish styles, it houses more than 58,000 residents with room for another 120,000. It's a 3.5 acre city within the city.

"A city of the dead," writes Chuck Palahniuk in *Fugitives and Refugees*. He acknowledges that he used the mausoleum "as the basis for [his] second novel, *Survivor*. Part of the book [he] even wrote here." What's noticeably lacking are epitaphs, which apparently aren't permitted.

The only one I saw was for an eighteen-year-old girl murdered in 2003, Cassondra Brown, whose vault reads: "Beloved sister to women and dogs." Cassondra's vault is laid sideways rather than end-to, in itself not that unusual; what's unusual is that they allocated her two vaults, both of which are covered with mementos.

Look for the family vault of noted architect John Yeon. The mausoleum has gained a certain amount of local fame of late for an enormous mural, which has been painted on the Oaks Bottom side of the building, depicting a wide variety of birds.

Willamette National Cemetery

From SE Foster Road, take 110 Drive south; it will become 112th and take you to the cemetery entrance. Or take Flavel east from 82nd Avenue, which will become SE Mount Scott Boulevard and will terminate at the cemetery entrance.

Willamette National is as close to Arlington as you're going to get in these parts, without the uprights. If you have a whisper of a patriotic bone in your body, and even if you don't, you should make the journey. These people put it all on the line for you. And some of them paid dearly.

With some 120,000 interments, Willamette National is among the largest cemeteries in the region, while also being one of the youngest. Military stones and markers are ubiquitous in almost all Oregon cemeteries; the record of our military engagements has been written on the stones of the dead. But it is at Willamette National where the toll weighs most heavily. Even now, markers are added bearing the words "Iraq" and "Afghanistan"—the full price has not yet been extracted.

Willamette National occupies the crest and a flank of Mount Scott, along with Lincoln Memorial Park and the Portland Chinese Cemetery. It has some wonderful specimen trees, but the overall experience is one of sweeping vistas and broad lawns. One can see forever from up here, a perfect place for a cemetery.

There is an immense amount of activity here on a daily basis. Several funerals are performed every day, and a steady stream of visitors' cars trickles through the front gates. The VA is going through a major period of expansion and renovation of the cemeteries under their administration, and the handsome results are on display at Willamette in the new entrance, administration buildings, and the open-air amphitheater higher on the hill. But the *crème de la crème* is columbarium number three, the newest, and the adjacent committal shelter (the term for small buildings where ceremonies are performed, as they're not allowed on the grounds proper). The shelter is easily among the finest pieces of modern architecture in the Portland area, and the columbarium facing the woods was once an emotionally powerful place where survivors of the deceased hung memorials to their loved ones. For a while, the cemetery permitted personal memorials to be hung in the woods behind the columbarium, but that has since, unfortunately, been discontinued.

As significant as the renovation efforts are at Willamette, perhaps more important is a policy change implemented in 2001. Prior to that time, the VA would only pay to have one's marker inscribed with name, rank, dates, and conflict, if relevant. Any further epitaph was at the survivors' expense. Noticing their increased popularity, in 2001 the VA began covering the costs of short epitaphs; the result has been a flowering of sentiment where there otherwise had been silence. I have a database of over 120 epitaphs from columbarium three alone: some are touching, some are amusing, and some are downright inscrutable.

TIGARD

Crescent Grove Cemetery

9925 SW Greenburg Road, behind Washington Square.

This is the largest, nicest cemetery flying under the radar. There are larger cemeteries around—River View, Skyline Memorial, Lincoln Park, to name a few—but at 21.4 acres Crescent Grove is reasonably sized, and it maintains two mausolea with an attractive stone memory court and a set-aside for children's graves as well. There is a considerable diversity of cultures represented among the new stones. In spite of its proximity to ten thousand frantic shoppers and being fronted by busy Greenburg Road, Crescent Grove remains an island of calm, and in spite of its size, it remains pretty much a secret.

As a private, non-denominational cemetery in operation since 1852, it is one of the earlier cemeteries around. Not as artfully arranged as River View, it's more on the Lone Fir model but without the odd eccentricities. Due to tradition, it still allows uprights; and in the modern tradition, more and more stones bear lengthy inscriptions, something that disappeared in the interregnum between the introduction of granite and the mechanization of stone cutting.

Crescent Grove has a lot of good reads, but in particular it boasts a remarkable sculptured bronze head of Andrés Peacock (1973–1995), one of the more dramatic markers in the region.

Sunset Pioneer Cemetery (Tigard Evangelical Cemetery)

Road to the cemetery is directly across from where Bull Mountain Road takes off west from Highway 99W in Tigard. It can only be approached from the south (coming toward the city).

Appearing abandoned, there's a grave from 1983 here as well as one from 1897. Everything well overgrown and under a canopy of tall firs, the cemetery is bisected by a well-worn foot path from a set of apartment complexes to a bus stop on the highway. Paths lead to most of the stones as well, though many have been vandalized. The edges of the cemetery are hard to define, so if you go looking, persevere.

This cemetery has been termed Sunset Pioneer as well as Tigard Evangelical. One of the most disturbing aspects of this cemetery is the number of deep holes in front of headstones.

TROUTDALE

Douglass Pioneer Cemetery

SE Henley and SE 262nd Avenue between Troutdale and Gresham.

Metro's list of fourteen cemeteries runs the gamut from a highly publicized, central-city pioneer cemetery to hidden cemeteries in quaint rural outposts. While Metro runs a cluster of cemeteries in Gresham, Douglass is Metro's real representative in East County. The nine-plus acre Douglass is actively in use, has considerable new room in which to grow, boasts a columbarium (unused), and houses a cemetery within a cemetery, that of the East Side Jewish Community of Portland.

The shape of Douglass is roughly that of a lumpy T, with the crossbar being new, open land where the stones all lie flat. The T stem bears the upright memorials and older stones. The Jewish quarter, recently delineated with small evergreen shrubs, is wedged out of the new ground. The columbarium sits forlornly by itself.

Mind you, East County has never been a hotbed of flamboyance, and the headstones in Douglass reflect that modesty, but if you scan the new areas, you'll find many graves surrounded by piles of memorabilia. Glassed photos are making a comeback, and laser-etched likenesses are popular here. If Douglass excels in anything, it's in etched vehicles: tractors, train engines, trucks, planes, etc.

By all reports, theft is a serious problem at any cemetery. While thieves may take everything from the headstone to the body itself, it's the trinkets and embellishments that disappear more easily. Most of us are oblivious to the problem; if you don't know what was there, it's hard to know what's missing. But a child's grave in Douglass, heaped high with toys and artificial flowers and whatnot, was accompanied by a profile photo of the girl wearing a garland next to this note:

"Please, Stop stealing from my grave. I was only 5 years old when I passed away, and the small gifts are all my family can give me for my birthday and holidays. My death is very painful for my family, please do not cause them any additional pain."

Santiam Basin

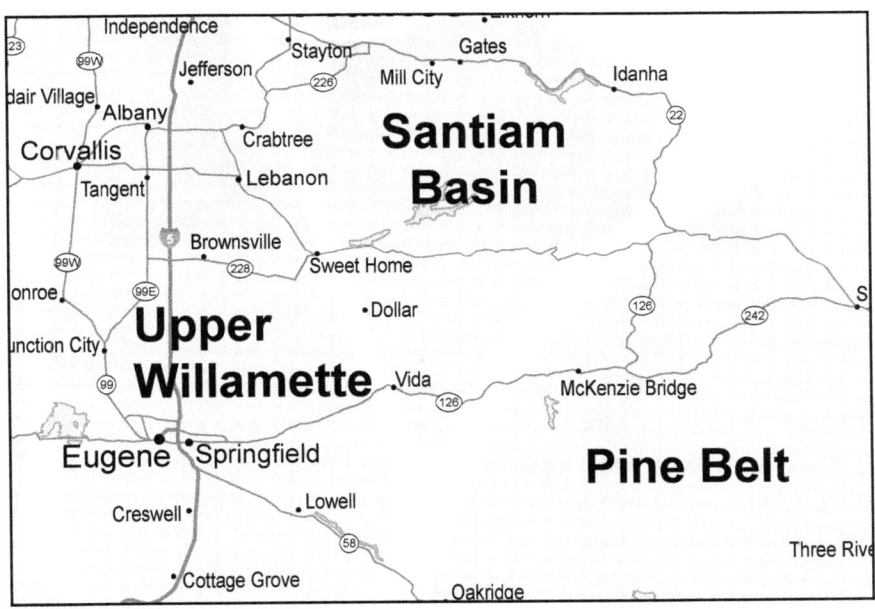

—Santiam Basin—

Albany

Riverside Cemetery

On the north side of the west end of Seventh Avenue SW in Albany.

Like everyplace else, the cemeteries of Albany mirror the city, and Riverside is an old pioneer cemetery of twelve to fifteen well-packed acres. It's still being used, but not heavily, partly because there's no room. A drive through downtown Albany and its core neighborhoods will quickly convince anyone of the town's influential past. The Victorians lining the streets would make any town jealous, and, were the town still as prosperous, it would be the jewel of the valley.

Albany is capital of the Santiam Basin, and its location near the confluence of the Santiam and Willamette Rivers was the reason for its early success. For a while, being a riverboat town on the Willamette meant something—until railroads and highways absorbed the freight. Albany was also an early rail hub for the valley, which helped propel it. In the end, it became the capital of the forgotten part of the Willamette Valley.

Riverside Cemetery reflects that picture. It has a good collection of older stones, but two things are immediately noticeable: One, none of the older stones is extravagant; if there was wealth in Albany, it didn't go into tombstones. Second, the stock of new stones is thin.

There are a number of white bronze markers here, with their usually crisp details. In a push to get with the times, the cemetery operators have installed a small, off-the-shelf columbarium, but the cemetery's best feature is a white columned, brick entrance portico. It's nonfunctional, but it spices the site up visually.

Waverly Jewish Cemetery (Saint John's Cemetery)

It occupies the SW corner of Waverly Memorial (see below for directions).

There's no synagogue in Albany these days, which accounts for the forgotten character of Waverly Jewish matching the general scratchiness of the greater Waverly Cemetery (below). It does have a few recent graves, the one great mystery about this cemetery being that it was once known as Saint John's Cemetery. Since it has been Jewish since its inception, one can only wonder.

Waverly Memorial Cemetery

On the north side of the east end of Salem Avenue, across the street from Waverly Park and Houston Cemetery.

Clearly a pioneer cemetery dating from the nineteenth century, the word "memorial" didn't get appended to cemeteries' names until after the creation of Forest Lawn Memorial Park in 1911, so there has likely been a name change somewhere along the line. Waverly is still in use, with new stones flush with the ground (à la Forest Lawn), and oaks restricted to the oldest section.

JEFFERSON

Jefferson Cemetery

Take North Avenue east from where it intersects with Jefferson Highway on the north edge of town. It becomes Cemetery Hill Road, which takes you to the cemetery.

Poised between Salem and Albany/Corvallis, Jefferson has become a bedroom community for both. With eight to ten open acres sloping uphill, the cemetery has a layout that is unique in my experience. The entire cemetery is crisscrossed with double parallel cement tracks, spaced apart roughly the width of a hearse's wheels, resulting in plots perhaps twelve feet square—a profligate use of space that would drive a modern cemetery superintendent mad.

LEBANON

Lebanon Odd Fellows and Masonic Cemetery

Cemetery Road enters Highway 20 from the east on the north side of Lebanon. Turn there; the street ends at the cemetery two blocks down.

Lebanon has had its ups and downs. Gaining original currency as a wagon-outfitting town, its greatest size came during the lumber boom of the mid-twentieth century, but when the mills went bust in the 1980s, the town's fortunes went with them.

Lebanon Odd Fellows and Masonic Cemetery houses a gorgeous new stone with a painted flag draped over its top, as if left there after a service. The stone commemorates a twenty-nine-year-old policeman and has a lengthy poem inscribed on its reverse: a children's book in verse celebrating the duty and honor of our men in blue and how one officer in uniform can inspire children to follow in his footpath.

Unlike many fraternal-order cemeteries that have been turned over to other authorities, it appears this one is still run by the brothers and is the major cemetery in town. The only one, really, as the Lebanon Pioneer Cemetery is no longer used. This one has a functioning sales office with a Pepsi machine outside, a work shed, and a columbarium. Couldn't be more up-to-date. There's not a lot of greenery other than a well-maintained lawn, but uprights are still permitted; consequently, it's visually more interesting than most of its modern equivalents. Mirroring a local proclivity for decorating front yards with old cars and miscellaneous matter, many graves are heaped high with plastic flowers, ceramic fawns, and bedraggled teddy bears. It's not a good place to see homemade stones, but it is a good place to visit decorated grave sites.

Sandridge Cemetery

Steckley Road enters Highway 34 from the south a couple miles west of Lebanon. Take it, and after a mile take Sand Ridge Road, which turns due south. After another mile, the cemetery road enters from the east; there is a sign.

Sandridge is sweet. Holding forth on a fir-covered hummock surrounded by lush fields, from the very turn down the drive it promises more than the average cemetery, and it doesn't disappoint. A diverse collection of trees and shrubs joins a succession of spring bulbs enlivening the upper half of the cemetery, while a newer, down-slope section still awaits the landscapers.

The landscapers, meanwhile, have been busy maintaining the place, and everything is shipshape. At twelve-plus acres, it qualifies as a large pioneer cemetery. A 1936 plaque dedicates the brick cemetery entrance to "the founders and builders of the Plainview Church and to their successors."

Looking east from Sandridge offers a full yet intimate view of Peterson Butte. Undoubtedly, the cherry-picking view is one reason the place has been so well loved. Located at the end of a long drive, the combination of charming grounds, inspiring view, and splendid isolation make it an ideal stopover.

Lyons

Fox Valley Pioneer Cemetery

Take Mill City/Lyons Road east out of Lyons. Cemetery about a mile out of town on your left (north).

What makes this four-acre cemetery in a hardscrabble timber town so appealing is not the imagination of the engravings nor the cleverly worded epitaphs but the wonderful plantings: rhododendrons, holly, cedar, fir, plus bushes, flowers, and an arbor vitae hedge between the cemetery and the road. As an added bonus, the place smells of the deep Cascades. An outfit called Santiam Canyon claims maintenance responsibility for the place; kudos to them. Curbing and small fences are popular here, with brand-new cement. It's a charming cemetery, worth a visit.

Scio

Franklin Butte Cemetery

On the west side of Highway 226, a mile-and-a-half or so south of Scio, a short side road paralleling the highway enters the highway in both directions. There are signs announcing the cemetery at either entrance.

At times in its past a more bustling place, Scio has never had a larger population than it has now, some 700 souls. Scio maintains a small clutch of Victorians and, as a bonus, a river (Thomas Creek) runs through town.

Scio rides the southern edge of the Santiam Basin, separated from the Southern Santiam by a push of low hills extending from the Cascades. A noticeable feature of the basin is the looming presence of the Cascade wall, as if the mountains had forgone their foothills and dragged the valley floor right up to their petticoats. Franklin Butte Cemetery holds down the rounded crest of the separation hills. The cemetery proper covers eight to ten acres, thanks in part to a recent land donation.

Sublimity

Hobson-Whitney Cemetery (Sublimity Graveyard)

Take Church Street east out of Sublimity. Shortly it intersects with Boedigheimer Road, after which it becomes Coon Hollow Road. Turn north on Boedigheimer. A few hundred yards down the road is a paved drive leading east to an enormous and very visible water tank. Take that drive as far as it goes, then head into the woods behind the tank on foot. You'll find it.

Sublimity was named for the sublime views, of course; this cemetery, also known by the euphonious name Sublimity Graveyard, was "lost" until supposedly rediscovered in 1979, according to an article in the *Capital Journal* from that year. According to the article, the cemetery had been cleared of brush at that time. While brush doesn't cover everything today, it's making a comeback. Trees cover the site, and it takes diligence to find all the extant stones. Due to their dispersed nature in the tall grass, it's hard to tell the dimensions of the cemetery or how many might be buried there. Nonetheless, despite its feral existence, Gladys Mayden (born in 1912) was buried there in 2004, proving that someone still has faith in the old burial ground. The earliest grave belongs to Salem Dixon (1838–1853) who "died by accidental shooting," according to his stone, which is carved with the old platitude: "Death is certain, the hour unseen."

Saint Boniface Cemetery

On the north side of Church Street as it exits Sublimity to the east, across the parking lot from the church.

At Saint Boniface, not only do you get a cemetery of unusual design, but you get a white-steepled pioneer church as well, ranking among Oregon's finest. Leading up to the church's steps is an allée of trees, and Saint Boniface has a wooden tower similar to those seen on some early Oregon farms.

Separated from the parking lot by a hedge, the three- or four-acre cemetery is largely open but has a few smaller trees. Its unusual design offers precise rows defined by cement strips running the length of the cemetery and upon which the headstones stand; it's a sober cemetery without undue ornament or wordiness and with a fair collection of stout, stubby, cement crosses. It also has a couple of iron filigree crosses, scarce in the Willamette Valley.

SWEET HOME

Gilliland Cemetery (Sweet Home Valley Cemetery)

From Highway 20 leaving Sweet Home in an easterly direction, take 49th Avenue south. There are signs to the cemetery—which is quite close—from that point.

Spread out over twenty or more acres atop rolling hills, the cemetery is decidedly flat-stone, save for one small corner at its rear left, where uprights appear. The lawn cemetery that dominates Gilliland wasn't "invented" until 1912, suggesting that only the rear corner with the uprights is the part of the cemetery dating back to 1854.

Turner

Cloverdale Cemetery

Find Parrish Gap Road west of Turner by taking Delany Road out of town. Parrish Gap Road will come down from the south about a mile and a half from town. Cemetery Road enters Parrish Gap from the west roughly two miles from the junction of Parrish Gap and Delany. Take it to the end.

One has to begin by giving thanks to Ruth Drager-Feitelson and Emma Drager, who are commemorated on a plaque for their volunteer labor in maintaining this superb little cemetery. The same plaque will tell you that the land was set aside from Simeon Smith's Donation Land Claim (DLC) property as a cemetery in 1856 and fifty-one years later was deeded over to the Turner IOOF, which held on to the land for another sixty years before turning it over to the present owners and marvelous caretakers, the Cloverdale Cemetery Association, bless their hearts. When I visited, all grave markers had been edged of vegetation to a distance of three to four inches, the grass was clipped short, and the place was quite shipshape, including a pristine white shed at the back. A few spreading oaks hugging the perimeter join a few more in the rear. From this rise, there's a view of the broad Santiam Basin below and the Cascades beyond.

Cloverdale is anything but pretentious. While it isn't richly stocked with fine graphics or inspired epitaphs, it does have a selection of photo-ceramics and one World War II veteran who was a "sharpshooter" during the war.

—Santiam Basin—

Whiteaker

Union Hill Cemetery

Take Highway 214, the Silver Falls Highway, east from its beginning southeast of Salem off Highway 22. Follow it six or seven miles until Union Hill Road comes in from the north. Take union Hill to the top of the hill, where the road bends around the cemetery.

Valleys, it goes without saying, are defined by hills. In gross anatomy, the Willamette Valley is defined by the Coast and Cascade Ranges, between which it lolls, but I would argue that the hills that give the valley its character are not the mega-ranges but rather the smaller clusters that fracture the valley into its separate enclaves.

Of the named clusters, the Waldo Hills are the least known, despite the fact that they cut the valley in half, force the Willamette River to the west, and are skirted by I-5 and the Santiam Highway. The Waldo Hills have their own peculiar history and geography.

The views make Union Hill Cemetery unique. Cemeteries are often built on hills; if not the top, then down the side—but it's the crests that lend cemeteries special dominance. Ostensibly, they're built on hills for drainage purposes, but one suspects that views enter into it. Consequently, cemeteries often own superior panoramas. Union Hill offers a spectacular display: 360 degrees of awe. Prior to discovering Union Hill, Mount Angel got my vote for the best view in the valley. Not any more. From Union Hill, you can see forever. If it weren't for valley haze (I'm being polite here), you could see six miles past forever. Above and beyond the sweep of the valley, there's the wall of the Cascades, and further in the haze is the shimmer of the Coast Range.

Siskiyous

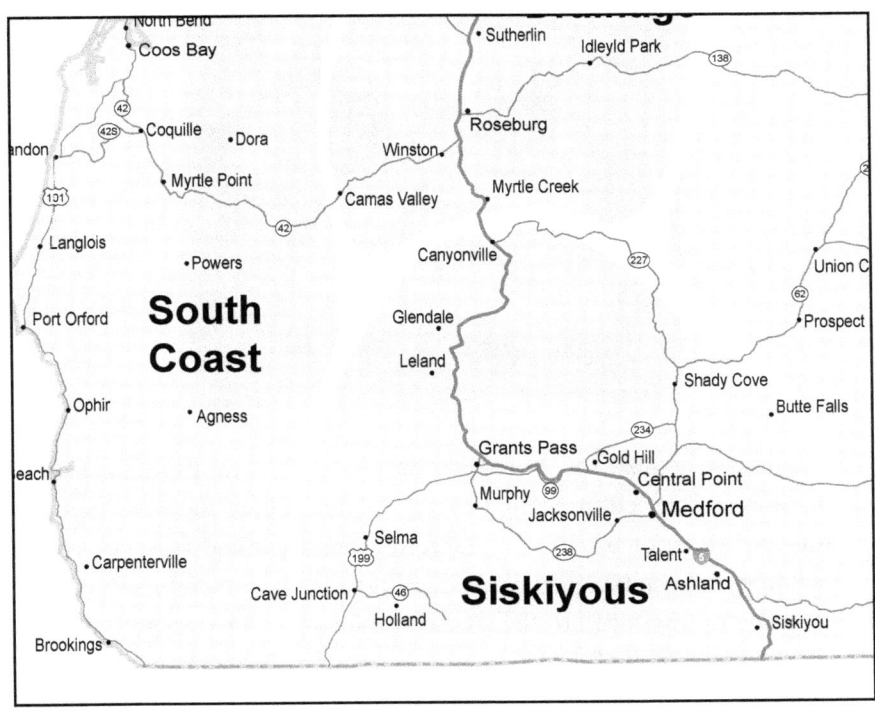

—Siskiyous—

Ashland

Mountain View

Almost in downtown Ashland, the cemetery is on Highway 66 (Ashland Street).

The region is notable for its rugged terrain and its far-flung pockets of population and agriculture. Here and there throughout the area are communities of superior beauty and interest, often separated from the rest of the world by inhospitable geography. Ashland is the personification of that phenomenon. Ensconced in the southern folds of a rich agricultural paradise ringed by densely forested wilderness, it shares a valley with the local commercial center, Medford, and the historical birthplace of the American community in southern Oregon, Jacksonville. Those towns may be blessed with money and history, but Ashland was gifted with the arts and education as the home of both Southern Oregon University and the Oregon Shakespeare Festival; consequently the town brims with creative and whimsical folks. Mountain View is an approximately four-acre cemetery with a thick covering of old trees, a good proportion being California madrone.

EAGLE POINT

Antioch Cemetery

Antioch Road crosses Highway 234 some five miles west of Highway 62. Take it north, and the cemetery will appear on the east side of the road after about a mile.

The Antioch Cemetery grounds were part of the lands developed by the Army, which in 1941 commandeered 43,000 acres of the Medford Valley for a World War II training facility. The cemetery was located smack-dab in the middle of the gunnery range and was constantly bombarded by live shells, which, as you can imagine, is not good for tombstones. Or much else, for that matter. To the Army's credit, they mitigated the damage by laying all the tombstones flat and burying them under six feet of sand where they remained for the duration of the camp. When they left, they took the sand with them and returned the uprights to their proper locations.

It was a volunteer groundskeeper for the cemetery who told me about its history, then jested that she was "a little concerned that [she] might yet run across an unexploded shell." Whatever spurred the volunteers to recover this fairly sizable cemetery, it's been working. The grasses are kept at bay and it's dotted with oaks and laurels and rhododendrons; it's actively being used and is quite lively for a cemetery of its kind. It also offers a fair amount to read and a good excuse to while away some time.

Eagle Point National Cemetery

Stevens Road heads east out of Eagle Point. Take it. Shortly out of town, it meets with Riley Road coming from the south. Take it, and the cemetery will soon appear.

Typical national cemeteries tend toward lawn cemeteries, which is partly true here, though there are also uprights; their stark uniformity provides a peaceful dignity that's mesmerizing. The carillon was playing when I visited, which certainly enhanced the sojourn. The long views of the surrounding hills and forests give visitors a sense of fullness and fecundity appropriate to the purpose.

JACKSONVILLE

Jacksonville Cemetery

From downtown Jacksonville, head north on North Oregon Street. When you hit E Street (three blocks up), turn west. The drive to the cemetery is at the end of the street, one short block.

While there are numerous delightful, rustic graveyards scattered throughout the state—we are blessed—these three are unmatched for size and variety of monuments: Lone Fir (Portland), Camp Polk (Sisters), and Jacksonville. These three say "Oregon" loud and clear. Not big. Not showy. Not elaborate. A little off-center. A little left foot. The box has yet to show up that we're supposed to think outside of. We don't march to our own drummer. We have no drum.

Jacksonville goes out of its way to get you to visit its cemetery, beginning with a spiffy black-and-white sign on the main drag and a wrought-iron entrance arch visible from the drag as well. The cemetery is the town's crown jewel, and other than the Britt Festival, it's arguably the best reason to visit this town preserved in amber. A stroll around the grounds offers ample testimony to the community's involvement, not the least of which is an "interpretive center" established there in 1991, amplified by several other interpretive signs located throughout. There's a lot of story to tell, and a lot of it is told through the cemetery.

Notably, the cemetery is an amalgam of six separate cemeteries: city; Catholic; Masonic; Odd Fellows; Red Men, both Improved and Independent Orders; and Jewish. Combining cemeteries is common, but to have so many sections for such a tiny town attests to its erstwhile luster. But the Jacksonville Cemetery, it's important to note, is not a cemetery frozen in time, and while the proliferation of relatively old stones (for the West Coast) is the advertised draw here, in my mind it's largely the active new stuff that merits attention. Admittedly, this place doesn't have quite the exuberant insouciance of Camp Polk, but it's a close second—and don't come here without expecting to spend a lot of time. The six sections must cover at least fifteen acres crawling up a madrone-covered ridge.

KENO

Keno Cemetery

Keno is 12 to 15 miles southwest of Klamath Falls on Highway 66. The highway crosses from the north to the south bank of the Klamath River at Keno. A couple of blocks after the highway crosses the river, Keno Worden Road peels off to the south. The cemetery appears on the east side.

The cemetery is a charming couple of acres under a resinous odor of ponderosa pines. There is a pervasive quality of light and smell particular to ponderosas, unmatched by any other forest in Oregon. It's a welcoming cemetery and a good place to hang your hat.

PLEASANT VALLEY

Pleasant Valley Cemetery

The drive to the cemetery heads east from Pleasant Valley Road north of its junction with Monument Drive. Pleasant Valley Road parallels I-5 on its west side about four miles north of Grants Pass. The drive is across the road from a mill, and there is a substantial sign at the roadway.

This cemetery is a conundrum wrapped inside a mystery. To begin with, it's huge. It sprawls across a feral wooded ridge line with roads cutting through the brush every which way. One could get lost in here! The size, tree cover, and random nature remind one of Camp Polk but with none of the activity or whimsical memorials.

The cemetery still gets used, but in most places, the forest runs free. What you do find more of here than in most places (though they're more common in the Siskiyous than elsewhere here) are sand-blasted wooden signs that look like business signs in resort communities.

Ruch

Logtown Cemetery

Maybe three miles southwest of Jacksonville on the east side of the Highway 238. It's right on the highway and hard to miss.

Logtown has, by any standards, one of the finest cemetery gates in the state. It's delicately decorated with yellow roses, which are the pride of the cemetery. Under a thick canopy of madrones and evergreens, the cemetery still bubbles with activity, and is evidently prided as much as the heritage rose.

It also has a superlative collection of memorials, both commercial and handmade. A plaque at the entrance says the cemetery was named after one Francis Logg and not the local industry. It notes that at one time there was "a livery stable, store, meat market, hotel, church, three saloons and two Chinese stores." Logtown isn't the only cemetery in the Applegate Valley, but it may be the best.

Williams

Sparlin Cemetery
Gotcher Cemetery

Take Watergap Road to Williams from Highway 238 (heading south). Sparlin Cemetery lies to the east just before town. Gotcher is just across the street.

If you're dying to get away from it all, Sparlin and Gotcher, two small cemeteries in Williams, might do the trick. Neither is large; both are typical pioneer cemeteries for this neck of the woods, and both are fairly long and narrow, with the majority of the graves in clusters along the edges farthest from the road, as if neither group wanted to have anything to do with the other.

Neither Sparlin nor Gotcher will likely make anyone's favorite cemetery list, unless they happen to know someone buried there, but at the same time, they're pleasant, well maintained rural enclaves that will probably avoid inundation by exurbia for a long time. There are a number of interesting markers here, several of which are homemade.

South Coast

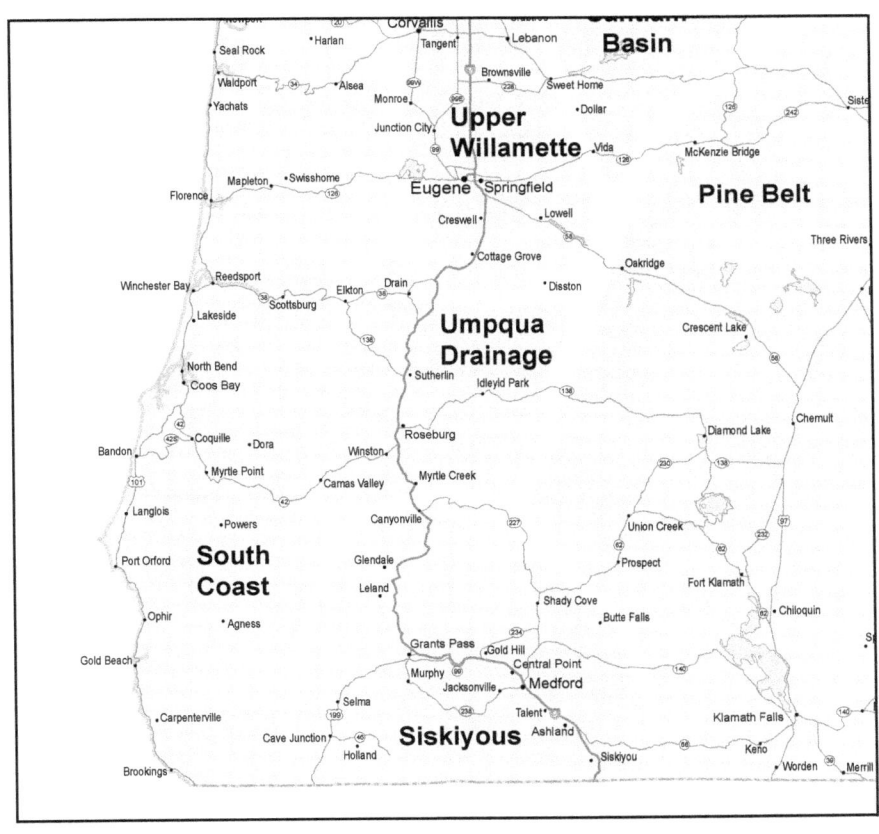

BANDON

Bandon Lodge #133 IOOF Cemetery

Highway 101 makes a few turns through Bandon, and it meets Highway 42S, which runs along the Coquille River. You want to take 42S toward Coquille, keeping a lookout on your left (north side of the road) because the cemetery will show up in about a block.

Not more than two acres, with a scattering of smallish trees, there are a couple of nice epitaphs here, as well as one "dog house," as half-height mausoleums are sometimes referred to. And don't let the modest cemetery prevent you from visiting Bandon-by-the-Sea.

COOS BAY

Marshfield Pioneer Cemetery

At the northeast corner of the intersection of Ingersoll and South Seventh, south of downtown Coos Bay. The cemetery fronts the imposing Marshfield High.

You'll need a key, which is available from the principal's office. Despite the fence and locked gate, fronting a high school invites plenty of vandalism, and almost no stone is spared. The cemetery comprises five open acres, with no trees to interrupt the sweeping view from the steps of the school.

—South Coast—

Coos River

Coos River Cemetery (South Fork Cemetery)

Getting there is half the trick. Take the Coos River Highway, heading east. Instead of going over the bridge to the north bank, take the shunt under the bridge, which follows the river on that bank, the confusingly named Coos River Road. After two or three miles, the road does cross the river. Immediately upon crossing the river, take the road entering from the left (north). Google shows it as South Coos River Lane. Follow this a mile or so until it takes a sharp turn to the right and becomes Landreth Road. The driveway to the cemetery (on the right) is prior to that turn.

This charming little three-acre cemetery is somewhat difficult to find but worth the effort. It's well maintained, interesting, and delightfully located on a dead-end road. It will probably be peaceful here forever. The cemetery is on a point of land where the Coos River divides into southern and northern branches, and occasionally it's referred to as the South Fork Cemetery.

COQUILLE

Coquille Masonic Cemetery

On the north side of West Central Boulevard in Coquille. West Central is Old Highway 42 and basically the main drag through town. The cemetery is west of downtown.

Coquille Valley, unique to the Oregon Coast, owes its remarkable fertility to annual flooding of the river. Farms can be cut off from the rest of the world for days or weeks at a time, but they're used to it and are set up to handle it. The valley in full flood, with fields marked by fence-lines poking above the water, conjures other times and distant places. The valley harbors a culture of its own, tied to Bandon at the river's mouth by geography and to Coos Bay by money and population.

This cemetery comprises three-plus acres with a clutch of older stones and not a lot of new stuff. Given that there's another cemetery behind this one, it merits a stop if you're passing through.

DEADWOOD

Deadwood Cemetery

Deadwood is, essentially, where Deadwood Creek Road coming from the north meets Highway 36. Take Deadwood Creek Road. The driveway to the cemetery is the first drive to the east (right) after turning onto Deadwood Creek. There's a house prior to it, but then the drive comes up almost immediately. There is no sign at the road, but the cemetery is at the end.

Deadwood Cemetery is a pleasant couple acres under moss and ancient cedars and is fairly modest in its markers. There are a couple oddities, and the bench is very well done; all in all, it's quite subdued. Either not enough people have died or they're getting buried elsewhere or cremated, but they haven't taken advantage much of this community resource.

SCOTTSBURG

Scottsburg Cemetery

The cemetery is east of Scottsburg. Look for Golden Drive heading to the east from Highway 38 and take it. Cemetery Road takes off from Golden about 200 yards from the highway.

Founded quite early for these parts, in 1850, Scottsburg once had ambitions to be the major burg on Oregon's southern coast. Dug into the gorge of the Umpqua with no flat land to build upon, Scottsburg today boasts a modest population. Herds of elk live along the western extremity of the gorge, to the delight of passersby, and from the middle, a road claws its way up the hillside to the naturally dammed Loon Lake and the hidden Ash Valley beyond, which only got telephone service in the 1970s.

The Umpqua is a fabled river; the only Oregon river to run through both the Cascades and the Coast Range, it's a free-flowing, catch-and-release river that curls out of the mountains from the neighborhood of Crater Lake. Its upper reaches are remarkably free of development, and its central valleys hide exquisite, vineyard-cloaked nooks and crannies. The treeless cemetery is divided into older (uprights) and newer (lawn) sections, with an access road splitting the two.

Tualatin River Valley

BLOOMING

Blooming Cemetery

At the corner of Nursery and Iowa Hill Roads. Approximately two miles south of Cornelius.

Blooming is the tail of a trail of German communities in the western Tualatin Valley that runs south from Germantown and Cornelius Pass Roads, and many old grave markers feature German rather than English text. Blooming has never been more than a clutch of homes stretched out along Iowa Hill Road, centering on Saint Peter's Lutheran Church (Saint Peter's Lutheran was also the cemetery's name at times). Surrounded by fields supporting a variety of crops, the name Blooming Cemetery Road was changed to Nursery Road because Hines Nursery occupies much of both sides of the short lane. The 1849 date theoretically represents the earliest grave, although there's speculation that the earliest grave could be from 1856.

BUXTON

Buxton Community Cemetery

When you reach the sign for Buxton on Highway 26 heading toward the coast, turn in the opposite direction onto Fisher Road. At the T at Staley Road, turn right. Cemetery is a short way down on your left.

Getting to this cemetery on dirt roads doesn't prepare one for the order, scope, and almost military precision of the Buxton Cemetery. Well-mannered rows of often curb-delineated family plots march up and down the field (despite current regulations of "no curbing of any kind").

Beverly Swanson's (1929–1985) marker has the faint impression of an ashtray and a couple of cigarettes. Did she have them put there because they were two of her favorite things—as is common—or was she trying to tell us what killed her? Or both? Next door, Marvin Swanson's (1918–1982) handmade marker in the shape of a dove holding its wings above its head to form a circle is rapidly crumbling away.

FOREST GROVE

Forest View Cemetery

Off Ritchey Road at the west end of Forest Grove. When Highway 8 bends north from Pacific Avenue heading west, the street that keeps going straight is Ritchey Road.

Both major cemeteries in Forest Grove are on hills at the west end of town, and I'd like to think one of them held the original grove of white oaks the town was named for. If this one didn't, the view is fine enough. State records list the cemetery as some thirty-seven acres, and its founding date of 1846 makes it one of the earliest cemeteries in the region.

Forest View comes complete with a forty-eight-niche columbarium and a mausoleum. The grounds are broken into areas named after trees: cherry, fir, etc. Despite its age, Forest Grove shows signs of having kept up with the times, the mausolea being only the most obvious examples. A large section is devoted to a lawn cemetery.

Mountain View Memorial

Heading west out of town on Highway 8 (Gales Creek Road), take Thatcher Road where it angles off to the north. Watercress will appear quickly on your left. Take it. Cemetery will shortly appear on the right.

This ten-acre cemetery holds some gems; being off the beaten path doesn't mean languishing. The cemetery is very active and is smartly cared for in a commanding position, with great old stones and wonderful new ones.

GALES CREEK

Gales Creek Cemetery

Turn west onto Old Wilson River Road at the Gales Creek Store in Gales Creek on Highway 8. Soda Spring Road intersects from the left. Take it. Cemetery is on the west side of road.

The Gales Creek Cemetery is nicer than your average cemetery—and your average cemetery ain't bad. This four-plus-acre cemetery was named after an early pioneer and person of note in the Oregon American colony, Joseph Gale, who had the distinction of being the master of the first ship built in Oregon, the Star of Oregon, launched in 1842, a year before the first wagonload of immigrants scraped across the Oregon Trail. He had landed in Oregon in 1834, coming, as almost everyone did then, by sea.

Gales Creek cuts a fanciful path from the edges of the Coast Range into the far western Tualatin Valley. The cemetery occupies a bend where the road leaves the valley. It's curious that, with Gales Creek's air of past gentility and a namesake settler from such an early date, the age of the cemetery only harkens back to 1874: hardly a grown person, as cemeteries go. Where was everybody buried before then?

Youth doesn't mean a dearth of early stones, but Gales Creek is definitely a cemetery where the new outshines the old; there are no diatribes here or dissertations on the love of one's mother. Cosseted by fir-bedecked ridges, the view from the cemetery is one of gentle accord, and the sentiments on the headstones reflect a comfort with place. Most are clustered together in the old part of the cemetery, but there is considerable open ground with only a few recent burials. It's worth walking over to visit these "outpost graves," well away from their fellow residents.

HILLSBORO

Masonic-IOOF Cemetery (Hillsboro Pioneer Cemetery)

North side of Highway 8, Baseline Road, as it departs Hillsboro to the west.

My map says both a Masonic and an IOOF cemetery are here, but where one starts and the other stops is beyond my reckoning; all I know is that the Masons are to the east while the Odd Fellows are to the west.

Most prominent of the Masons are the Tongue Family, whose obelisk is the grandest in the cemetery, as well as having the best plantings and an entrance gate all of their own. A number of prominent early settlers are buried here, among them Desire Griffin (1806–1884) of Boston, "missionary to native tribes, 1839," who was the "first white woman in Tualatin settlement, July, 1841. First white mother in same, Nov. 8, 1842." But my heart goes out to Rachel Johonet Spalding (1803–1880), also of Boston, who "with her husband, Rev. H. H. Spalding,/ was successful in modest/ but enduring labors among/ Native Tribes. — Let daughters of Oregon share the work,/ and the Eternal rest."

Tualatin Plains Presbyterian Church Cemetery (Old Scotch Church Cemetery)

Head east on Old Scotch Church Road from its intersection with Glencoe Road north of Hillsboro. Cemetery is less than a mile down the road on the north side.

Cloistered underneath tall redwoods and weeping birches, the Tualatin Plains Presbyterian Church (also known as the Old Scotch Church) and Cemetery are, without serious competition, the most delightful church/graveyard combination in the region. The white-spired rural church could not be more quintessential were it in a New England village. The new entrance plaza and the even newer columbarium are of exquisite and complementary design. The church remains active (as does the cemetery) with people coming and going on all days. Like the rest of the valley, this will soon be surrounded by monolithic developments, but thanks to the canopy of trees, the cemetery should be spared the worst ravages of urban expansion.

The church, of course, is an added bonus for the tapophile; the ten-plus acre cemetery is interesting enough to stand alone. It's filled to the gills with old and new markers, the most prominent of which is unquestionably that of Joe Meek and family. Joe (brother to Stephen Meek of *Meek's Cutoff*) was one of the more colorful of the footloose mountain men that helped found the modern state of Oregon. Meek and his family weren't originally buried at Tualatin Plains, but their remains were moved there after a freeway disturbed their first resting place. I'd like to think he'd find it fitting. The graveyard at Tualatin Plains is anything but rooted in the past. There are older and more historic cemeteries in the vicinity, but none of them lives so vibrantly in the present.

Valley Memorial Park

North side of Highway 8 as it heads toward Portland, southeast of Hillsboro.

Every once in a while a cemetery comes that can kill you just getting there. Put this one high on that list. You'd be safer arriving dead. Located on the inside of a bend in the busy TV Highway, there's no stoplight nearby, and the traffic plows past madly. And once you've successfully extricated yourself from the highway, its sounds dominate the roadward side of the cemetery.

Fortunately, there's another side to it, a side that slopes down to a horseshoe-shaped pond screaming with wildfowl. It's here where cemetery director

Kim Kaufold separates his operation from the pack in the lower valley. It's here where Oregon finds its first "green" cemetery. A movement started in England, it has taken its time crossing the puddle but is on the verge of explosive expansion.

Green cemeteries, if you're not yet aware, are, in essence, ones without chemicals (good-bye, formaldehyde), impermeable coffins, or markers other than trees or bushes or, perhaps, GPS locations. Green cemeteries are often operated partly as nature preserves without the appearance of a traditional cemetery. In this country they're being touted by Tyler Cassity, who's best known for creating the Hollywood Forever cemetery and as consultant to HBO's *Six Feet Under*.

Valley Memorial is blessed with a large tract of land, most of which is undeveloped and home to an abundance of wildlife. Kaufold's intentions, like those of the industry, are to maintain the wild lands in a nature preserve with only limited access. To its credit, while Valley Memorial traditionally has been a lawn cemetery, it does reserve a small section for uprights.

LAURELWOOD

Hill(s) Cemetery

To the east of Spring Hill Road about a half-mile north of where Laurelwood Road intersects with Spring Hill. A small green sign on Spring Hill Road points to the cemetery.

ODOT gives Almoran Hill Cemetery as an alternative name to what they term Hill Cemetery, as do most other sources save for the sign at the entrance to the cemetery, which lists it as Hills.

In any event, the cemetery *does* occupy the crest of a small outrigger of the nearby Chehalem Hills and hosts a commanding view of the surrounding valley. It's a well-situated resting place that will probably be safeguarded against urban sprawl for some time, thanks to the protective wall of the Chehalems. You get a fine view from up here; to the west, the cemetery overlooks the whilom seasonal Wapato Lake Bed. Wapato was an important pre-Euroamerican foodstuff and trade item in the Columbia Basin, and Wapato Lake Bed was a major gathering (in both senses) grounds for all the local tribes. The Chehalems peter out not far from here and the lake bed is on the pass between the Tualatin and Yamhill Valleys.

Surely, the most important person interred in Hills is Peter McIntosh (1861–1940), the "Father of the cheese industry in the Oregon Country." He brought the recipe for cheddar cheese to the dairymen of Tillamook from the exotic state of Washington.

MOUNTAINDALE

Raffety Cemetery

Off Dairy Creek Road a half-mile north of its intersection with Mountaindale Road. Cemetery sign visible from road.

The drive to Raffety Cemetery looks like the driveway for a house and garage, but a gate across the drive gives the name of the cemetery, which is probably another quarter mile past the gate.

The Raffetys erected an impressive obelisk in the center of circular curbing whose entrance gate is flanked by two redwoods slowly beginning to dominate the site. As to the rest of the site, one has the feeling that it was nice of the Raffetys to let other people be buried here. The cemetery is still being used, has land to expand, and is moderately well maintained.

SHADYBROOK

Shadybrook Cemetery

Take Glencoe-Shadybrook Road east out of North Plains and keep following when it becomes Dixie Mountain Road. The road to the cemetery comes up shortly on your right. There is a sign.

The gravel drive to the cemetery is through a farmer's property, and it feels like you're going up to an old orchard between fence rows. When you get there, you find a tiny cemetery bursting with vigor, including, seemingly out of place, a brand-new columbarium. The drive continues on through the parking lot to circle around a sapling in the middle of what's, obviously, an expansion area. Many of the graves are thickly planted and a spring visit would be glorious.

VERBOORT

Visitation Cemetery

From Highway 47 heading north out of Forest Grove into the Tualatin Plains, take Ostermann Road to the east. Entrance to the cemetery is about three quarters of a mile down on the north side of the road.

The earliest death date I saw, which doesn't mean there weren't earlier ones, was 1875, the same year the Visitation Church, with which the cemetery is associated, was founded by the Reverend Verboort, after whom the community was named. The reverend, who was born in Holland in 1835 and emigrated to Wisconsin in 1848, died a year after coming to Oregon and organizing the Visitation Church.

It's a two-acre cemetery rapidly filling up and without much hope of expansion, unless there's a major change in the law, according to the groundskeeper who's been maintaining the place—and quite well, I must say—for thirty-eight years. He was among the crew that planted the arbor vita lining the entrance drive—trees he's had to trim back five feet on three different occasions. He said that by law, the cemetery cannot expand its acreage by more than 10 percent, which, of course, would be useless to them. Its ultimate fate remains uncertain.

Aside from its orderliness and the profusion of little crosses on the tops of many of the headstones, the overwhelming preponderance of Dutch names is what's striking about the Visitation Cemetery. The cemetery is also somewhat unusual in having a paved walkway bisect a rectangular plot, in the middle of which is a large white cross and a small columbarium. At the farther end is a statue of the good Reverend Verboort himself.

Umpqua Drainage

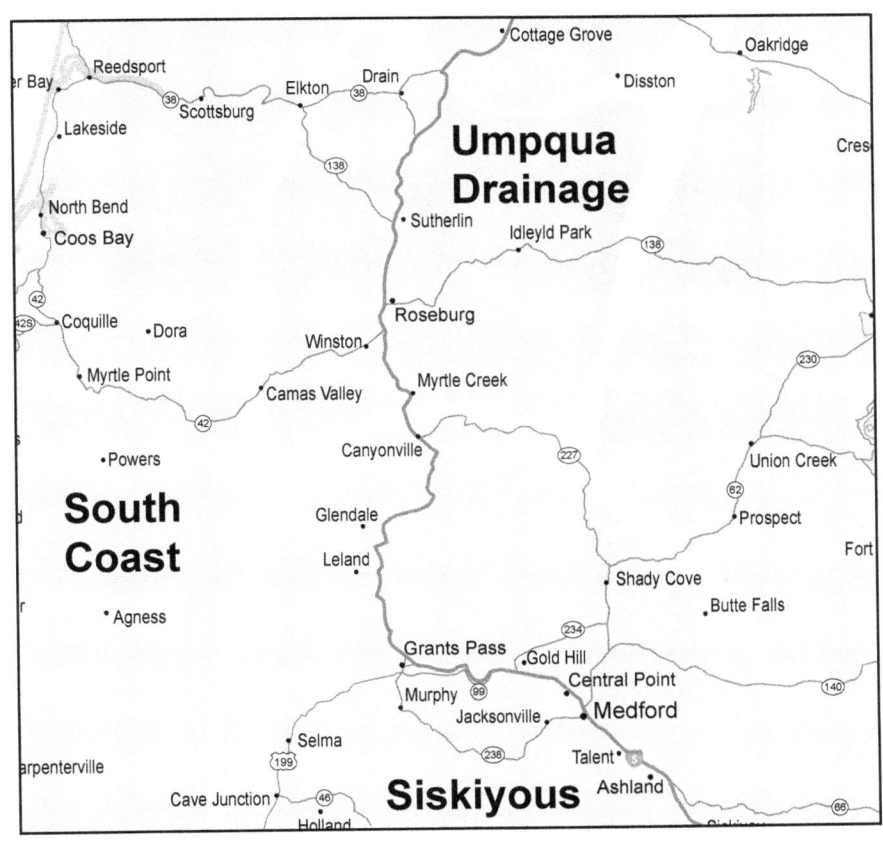

DRAIN

Drain IOOF Cemetery

Find Alta Vista Avenue, on the east side of town, and follow it almost one mile eastward to its end at the cemetery.

If you're heading from the Willamette Valley to the south coast, Drain is the first community you'll hit in the Umpqua Drainage. It's a tiny town famous many years ago for Arlene's Cafe, well known for its enormous portions.

Apparently the cemetery of choice in the neighborhood, the IOOF cemetery is twice the size of the Drain Cemetery and has more current activity as well. The cemetery is divided into a two-acre older section, covered with uprights and large trees, and a two-acre modern lawn cemetery. This far from town, it's blessedly quiet—a fine place to settle down.

LOOKINGGLASS

Lookingglass Community Cemetery

Access to the cemetery is off Coos Bay Wagon Road, a few yards west of its intersection with Lookingglass Road.

This is a typical pioneer cemetery with a surround of large trees, though it gets more use than many other rural cemeteries of comparable size. Perhaps it has to do with the community, as the Lookingglass Valley is a unique place, one of Oregon's hideaways. In ranch country with wineries just around the corner, Lookingglass anchors the eastern end of the Coos Bay Wagon Road, the original road between Coos Bay and Roseburg, and is one of the great trans-mountain routes, albeit a slow one. A goodly chunk of it is dirt, but still, the drive up Brewster Canyon is deep Coast Range.

MYRTLE CREEK

Myrtle Creek Pioneer Cemetery

From Highway 99 south of town, Pioneer Way enters from the west. Take it. There is a sign.

This one-and-a-half-acre cemetery under a canopy of madrones is a model of preservation boasting a stunning new gate worth the detour alone. No longer active, it remains a well-maintained museum piece. Almost every stone shows signs of vandalism, but at the same time, every stone is meticulously preserved. It's an utterly charming place to visit pioneer graves, the only distraction being highway noise. An information kiosk provides highlights of some of the people buried here.

Oakland

Oakland Masonic and Old Town Oakland Cemeteries

Take Old Highway 99 north and turn right on North Old Town Road. In roughly four miles, you'll turn left. There is a small sign.

It's got a bright new fence and gate, but I doubt the Masons are involved; a sign noting contributions toward the new hardware doesn't mention them. Despite the new equipment and evident upkeep, no one appears to be using the cemetery anymore. Pity, as there's lots of room left, and the location's not bad for this four-acre graveyard lazing up a gentle slope, for the most part sans significant timber.

Standard issue pioneer cemeteries, this and the erstwhile Oakland IOOF Cemetery (now Cedar Hills) speak to the former glory of this small town. The town is on the National Registry of Historic Places and is well worth a detour.

Roseburg

Roseburg National Cemetery

In Roseburg, head west on West Harvard Avenue from its intersection with I-5 (exit 124). The cemetery will appear on the north side of the street.

At four-and-a-half acres, this is a tiny cemetery as far as veteran cemeteries go; consequently, it's pretty much filled up. The older burials have uprights, but more recent burials warrant flush markers only. The cemetery is flat and sans trees, but it's next to a park.

TENMILE

Tenmile United Methodist Cemetery

Tenmile is some seven or eight miles west of Winston on Highway 42. When you see Coates Road come in from the north, take it. Turn west (left) on Tenmile Valley Road, and the cemetery will appear shortly.

A comfortable, small, charming cemetery of only a few acres, gracefully accompanied by a scattering of young and youngish trees, not only does it harbor a concrete picnic table and a parking canopy but it also has a hexagonal gazebo-cum-committal shelter. The land is a modest rise in a rumpled part of the Coast Range.

UMPQUA

Coles Valley Cemetery

Take the Umpqua-Sutherlin Road west out of Sutherlin until it crosses the river and becomes Hubbard Creek Road. A mile past the bridge, Melqua Road enters from the south; take it. Cemetery is on a hillside on the west side of the road.

This cemetery sits comfortably on a slope edging the fertile Coles Valley, the last riverine agricultural valley before the Umpqua plunges into the Coast Range. There is no river in Oregon like the Umpqua, which enfolds a special mystique of its own, from the pure upper reaches through the serpentine farm valleys to the majestic tidewater run to the sea. It is an enchanted river, and the Coles Valley Cemetery will lead you into its middle haunts. There is a soft amber light here unlike anywhere else in the state.

WINSTON

Civil Bend Cemetery

Highway 42 (Douglas Boulevard) heads west from Highway 99 in Winston; take it. Almost immediately, Civil Bend Avenue enters from the south; take that into the cemetery.

The "bend" referred to is one in the Umpqua River; the cemetery comprises four or five long acres on top of a gentle knoll under a spread of older trees, with a number of the graves enlivened by flower beds. Its entrance is announced by a large rock with carvings of a horse-drawn hearse. Decades ago, this cemetery was much more rural than it is now, but in any event, it's encouraging to see one more rural cemetery being well looked after.

Upper Willamette

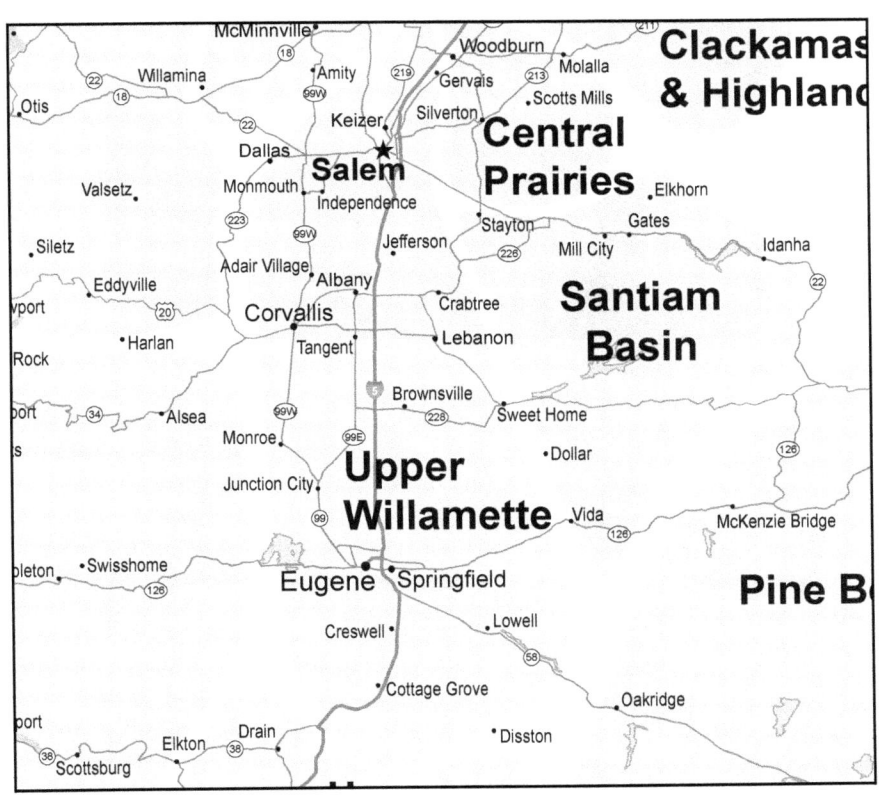

Alpine

Alpine Cemetery

From downtown Alpine, i.e., the intersection of Bellfountain and Alpine Roads, head west on Alpine Road. Cemetery road will enter Alpine Road from the north a block or two down. Take it to the end.

Make no mistake, this is the Alpine Cemetery. The sign on the archway says "Simpson Chapel, 25600," but no one else is going to know it by that name, and I have no idea where it came from.

You'll have to undo a gate to drive up here, but when you get here, you'll find four fairly pedestrian acres housing two big oaks and a border of firs and redwoods. There is a cute weathered shed in the back and a lot of room left on the lower slopes; it doesn't look as if Alpine will be filling it anytime soon.

Bear Creek

Rest Lawn Memorial Park

On the east side of Territorial Highway about a half-mile north of its intersection with High Pass Road, west of Junction City.

Rest Lawn couldn't have been named Rest Lawn Memorial Park when it was founded: The graves in this six-acre cemetery go back at least to 1880, and the world's first "memorial park" wasn't founded until 1912. Fortunately, although adopting the nomenclature of the memorial park, Rest Lawn didn't adopt the style, i.e., a lawn cemetery with no uprights. Instead, this is an old-fashioned Odd Fellows cemetery with a gussied-up name but, thank heavens, no gussied-up nature.

A line of firs marches down the center drive of the cemetery, joined by miscellaneous other trees and a humble collection of grave markers, one of which, the one for "Sunny" Hogan (1915–2003), merits a detour. It's a burnished steel silhouette of the "End of the Trail" against a coal black stone.

Like so many indigenous Oregon cemeteries, this one rolls up a hill to a grand view. It appears as if the original interments spread themselves out randomly over the entire cemetery, and the Johnny-come-latelies have been filling in the gaps ever since. Whoever has taken on the duties of maintaining the cemetery has done landscaping as well. It is a fine cemetery, and it's just around the corner from the exquisite Danish Cemetery.

Danish Cemetery

On High Pass Road, west of its intersection with Territorial Highway, west of Junction City.

Not much more than two acres surrounded by stately firs and graced by perennials, the Danish Cemetery is a tidy lot and quite definitely Danish, as most occupants have last names ending in "-sen"; however, one of the most interesting persons interred there is the decidedly un-Danish Eugenia Rett-Wilczkowiak, who was a "member of the Polish Underground Home Army," participated in the Warsaw Uprising of 1944, and won the "Bronze Cross of Merit with Swords."

Stark black lettering on a white arch of hand-laminated wood surmounting pillars made of concrete blocks reads in Danish, "*Kampen er til ende bract,*" which is translated on a plaque at the cemetery as "The struggle is finished."

BELLFOUNTAIN

Bellfountain Cemetery

The road heading due east out of the hamlet of Bellfountain is Dawson Road. After a half mile, Dawson meets Occidental Lane heading south, but a spur at that point heads north. The cemetery is down the spur.

Bellfountain is easy to overlook because it's not on the way to anywhere, unless you're fond of taking back roads between Corvallis and Eugene. But even getting close to Bellfountain demands a nod.

The graveyard, is a tale of two cemeteries, one an older, two-acre section with upright stones and covered with large firs, laurels, rhododendrons, and holly, while the larger, newer section is trying valiantly to be a lawn cemetery demanding flat-laid stone, many of which are actually "pillows," as they say in the trade, and rise significantly above the ground, obviating the gains supposed to be accrued with a lawn cemetery. Bellfountain has plenty of new stones and modern graphics; most unusual are the many pairs of small, pink and purple wooden crosses dotting the landscape.

BROWNSVILLE

Brownsville Pioneer Cemetery

At the eastern end of Kirk Street in historic Brownsville.

Noticeable right off the bat upon entering the cemetery (past the "cemetery parking" sign) is a chainsaw-carved bust of, one can only presume, Indian Lize, who has a neighboring stone in her honor as being the "Last of the Calapooyas," who died in 1921, "age about 100 years." Next to her are two flat markers: one for Susan Indian (d. 1921), and one for L. B. "Alva" Indian (d. 1892).

The Brownsville Cemetery is also unusual in having a matched pair of Woodmen of the World tree-trunk markers. Furthermore, the cemetery has a number of homemade or hand-decorated grave sites of merit, including one very simple, very pure, very stainless-steel cross.

BUENA VISTA

Buena Vista Cemetery

Take Riverview, the middle of the three streets in Buena Vista, to its northern terminus at the top of a hill overlooking the hamlet.

The view from the cemetery is quite lovely, overlooking the fairy-tale Willamette Valley and the nearby patriotically named American Bottom, not to mention the river. As cemeteries go, this is archetypically pioneer, without a lot of modern stuff. Someone has been cleaning the stones of late and maintenance in general is pretty good, although a few more trees might help.

Coburg

IOOF Cemetery

Taking Coburg Road north out of Eugene, the road to the cemetery is the first drive to the east past the bridge over the MacKenzie.

As cemeteries go, 1882 is young for an Odd Fellows endeavor, and at three acres it's not terribly large, but it's a pleasant diversion. Its main drawback is that it backs nearly onto I-5, and the traffic noises are constant. Many of the individual plots are planted with bulbs, a gift from volunteers.

CORVALLIS

Armstrong Cemetery

The cemetery is off Bellfountain Road, south of where it meets Airport Avenue. Airport Avenue heads west from Highway 99W a couple miles south of Corvallis.

Not more than an untended quarter-acre with a handful of old graves underneath old trees. Surely an abandoned DLC cemetery. The living have long since left this place, and the dead are thinking about it. It's next to a pond, and an old hammock is strung between a couple trees down at the shore.

Crystal Lake Cemetery

SE Crystal Lake Drive heads east from Highway 99W in Corvallis south of the highway's junction with Highway 34. There is a cemetery sign at that intersection.

Crystal Lake Cemetery is the city's one-size-fits-all cemetery and is more or less the equivalent of Portland's Lone Fir. On a flat table of land overlooking Willamette River bottoms, its older sections harbor a few respectably old trees, and the place is, fittingly, on the National Registry of Historic Places.

Unlike Lone Fir, though, Crystal Lake incorporates modern elements of cemetery design in its newer sections, which are the first sections one encounters coming through the southern gate.

There is a signboard with a protected pocket for brochures giving a bit of the history of the cemetery, evidence of more than average concern for one's past. The brochure is issued by the Benton County Natural Areas and Parks Department, which, presumably, is the current caretaker of the property. The cemetery is still in use.

Crystal Lake is a good example of the indigenous DLC cemetery as developed with the opening of the Oregon Territory. Probably the most common way for Oregon cemeteries to have begun were as family cemeteries on a corner of someone's DLC, a corner that eventually grew and became dedicated as a community cemetery.

Both Crystal Lake and Lone Fir began in this fashion. Many of those DLC cemeteries remained private and many of them have subsequently disappeared. Others, though, were deeded over to civil authorities or, as with Crystal Lake, to a fraternal order—in this case to the Masons—and survive to this day.

The cemetery has one notable statue, that of a Civil War soldier on a pedestal erected in 1908, that reads "...in memory of the men who bared their bosoms to the storms of battle."

Corvallis, originally a transportation hub for the gold mines to the south and Portland to the north, is a charming and peaceful (except on football weekends) town that really could be the "heart of the valley."

Saint Mary's Cemetery

At the intersection of NW Grant and NW 36th Street in Corvallis.

Acre for acre, there may not be a prettier cemetery in the state. There are certainly ones with better views, but for comfortably laid out grounds, this is hard to beat—and it's not easy to accomplish on a five-acre triangle of land clawing its way up a hillside so steep that the highest rungs of the cemetery are terraced, which only adds to the ambiance. Keeping up with the times, there is a small, upright columbarium on a cement pad, and there is a good mix of old and new stones, enough so that the place becomes a treasure hunt for notables.

What truly distinguishes the place are rich plantings of shrubs and flowers that create virtual rooms up and down the incline. When I visited in the spring, the flowering trees were at their peak, and the sun was strong. The park-like setting was at its most superb. To top it off, three deer slowly nibbled their way across the lawn. One lay down next to my car for awhile, and none seemed too concerned about my intentions.

COTTAGE GROVE

Fir Grove Cemetery

Cemetery Road, which leads to Fir Grove Cemetery, heads north from Main Street at the west end of Cottage Grove.

A very nice, well-maintained, six-acre cemetery climbing a steep hillside, this is the cemetery of choice for Cottage Grove, appropriate for one of Oregon's best-preserved towns, which has twice won an "All American City" award.

The cemetery isn't just maintained but is landscaped and modernized with the addition of a columbarium; thankfully, it is not modernized to the extent of carrying a flat-stone requirement. The view of the surrounding hills is magnificent, and the upkeep is top-notch. It may not be a lawn cemetery, but it has a great lawn nonetheless. While not an excessive cemetery, it has its share of interesting stones, including one carrying a rendering of Sylvester the Cat saying, "It's 4:20," apparently in reference to the California penal code number for marijuana possession.

McFarland Cemetery

In a wedge of land between Holly Avenue and Kalapuya Street in Cottage Grove.

You'll note when you get there that the wedge between Holly and Kalapuya is a forested hill, up which a set of stairs has been laid. The cemetery is at the top of the stairs, under the brush and weeds. You'll be able to see the tops of the few un-vandalized stones above the vegetation. The poignant part is a dedication plaque from 1978 that you can find if you look. It thanks "the Community Service Classes of Cottage Grove High School and to all others who helped in the restoration of the McFarland Pioneer Cemetery…May all who shall be interred here now rest in peace."

CRAWFORDSVILLE

Crawfordsville Union Cemetery

The drive to the cemetery heads south from Highway 228 on the east edge of Crawfordsville. There is a clear sign at the highway.

The Crawfordsville Cemetery has much to recommend it, besides its estimable view. Its founding date, 1851, is early and speaks to the attraction of the Calapooia Valley to the settlers. At five to six acres, it was designed for a larger population than it now warrants, which only means there are plenty of good lots available. It has a few large trees and shrubs and is distinguished by a plethora of signs (among them "All stones set flat," despite all the upright older stones). It is a comely cemetery with a unisex privy—the sign reads "Men or Women"—and a work shed, and it offers a sweeping view of the Calapooia Valley.

CRESWELL

Creswell Pioneer Cemetery (Creswell Association Cemetery)

The driveway to the cemetery heads west from Howe Lane west of Creswell.

This cemetery is a secluded oasis of enchantment far from the distant din of traffic, surrounded by woods, with a deep peace settled over the place like a fog. After a long drive from Howe Lane, the cemetery begins inauspiciously with a collection of flat stones on a small plot, playing its way uphill to a dogleg right. Only when one rounds the corner does one appreciate the scope and ambiance of Creswell Pioneer. Here under a canopy of maples, firs, and madrones augmented by smaller bushes rests a serene community of erstwhile Creswellians peacefully guarding the passing eons.

The stock of interesting and thoughtful grave markers was truly surprising, including a number of homemade displays—the steel cross with the calf-roping rider watching over R. Gregorio Rodriguez (1960–2003) is outstanding. The cemetery can't be more than three acres in size, but given the quality of its markers and location, it plays much bigger. If you have a nice day and time to spend, this would be an excellent choice for a picnic.

DALLAS

Dallas Cemetery

On the west side of Highway 223 a few blocks south of Dallas.

Dallas has a knockout cemetery running the gamut from early pioneers to modern imaging. At fifty acres, it's enormous for a community of this size; chunks of it are not only not filled but still covered in woods and brush. Originally an Odd Fellows cemetery, it was taken over by the City of Dallas in 1952.

A stone carver was adding a new date to an existing stone when I visited. He was lying on a tarp to protect himself from the damp ground, surrounded by chisels and mallets, and had a black mastiff chained to a pipe stuck in the ground. "Nobody carves letters by hand anymore," he said. "I just can't afford the tools right now, so I do this."

Eugene

Eugene Masonic Cemetery

At the southern terminus of University Avenue in Eugene.

At first glance, The Eugene Masonic Cemetery looks like one more cemetery given over to despair, with headstones disappearing beneath a tangle of wild plants—but upon closer inspection, one finds strange goings-on, such as paths to various tombstones mowed through the weeds, signs here and there identifying the riot of plants you see not as weeds but as native plant species, and other signs offering short biographies of some of the people interred here. In fact, the more one looks, the more paths and signs one sees.

A constant flow of visitors and dog walkers passes through the grounds; the cemetery is a nature park and a wildlife preserve as well as a cemetery. The Eugene Masonic Cemetery is unique to the state of Oregon; there's nothing else like it. From its inception in 1859 until 1993, it was a Masonic cemetery in the typical mode of fraternal order cemeteries and, like many fraternal order cemeteries, fell into disrepair and disuse as operating funds dried up. In 1993, ownership of the property transferred to the nonprofit Eugene Masonic Cemetery Association, which brought the cemetery back to life as a nature preserve as well as a burying ground. This cemetery also gives a nod to the "green" cemetery movement, in which the dead are buried without markers in a natural setting.

There are very few cemeteries in Oregon on the "must see" list; this is one of those.

Eugene Pioneer Cemetery

Behind the University of Oregon, running alongside University Avenue and 18th Street.

This sixteen-acre cemetery could be mistaken for Eugene's answer to Portland's Lone Fir, but don't you believe it. It's not even Salem's City View or Corvallis's Crystal Lake. But it's a great place for university students to hang out, make out, or do whatever else university students do in the woods these days. It does resemble Lone Fir in having a bunch of old stones and a canopy of large, old trees, but the place has become frozen in time and lacks the vibrancy of a living cemetery. And as a consequence, Eugene Pioneer (known also as Pioneer Memorial) hasn't enjoyed the community support that Lone Fir inspires. For that sort of support, see the Eugene Masonic Cemetery, above.

FALLS CITY

Falls City Cemetery

Across the road from the Falls City IOOF Cemetery is a drive going up the hill next to someone's driveway. That drive leads to the Falls City Cemetery, but it is unmarked.

A small, rough hewn cemetery under trees, there are interesting markers here, including the marker for Art Inman (1932–2003): a painting under glass of a bull elk, ankle deep in a blue lake fading to a fog-drenched forest on the far shore. Also of note is a square block of granite, the upper portion of which has been carved into a cylinder, atop of which is affixed a sundial with four names marking the quadrants and the "epitaph": "Be like this sundial/ Count only the sunny hours."

Independence

Hilltop Cemetery (Cemetery Hill)

About three miles south of Independence on the east side of Corvallis Road.

Everybody lists this as Cemetery Hill Cemetery, except the entrance sign, which calls it Hilltop. Once an Odd Fellows cemetery, it is currently owned and maintained by Polk County, along with the Buena Vista Cemetery.

It remains an active (more so than Buena Vista) and cared-for cemetery. There are benches here and there, awning shelter tents, and new graves. It's goodly sized for a rural cemetery—possibly a half-dozen acres, mostly unwooded, though with a large central oak. There is a bevy of new graves at the north end of the cemetery, unquestionably the most colorful collection of graves in Polk County outside of Grand Ronde: homemade altars, shrine houses, and crosses; plastic flowers and photographs; a cross and arch covered with hundreds of crocheted flowers. These are people who did not go gentle into that good night. They laughed and danced and had a beer here at the dying of the light. Why they've let their hair down here unlike at other cemeteries in the valley is beyond my ken.

Downtown Independence retains its fine Victorian buildings, and there's one treasure here that pays for the entire trip: Corvallis Road. It's tied together with ninety-degree turns and is slower than a pea-picker in January; but you'll have it mostly to yourself, allowing you to putz along and admire the how-green-was-my-valley at a pace God intended you to.

Oakville

Oakville Cemetery

Oakville Road snakes and jerks its way south from Highway 34 east of Corvallis. Four or five miles down the road, the drive to the cemetery will appear on the west side of the road. There is a sign.

What a nice and well-loved cemetery this is: four acres protected by redwoods and evergreens centered around a plot kiosk, with a plot map and a heavily laminated plot book, destined to withstand any weather. A note above the map says the kiosk is "In memory of Norman Coon in appreciation for his years of service to the Oakville Cemetary Association."

With a number of benches scattered around, this is as good a place as any to contemplate the richness of the pastoral countryside, where sheep far outnumber people and the walls of the Cascades and Coast Ranges begin to gather in. There's a good stock of epitaphs, both old and new, and an assortment of new and old artistic details; including an enigmatic one, seen twice, of a house cat sitting on what looks like a hank of rope and surrounded by what looks like a belt. One of the "belts" is inscribed with a slogan: "Touch not the cat bot a glove."

PALESTINE

North Palestine Cemetery (Palestine Memorial Church)

On the north side of Palestine Avenue between the Independence-Corvallis Highway and Scenic Drive, northwest of Albany.

Both the graveyard and the old Palestine Memorial Church next to it are maintained by the North Palestine Cemetery Association, to which we should extend our thanks for doing a commendable job. The church and cemetery occupy the best of the summit of Kay's Hill and offer a broad view of the Willamette bottoms below.

It's a small, cozy cemetery watched over by mature trees. It is still used by a well-chosen few who appreciate its beauty and prospect. One of those was Scott Smith (1950–1999), whose blue and white, handmade mosaic marker is gorgeous.

Recently, the cemetery has been enriched by the addition of a polished black granite slab for Barbara Nored (1945–2005), which has a gaping cleft at the top surmounted by a gold ball. "Nored" is spelled out in high relief gold lettering and each side of the slab is adorned with four gold leaves floating above the surface as if blown there by the wind. It's an exquisite piece of art that will never show up at your local museum; you'll have to come here to see it. A plain white, steeple-less church crouching under dark firs is the fitting accompaniment to this vernacular cemetery.

PEDEE

Womer Cemetery

Take Highway 223 south of Pedee. At the intersection of Burbank Road and Womer Road, take Womer Road north; the cemetery will soon appear on your left.

Between Dallas on the north end of Highway 223 and where it meets Highway 34 in the south near Corvallis, there is only one community of note: Pedee. Pedee has a school, a store, and a church. What it has mostly is quiet isolation and the murmur of the coastal forest. Highway 223 doesn't see much besides local traffic, and if you go, you'll have it largely to yourself. Though Womer shares its hill with the private Edwards Cemetery, Womer appears to be the local "cemetery of record" and is a modest, if still active, cemetery.

PEORIA

Pine Grove Cemetery

South of Peoria, take Pine Grove Road west from Peoria Road.

Peoria is one of a string of Willamette River towns diminished when the railroad came through the valley. Peoria Road, though, remains one of the finest agricultural drives in the Willamette and cuts through the heart of the upper valley. The northern stretch is enriched by the commercial Peoria Gardens and a state agricultural station. The cemetery is associated with the historic Pine Grove Church; both are plain but comforting.

PHILOMATH

Mount Union Cemetery

At the intersection of Mount Union Avenue and Benton View Drive east of Philomath and south of Highway 24/30.

A plaque fixed to a boulder inside the cemetery reads, in part: "On May 11, 1861, Reuben and Mary Jane Holmes Shipley, former negro slaves, deeded from their farm purchased from Charles Bales' Donation Land Claim the original plot for this cemetery."

I know of no other Oregon cemetery founded by African-Americans. About five to six open acres, it's still in use, though minimally maintained; one would hope that, given its unique provenance, it will eventually see better care.

SAILOR

Sailor/Noti Pioneer Cemetery

The road to the cemetery goes north from Highway 126 about four miles west of Veneta and approximately a half-mile west of where Suttle Road meets Highway 126.

This slim, two-acre cemetery would be undistinguished were it not for a fraternal order associated with it. Unlike the Masons or Odd Fellows, this order didn't found this cemetery, nor do they manage it now, but like any other order, they are clustered together. Members from as far away as Washington and Idaho choose to come and be buried here among their brethren, among them Shovelhead, Fast Fred, Big Carl, Ole Sweetheart, Wolfman, and No. 9. Welcome to the motorcycle club known as the Free Souls. The Free Souls run a ship-shape shop; some of their markers are homemade, but most are standard-issue stone, and their grave sites are kept clean and orderly. Even given the cemetery's small size, there's plenty of room for more residents here, as the entire upper half of the cemetery is unused. The occupied portion has grown a few small trees and bushes. As for the chain-link fence around the graveyard, don't blame the bikers; chain-link is the fencing of choice for rural cemeteries.

WALKER

Walker Community (Union) Church Cemetery

Take England Road west from Highway 99, three or four miles north of Cottage Grove. The church is clearly visible from the intersection.

Here you'll see a near-perfect combination of white country church and sheltered graveyard. There are both newer and older sections, each about an acre, with the newer section higher on the hill and open to the sky. The older section is settled down under a ceiling of intertwined oak branches; perennials color the grounds, but it's the protective dappled light filtered through the oaks that lends this cemetery a timelessness appropriate to its cause. It's unusual in its topography in that the lower portion wraps around a gully, a feature usually only seen in larger cemeteries. If there's any drawback to the cemetery, it's that it overlooks Highway 99, Interstate 5, and the railroad tracks, all within a mile of each other.

Yamhill Valley

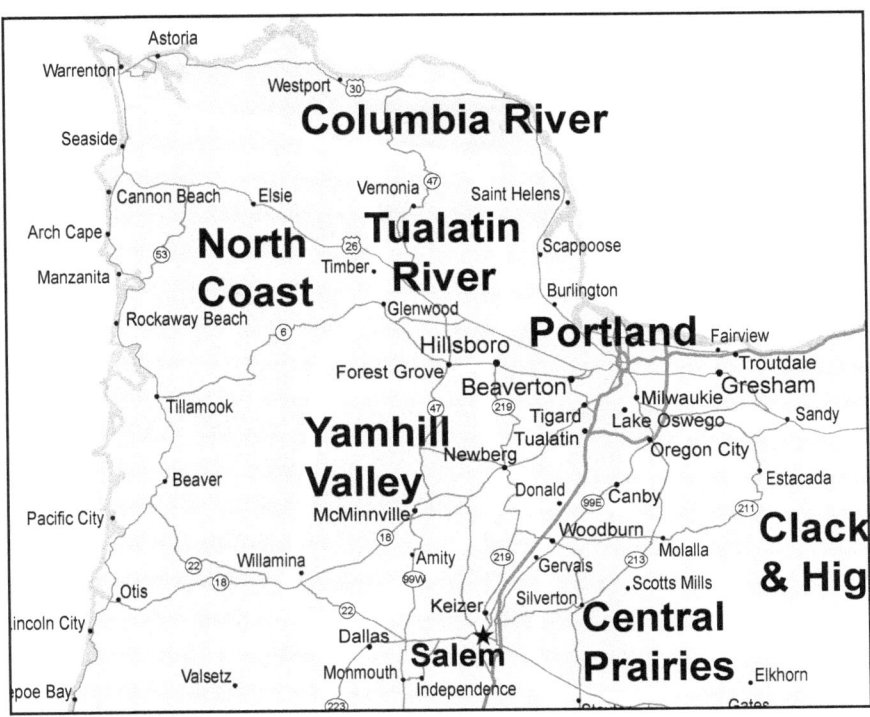

AMITY

Amity Cemetery

In Amity, take Bellevue Highway west out of town. Turn south on Woodland Way and there you are.

Named after a school that began in 1849, Amity is a pleasant little town with a stock of nicely preserved older houses—visually, the ideal of a small Oregon town. The cemetery is much like the town: pleasant and sturdy. Four to five acres in size, the older portion is tree covered while the newer lies open. It's not a cemetery with a lot to say—folks aren't as vocal here as they are at North Yamhill, below—but there's a surprising amount of well done, personalized graphic detail on some of the newer stones, and there are a few handmade memorials worth digging for, as well as a statue of two cherubs holding hands over one tombstone.

BETHEL

Bethel Cemetery

At the corner of Zena and Oak Grove Roads, northwest of Salem.

Nestled into a cove of the west slope of the Eola Hills called Plum Valley, Bethel Cemetery sits on a rise overlooking the valley westward. Along with the Bethel Church (located nearby) it is among the last significant vestiges of the community. At three or four acres, it's a mid-sized pioneer cemetery with its share of older graves, including that of one Oscar Kelty, who was hanged in Dallas for the murder of his wife.

The cemetery itself is open and rather sparse; a "largish" pioneer cemetery in a great location, it has a clutch of new memorials off to one corner, near the trees. You can visit the wineries of the Eola and Amity Hills while you're here as well.

CARLTON

McBride Cemetery

Take Meadow Lake west out of Carlton. Turn north at McBride Cemetery Road, a couple miles out of town. Drive about a third of a mile up McBride Cemetery Road until you see three driveways together on the left. Take the one in the middle.

When you do get to the cemetery, several hundred yards up a one-lane road with a dogleg left, you'll find the McBride Cemetery sign with wood-burned lettering and embellished with a burned-in daisy design. It's sweet and childlike.

The cemetery is surprisingly large, especially for one so unannounced. It's not overly well maintained, but the weeds have been cut; if you don't step in the poison oak, you'll be okay. It has its complement of grown trees but is by no means overgrown.

The cemetery is named after Thomas Crawford McBride (1777–1857), for whom a modern stone has been laid. It proclaims McBride a "Pioneer Christian Preacher/ Among the first in Oregon Territory/ This marker has been placed/ by his spiritual heirs."

CHEHALEM VALLEY

Noble Pioneer Cemetery

On the west side of Kings Grade Road, about a half-mile north of its intersection with North Valley Road.

This well-maintained, two-acre cemetery, ringed by plantings of new maples and decorated with occasional rose bushes, is lorded over by a scattering of large, old fir trees. Worth visiting not so much for its collection of headstones, modest and terse, as for its location in the Chehalem Valley.

Like the rest of Oregon, the Chehalem Valley is intensely agricultural, and Noble Cemetery is across the road from a massive tree-seedling operation. The hundreds upon hundreds of rows of differing trees are as precise and neat as a Grandma Moses painting and lend a calming sense of order and peacefulness to the area. Lifting slightly over the valley, the cemetery is, indeed, an honorable place to rest. One particularly ancient and huge tree is preceded by three concrete benches describing an arc on one side, where the visitor is invited to rest and contemplate.

DAYTON

Brookside Cemetery

As you're leaving Dayton heading south on Highway 221, when the highway makes a slight jog to the left (east), another road continues straight, at the end of which you can see the stones of the cemetery.

Dayton is one of the few Oregon towns modeled on the eastern pattern of a town square and contains a replica of an old pioneer-era block house. The vicissitudes of Brookside Cemetery are exemplary of what can happen to any graveyard, especially small unaffiliated ones. The Brookside brook has long since disappeared from view, but it was unquestionably visible when Joel Palmer, Dayton's founding father, donated the land (he is also buried here). Longer than wide, with trees on the brook side, the cemetery no longer accepts recipients but wouldn't mind donations. Two signers of the Champoeg Accord hang out here, and there is a cenotaph to a third, whose body disappeared during the Cayuse Indian War.

When I first visited this cemetery, it was unkempt and heavily vandalized. During my most recent visit, I encountered a flock of grade-school children cleaning the place up as a class project. It is still heavily vandalized—emphasizing the need for donations—but at least now it's being cared for.

Dundee

Dundee Pioneer Cemetery

At the end of NW Viewmont Drive. From 99W in Dundee, take First Street north up the hill to Dogwood to the T; turn right (east) on Dogwood. Take Dogwood to Viewmont Drive and turn back north (up the hill) on Viewmont.

This is a fairway twenty-five to thirty yards wide, littered with tombstones; it thinks it's a cemetery. But do come up for the view. Gaze out over the broad expanses of French Prairie to the distant Cascades. It's a wonderful place to be buried.

—Yamhill Valley—

The stone that drew my eye, when I visited the day after Memorial Day, was a small, naturally shaped, pyramidal stone sunk into a square of concrete with words written on the concrete in tiny lettering: "Indian Unknown."

LAFAYETTE

Trappist Abbey of Our Lady of Guadalupe

At 9200 NE Abbey Road, which heads north out of Lafayette. Abbey is on the east side of the road a couple miles out from Lafayette.

A more serene spot could hardly be found in the lower valley. It doesn't have the commanding presence of Mount Angel, but it doesn't have the traffic, either. The Trappist monastery began in Pecos, New Mexico, in 1948 but moved to the Pacific Northwest in 1955 in search of better farming. There is a bookstore at the reception desk, which will be evident once you're there, and models and drawings of planned expansions are shown there. The caveat is that, unlike the graveyards at, say, Mount Angel or Marylhurst, this is behind a closed gate, and you'll have to ask permission to visit it.

McMinnville

Evergreen Memorial Park

In the northeast corner of the intersection of Highways 47 and 99W between Lafayette and McMinnville.

Having been founded in 1970, this is one of the newer cemeteries in this region and recent enough that they should have known better than to situate their cemetery at the intersection of two busy highways. Be careful when approaching this one—and do approach it, as it's one of the more interesting cemeteries in the region, new or not.

The ODOT survey lists it at fifty acres, but, if that's so, I don't know where they are hiding them all. For the most part it's a standard, unimaginative cemetery with stones lined up neatly sans distinguishing characteristics; but suddenly, in the last decade or so, extending out from the left of the rear mausoleum, pandemonium breaks loose and the rules are tossed away. Stones leap up in size and shape. Laser etchings tell mini-stories. The modern era has begun.

It echoes the old adage: the more things change, the more they remain the same. Evergreen has several good examples of modern-day equivalents to the era of chapbook inscriptions, when the same pious sentiments were copied from grave to grave. Today's epitaphs are as likely as any to be cribbed from elsewhere, though the sources may reach more widely now.

Masonic Cemetery

Find Hill Road west of McMinnville, then find the entrance to Chemeketa Community College off Hill Road. Across the street is a new housing development. There are signs to the cemetery at that juncture. Take Horizon street into the development and follow the signs.

ODOT lists this as a five-acre cemetery, but it feels more like fifteen going on twenty. An open cemetery with concrete curbs around many family-sized plots, it's still in use, though not as active as one would think for a cemetery of such size. Gnarly weeds have replaced much of the grass; not only is it mowed, but there's a live-in caretaker and a large open-roader jacked up in the center of the cemetery with a scattering of lawn furniture here and there. When I visited, a mother deer and two spotted yearlings were cropping the crabgrass. They took one look at me and my camera and decided I was harmless enough and continued their munching.

The cemetery has an interesting new "construction" next to the open-roader: a concrete pad backed by five flags, one for each major branch of service and a taller one for the United States. In front of the flags are two sarcophagi with writing on most sides: largely names, dates, and a few words about a variety of people from three pioneering families.

The memorial is similar to other memorials springing up in cemeteries throughout the region, largely reflecting a strong burst of patriotism. This pad is new, post 9/11. A side of one sarcophagus extols the virtues of the armed forces and manages to intertwine the pioneer story with military history: "The pioneers of Oregon extended our nation from the Atlantic to the Pacific. It is the constant vigilance and valiant service of our veterans that allow us to remain one nation under God with liberty and justice for all. We must remember and be eternally grateful for their sacrifices."

Another side outlines "Oregon Before 1843" in three short paragraphs:

"The Treaty of 1818 guaranteed the United States and Britain equal access to the Oregon Country, but neither claimed sovereignty. The area now comprises Oregon, Washington, Idaho, plus some of Wyoming, Montana, and British Columbia.

"In 1842, less than 100 white men, a majority of them Canadian, lived in the Willamette Valley, where the English owned Hudson Bay Company dominated commerce.

"The signers of the 'Wolves Letters' and the one hundred settlers at Champoeg in 1843, had sparked the founding of the Oregon Territory and State."

South Yamhill Cemetery

From Highway 18 about two miles southwest of McMinnville, Masonville Road departs to the west. Follow Masonville Road until it reaches the base of the hills and jogs to the right. McCabe Chapel Road intersects there from the south. The drive to the cemetery is there at the corner off McCabe Road; there are signs.

Only a tad off the beaten path, just before the road heads into the hills, South Yamhill Cemetery hides behind the trees like a demure lady concealing her charms. Go ahead, part the branches and see what she has to offer: You'll find one of the outstanding gems of the lower valley. I don't know what it is about Yamhill, but both this and North Yamhill combine to make a brace of exquisite rural cemeteries second to none.

This is not a large cemetery, only a couple acres spread out over a south-facing slope surrounded by mature trees. A grove of trees separates the cemetery from the road, in the center of which is a clearing where a Baptist church once stood (third Baptist church west of the Rockies, established in 1846). The church may be gone, but clearly a higher spirit calls this home, as well does a collection of monuments as rich in personality as any and many times the size. These are the cemeteries that earn the sobriquet Art Parks. They are hidden sculpture gardens you're allowed to visit for free. The pair of markers—one can't call them tombstones—for Paaolo Phung (1909–1989) and Maria Chim (1907–1987) stand out as unlike anything else I've witnessed, so stylized that one has to believe that somewhere in the world they are the norm, but here they're unique. The view is verdant. Cows wonder what you're doing here.

Newberg

Newberg Pioneer Cemeteries (Fernwood, Friends, Kilpatrick Post G. A. R. Cemeteries)

At the end of Everett Street in Newberg. Everett connects with Highway 219 coming in from St. Paul before it joins up with Highway 99W coming from Portland.

There's a cluster of three cemeteries in Newberg's historic cemetery row: Fernwood, Friends, and Kilpatrick Post G.A.R. Fernwood is on the National Registry of Historic Places.

While this triumvirate of pioneer cemeteries is somehow less than the sum of its parts, there are advantages in having three pioneer cemeteries together, and one would be foolish to come this far and not visit them. If the cemeteries are not enough, Newberg is a charming valley town with a wonderful stock of houses both old and new. The surrounding countryside is equally delightful.

None of the Newberg cemeteries is particularly old, with Friends weighing in at 1880. It appears to have considerable open ground left for interment, in the middle of which is a new columbarium. To my knowledge, it's the only Friends cemetery in the lower valley. The G.A.R. cemetery, with a white obelisk in the center, offers one of the few visible memories of the Civil War here on the coast.

SHERIDAN

Pleasant Hill Pioneer Cemetery

Take Christensen Road south from Highway 18, a couple miles northeast of Sheridan. The road immediately turns east. Soon Dejong Road comes in from the south. Take it a mile and a half to the center of the crossroads community of Ballston and turn right on Ballston Road Turn left (south) at the T and drive a quarter-mile until Pleasant Hill Road comes in from the west. Take it to the top of the hill (a mile or so) and the cemetery will be visible on your right.

Until the 1930s, the site was home to the Red Prairie Methodist Church but no longer has a religious affiliation. It is yet another example of spontaneous rural cemetery resurrection.

The cemetery has the largest collection of small headstones I've run across and is remarkable in that respect. The caretaker, a neighbor who volunteers her time, said they've unsuccessfully tried to glue some of the stones back together and have pressure-washed others. It's a labor of love at which they've been diligent. The results are manifest. Though recently revived, the cemetery doesn't boast many new graves. For the most part, this is a repository of the old. Despite the lushness of the surroundings, this is a simple graveyard without the trappings of prosperity demonstrated in, say, the Aurora Community Cemetery close to the Willamette River.

WILLAMINA

Buck Hollow Cemetery (Upper Willamina Cemetery)

Driving west on Highway 18 though Willamina, the road comes to a "Y," where the highway goes left and Willamina Creek Road goes right. Take Willamina Creek, which follows a secluded agricultural valley into the Coast Range. As the road begins to climb out of the valley, Buck Hollow Road appears from the east. Take it. The second drive on your right (south), unmarked, goes the short distance to the cemetery. If you miss the correct drive, try again. It's there. The cemetery can be seen from the road if one looks closely.

Just when you thought you couldn't get any farther from civilization and still be among people, along comes one of the finest rural cemeteries in the state. It's exquisite. There may be ones with better views—and the roar of heavy trucks passing on Buck Hollow Road is a bit loud—but no rural cemetery is more fun to visit. This is the *crème de la crème*, when everything else is skim milk.

As to be expected in a lobe of the valley where the soil begins to thin, it's not wealth and magnificent statuary that makes this hidden cemetery such a draw. On the contrary, it has the largest collection of handmade memorials in the region. Forget the stylized formalities of the stone cutter; real people have been buried here under the towering firs. Hand-poured concrete, hand-painted slabs, and wooden markers all find their way to this three acres of hallowed ground. Obviously, keeping up with the Joneses here means milking your own spirit. It's a long ways to Willamina (unless you happen to live in Sheridan), but it's worth every mile.

ODOT calls this the Upper Willamina Cemetery and dates it from 1866, though the sign claims 1917, which may be when it became the Buck Hollow Cemetery. The timber industry is well represented in the Buck Hollow Cemetery, where at least four stones display etchings of log trucks, and a plain handmade wooden cross for Gene Mosser (1933–2001) nominates him as "Heavens Trucker."

Log trucks aren't the only vehicles carved into the stones here; also represented are a muscle car, two race cars (on the same stone), and one converted school bus labeled "Oregon or bust."

Yamhill

Pike–North Yamhill Cemetery (Pike IOOF Cemetery)

Taker Hacker Road north from its intersection with Pike Road. The cemetery drive appears shortly on your left. There is a sign.

The best way to find Yamhill and Pike Cemetery is to take Highway 240 west out of Newberg through the Chehalem Valley, behind the Red Hills of Dundee, and over the hillocks separating the Chehalem Valley from that of the North Yamhill River. Orchards, berry patches, meandering creeks, wooded ridges, bosky dells, Victorian farmplexes, contented cows, and goats all share the countryside with burgeoning grape growers. Here and there, substantial new mansions dot the crest of hills, but the Chehalem and Coast Ranges buffer the Yamhill-Carlton area from the onslaughts of outer Portland. There's no big superhighway from here to anywhere, so it appears to be protected for the foreseeable future.

Records indicate that this marvelous cemetery covers only four acres, but it seems much larger than that. It rises up a gentle slope to a broad crest with a good command of the fields below and the hills beyond. It is a long way from encroachment, and the scene will undoubtedly stay serene for a long time to come. The cemetery is well maintained and actively receives new graves. Upright headstones are still allowed, and it has a handful of some of the best new markers in the territory. There are older stones here, as well, but it's the recent stuff that shines. Literally.

Yamhill-Carlton Pioneer Memorial Cemetery

Nearly halfway between Yamhill and Carlton on Highway 47, Fryer Road departs to the east. The cemetery is a third of a mile down the north side of that road.

The Yamhill-Carlton Cemetery sits on a small knoll in the middle of the northern Yamhill Valley and commands a surrounding view of some of America's most vaunted and valuable wine country and the forested flanks of the Coast and Chehalem Ranges.

The stones here are still fairly modest, which is not to say they're without interest but rather that the good times are yet to roll. As in other pioneer cemeteries, the long and short ends of Oregon's history are both planted here. Near each other are two fairly new stones marking a brace of the oldest graves, moved here in the summer of 1853 when the original cemetery, a half-mile south, was relocated. (For what it's worth, thirteen people were moved to the new cemetery, although the first burial in the original cemetery wasn't until January of the same year.) The two new stones are for Indian Clark and Indian Jim; a sign close by proclaims the two "worked with the early settlers and requested they be buried in the white man's cemetery."

The other end of the spectrum is anchored by a cenotaph for Staff Sergeant Thomas Hepburn Perry, born in 1942 and gone missing in action in Vietnam on May 10, 1968.

No cemetery is worth its salt without a good mystery. The most enigmatic epitaph survives because it is on a different surface than the vital statistics, which have all but been obliterated by moss. The stone probably came from early in the twentieth century. It tosses off lightly: "As to pleasant dreams."

Zena

Spring Valley Presbyterian Cemetery (Zena Cemetery)

The cemetery is on the east side of Brush College Road south of its intersection with Zena Road.

Zena, named after one Arvazena Cooper, is located below the flanks of the Eola Hills, with the Spring Valley Presbyterian Church and graveyard surmounting a hillock overlooking the whilom town. A 1961 sketch of the community shows a grist mill, post office, blacksmith shop, and grange hall, besides the church and cemetery, which are all that remain.

Spring Valley Cemetery (which the USGS calls the Zena Cemetery) fronts the historic pioneer church under spreading oaks. From here you can see heaven; it starts at your feet. There may be more impressive graveyards, there may be ones with more imaginative verse, there may be more beautiful churches, and there might even be more spectacular views—but few combine everything so neatly into one package.

The simple, white-spired church was built by volunteer labor in 1859, and, somewhat unusually, the driveway and parking lot approach the rear of the church, and it's not until you've walked around the building, away from the vehicular world, and gotten under the serenity of the trees that you see its face. From the steps you look out at the fertile bottom lands of the Willamette. The church bell, carried round the Horn from England, tolls still.

About the Author

Photo credit: David L. Minick

Most of Johan Mathiesen's professional life has centered around food, either making it, writing about it, or selling books about it. Over the years, he has run restaurants and bakeries, hitchhiked across the country, built a cabin without power tools, published an alternative newsletter, operated an alternative school, and tended his own garden.

He has published articles in the *Minneapolis Tribune*, *Simple Cooking*, and *Petits Propos Culinaires*, and articles from the latter two have been reprinted in anthologies. His cemetery photos have appeared in the *ASG* (Association of Gravestone Studies) *Quarterly* as well as in two books: *Grave Humor* and *Weird Oregon*.

Mathiesen currently lives in Portland with his wife, Kay, and has four children and five grandchildren. To learn more about his cemetery adventures, visit his blog at http://bloggingadeadhorse-dmt.blogspot.com.

www.ingramcontent.com/pod-product-compliance
Lightning Source LLC
Chambersburg PA
CBHW051034160426
43193CB00010B/943